Praise for *Brave(ish)*

"In *Brave(ish)*, author Margaret Davis Ghielme[...] the Technicolor riches of places and people with [...] As she discovers the world's splendors, however, from incandescent rice paddies to moonlit deserts, she also learns to navigate another landscape: the fiercely beautiful, sometimes rocky terrain of her own heart."

—Janice Deal, award-winning author of *The Decline of Pigeons*

"Written in lyrical prose peppered with insight and wisdom hard-won through travel and personal struggle, *Brave(ish)* is Margaret's continuation of her storytelling and one-woman shows that left audiences wanting more. In this uplifting, witty, and sometimes dark memoir, Margaret discovers her truths and her story, one destination at a time."

—Jen Cullerton Johnson, award-winning author of *Seeds of Change*

"*Brave(ish)* should be required reading for all perfectionists who are sick of people pleasing and ready to reclaim their own lives. You'll love traveling around the world with Margaret, and you'll root for her as she embraces her true self. By owning her desires and asking for help, she is able to become the type of authentic person we all hope to be."

—Nadine Kenney Johnstone, award-winning memoirist of *Of This Much I'm Sure*

"Margaret Ghielmetti shows us that sometimes you have to travel a long way to find a path back to your true self. *Brave(ish)* is intimate and honest—the two best words to describe a memoir."

—Arlene Malinowski Ph.D., award-winning playwright of "What Does The Sun Sound Like"

"Travel lover Ghielmetti sets her coming-of-middle-age tale against a vivid and alluring backdrop of beautiful and complex places such as Egypt, Singapore, Paris, and the Presbyterian Home in Evanston, Illinois. This culturally rich narrative makes us long to travel with Ghielmetti as she comes to understand that discovering her exterior landscape is secondary to discovering her interior one; that she can create momentum even when being still; and that living in these distant places in the world has brought her nearer to places of the heart, and of the spirit."

—Patricia Ann McNair, award-winning author of *The Temple of Air* and *And These Are the Good Times*

"*Brave(ish)* invites us on Margaret's amazing adventures, where treasures are unearthed—some from worlds beyond what most of us have or will ever experience. Women's lives often have a tipping point, and Margaret shares with us that moment of revelation where what she once dreamed and imagined no longer suffices."

—Laurie Kahn, director of Womencare Counseling and Training Center and author of *Baffled by Love*

"This beautifully written book invites readers to join the author on a parallel journey. A wonderfully rendered narrative of life and travel on multiple continents around the world, *Brave(ish)* explores the humor and humanity of the places Ghielmetti inhabits and chronicles a poignant interior journey and her struggle to transcend constraints of childhood rules. Told with love, warmth, and brave self-reflection, the victories and losses along these two journeys coalesce to form a nurturing path of being at home wherever your travels take you."

—Dr. Niva Piran, award-winning author of
Journeys of Embodiment at the Intersection of Body and Culture

"*Brave(ish)* is a breathtaking journey across the globe and into the soul. The author's adventures as a 'trailing wife' will captivate you with glimpses into the opulent world of first-class hotels and jaw-dropping travel destinations—but it's her determined quest to find home within herself that will hold your heart."

—MT Cozzola, author of *Boy Small*

"Ghielmetti's sure hand and clear prose guide us through her compelling story of breaking free from the straightjacket of perfectionism. If memoir is the art of making the personal universal, she has hit the mark and then some. You'll enjoy her often wise, often funny journey through an emotional and international landscape."

—Anne Laughlin, author of Lammy-nominated *The Acquittal*

"Reading *Brave(ish)* led me to an "aha" moment I had been unknowingly awaiting my entire adult life. A recovering perfectionist myself, I found solace in another woman questioning "What will I be if I'm not perfect?" Kudos to Margaret for asking tough questions and finding answers. Let us take her example and forge ahead towards being—at the very least—brave(ish)."

—R.C. Riley, author of the solo show "Wrong Way Journey"

"To use Ghielmetti's own words, reading her memoir is like an 'otter easing into a river.' It's easy to cry and laugh with her on her journey through both exotic places in the world and intimate places in the heart. At the same time, I was permitted to walk through the door of her complex family and marriage and witness firsthand the behind-the-door feelings of both. Rarely is a reader given such profound access to the humble humanity of another person."

—Adrienne Weiss, author of *Brand Buzz: 3 Breakthrough
Secrets for Building a Winning Brand*

"In her eloquently crafted memoir, Margaret Ghielmetti takes us along on parallel journeys. Each stop along the way of her 'sheroe's journey' back to self is set against a gorgeously painted backdrop that is her literal journey around the world."

—Rita Balzotti, Career Advancement & Alumni Manager, Cara Chicago

"Margaret shares a mosaic of intimate thoughts, souvenirs, and memories with a humorous and colourful writing style that compels you to read to the end of the story. This book should be a 'must-read' for anyone embarking on an international career as an expatriate—with all the good and not-so-glamorous aspects of it. Most importantly, this book is a love story about acceptance of oneself."

—René Beauchamp, founder of *Rise&Spice* blog and consultant hotelier

"What an inspiring book with memories of the glamorous life of a hotel general manager—and the trepidation of daily life trying to get the new culture and customs of each new move. The beautiful writing transports us on an expat journey and I would highly recommend this book for anyone about to embark on this life."

—Louise Beer, founder and director of PragArtworks Gallery, Czech Republic

"*Brave(ish)* is a revelatory and rich mix of memoir and travelogue. In this emotionally powerful book, Ghielmetti reveals the painful journey she takes to self-discovery with insight and humor. An acclaimed storyteller, Margaret writes with raw honesty, probingly and hilariously, about her adventures and struggles as a trailing spouse."

—Don Henderson, retired book buyer for Gallery Shops, National Gallery of Art

"*Brave(ish)* is an international journey and a glimpse into the interior of the soulful writer. Ghielmetti's candor gives context to her experiences and each of the places—and transported me there. With an openness to share without holding back, she allows the reader a firsthand experience into her emotional life—and in doing so allows the reader to be in touch with theirs."

—JoAnn Kurtz-Ahlers, president of Hidden Doorways, A KAA Travel Collection

"Margaret takes her readers on a tour of far-off, exotic locations through her beautiful storytelling. It's in these places that she comes to grips with her need to please. The unfolding and rediscovering of who she is in this world and the power of her story is a triumph."

—Deanna Moffitt, CEO of Luminant Leadership and transformational coach at The You Experience

"As one of live lit's most skilled and respected storytellers, Ghielmetti consistently weaves the perfectly crafted tale on stage, and *Brave(ish)* is as bold, fun, and fascinating as her spoken-word performances. Turns out this self-proclaimed 'teacher's pet' also has an adventurous streak!"

—Stephanie Rogers, producer and chief creative officer at Story Jam and Story Jam Studio

"In this intimate memoir, Ghielmetti takes us on several voyages at once. Through vivid sketches, we travel with her to France, Egypt, Thailand, Singapore, and India. Along the way, we see how she refashions her family's rigid code of behavior into more flexible guidelines. We watch the growth of her relationships with her husband, her aging parents, and her higher power. We're alongside as her self-concept evolves, from 'trailing spouse' to aspiring writer to confident story-teller to—at long last—published author. It's one woman's inspiring voyage of self-discovery and empowerment."

—Dan Richman, editor of *Drive or Die*

"*Brave(ish)* impacted me deeply. It made me laugh and cry out loud, sometimes simultaneously. While Margaret's journey is an unusual one that has taken her all over the globe, it is one so many of us can relate to while enjoying the wonderful travel tales. It made me think about my own 'family handbook' and how it has impacted my decisions and my life. Margaret reminded me that it's never too late to find yourself."

—Alexis Romer, VP-Sales, Luxury Travel Industry, Bulgari,
EDITION, Luxury Collection, Ritz-Carlton, St. Regis, W Hotels

"*Brave(ish)* traces a journey of life: learning the 'family handbook' of rules while we're young, then applying the rules religiously—until we evolve and shed layers to eventually get to our place of peace. Margaret reminds the reader that it's acceptable to 'kiss our good little girl good-bye' in order to unleash our essential selves into the world. This book inspires me to investigate my own family handbook, setting down the rules which no longer work for me and breaking free from their grip to accommodate who I am now."

—Michelle Sanford, leadership coach at
Impact by Design/Sanford & Associates

"If you've picked up *Brave(ish)*, you're about to journey to some of the world's most fascinating places, including those within. Admitted people pleaser and perfectionist Margaret brings humor, tenderness, and authenticity to the practice of releasing perfectionism. She is pure class without the 'act,' a guide who journeyed the world to find home."

—Lynne E. Sheridan, transformational trainer at Inspire Coaching

BRAVE(ISH)

BRAVE(ISH)

A Memoir of a
Recovering Perfectionist

Margaret Davis Ghielmetti

SHE WRITES PRESS

Copyright © 2020 Margaret Davis Ghielmetti

All rights reserved. No part of this publication may be reproduced, distributed, or transmitted in any form or by any means, including photocopying, recording, digital scanning, or other electronic or mechanical methods, without the prior written permission of the publisher, except in the case of brief quotations embodied in critical reviews and certain other noncommercial uses permitted by copyright law. For permission requests, please address She Writes Press.

Published 2020
Printed in the United States of America
ISBN: 978-1-63152-747-0
ISBN: 978-1-63152-748-7
Library of Congress Control Number: 2020906185

For information, address:
She Writes Press
1569 Solano Ave #546
Berkeley, CA 94707

She Writes Press is a division of SparkPoint Studio, LLC.

All company and/or product names may be trade names, logos, trademarks, and/or registered trademarks and are the property of their respective owners.

Names and identifying characteristics have been changed to protect the privacy of certain individuals.

For Patrick, *amore mio.*

CONTENTS

Author's Note

I've made every effort to accurately relate the substance of my experience during this time in my life, relying on personal notes and my memory of events and conversations. For privacy, I changed the names or descriptions of some individuals and places and omitted others; for the sake of the narrative, I collapsed time and condensed events in some cases, but only when these had no impact on the substance of the story.

PROLOGUE

"**H**ow *lucky am I?*" I keep telling myself that whenever I feel uncertain about our move overseas. I've quit my job, and now I'm officially a Trailing Spouse, following Patrick's career. We'll be in Paris for the summer of 2000: a temporary gig for my hotelier husband, helping relaunch the newly renovated Four Seasons there. Then, in autumn, we'll move to Egypt for three years for his new job as general manager. It's the promotion Patrick has been working toward his whole career: fourteen years of climbing the hotel world ladder from night shifts to now.

It's a big shift for me, too: from Corporate Worker to Corporate Wife, but I'm determined to do it not just well, but as perfectly as I can.

And I finally have the time to write the book I've dreamed of writing since I was a little girl!

One of the perks of the job includes living in Four Seasons hotels (which is going to be a welcome change after three years in a minuscule fourth-floor walkup in New York). Our furniture and household goods have been shipped off to storage somewhere in New Jersey. All we're packing are two bulging suitcases of clothing for each of us. While I'm not a big shopper, I *have* splurged on a few items appropriate to a GM's wife. Hello, white linen blouses, silky shawls, and tailored slacks. Farewell, uniform of twenty years' working 200 percent in customer service and sales: black skirts and jackets, pumps and pantyhose.

Tucked inside my carry-on is our wedding photo from seven years ago: Patrick and me at thirty-three, smiling serenely, my new Swiss husband's arm around my waist. Also coming on the plane is my well-worn, well-loved American passport, too many tourist guidebooks to Paris, and my brand-new turquoise-blue journal—the latest in a lifetime of journals for a wannabe Great American Novelist.

Oh, and The Family Handbook is coming, too. Not written with actual ink on paper, but bestowed upon me at birth by my parents, and engraved upon my consciousness. I've carried it—and carried it out—for all my forty years: from toddler to teacher's pet to teenager (between flute lessons and soccer practice). I carried The Handbook as I picked up my degrees in Arabic and French, then as I crisscrossed Europe alone with a backpack, a Eurail train pass, and the Thomas Cook train timetable. I carried The Handbook as a sales manager, crunching Altoids before sales calls, and slugging "Another Chardonnay, please!" during endless client dinners. I always assumed everyone had gotten a Family Handbook just like mine. My three older brothers had gotten theirs. Mother and Dad had gotten one at birth, too. I never gave it a second thought.

The Davis Family Handbook

I solemnly swear to abide by the rules, including, but not limited to:

Repeat "How lucky am I?"

Stay grateful and glass-half-full even when I'm already homesick for places I haven't left yet: my childhood Evanston, shaded by sturdy oaks; my grown-up Chicago, lapped by our mighty lake; New York City, where Patrick and I have "worked hard, played hard" for these three years. Definitely repeat "How lucky am I?" when I'm missing my interested-in-everything mother and my sweet, smart, silly dad. Repeat "How lucky am I?" even when I'm moving four thousand miles away from the best friends in the world, who are always up for hours of laughter. Sure, I'll keep in touch with the occasional expensive overseas phone call, but that's not the same as catching up over coffee.

Repeat "How lucky am I?" *especially whenever anyone tells me how lucky I am.*

If you want it done right, do it yourself.

Actually, do it yourself no matter what. Preferably yesterday, without any help.

I've just moved my parents from the big family house into a retirement home apartment. I've Excel spreadsheet-ed my way through the bid process for Patrick's and my international move. Since Day One of our marriage, I've managed our finances down to the penny and planned every one of our trips in excruciating detail. "Measure twice; cut once," I learned growing up. But I measure as many times as it takes to ensure *perfection*. This includes my novel-to-be. I'd already written a little book at ten years old: a tomboy with long brown hair runs away from home to tame wild horses in the wilderness—of Wisconsin! One day, though, I realized a fatal flaw in my plot: my heroine was sleeping outside under the stars, which would only be possible in *summer*. She survived on apples, which she could only have plucked from the trees in *autumn*. I promptly ripped my manuscript into a million pieces.

No gray areas for me.

Always put others first.

I love to make people happy! And my parents have reminded me that, in marrying a responsible and successful man, I have "hitched my wagon to Patrick's star." So of course his career comes first now. And, in any case, the Ritz-Carlton Hotel Company has never once suggested that I keep my sales job once I've moved an ocean away from my clients. That wouldn't work, and I can't work overseas anyway: I'll be on a "dependent's visa."

So, it's onward to the next career: what's known in international relocation circles as the Trailing Spouse. While I hate that term, I love that I'm earning the bragging rights that come with no longer being just a traveler. (I won't even *say* the word "tourist.")

Oh, and I'll be the Best Hostess to the World: *"I hope everyone will come visit us!"*

Don't air your dirty laundry in public.
I've hesitated sharing my heartbreak with my friends over losing a five years' infertility battle. They're busy moms, like I was sure I'd be by now. Why would I burden them with my impending homesickness or my uncertainty about my new role? I'm off to places people only dream about, while they're schlepping to the grocery store in a mini-van. *Just smile, Margaret.*

Above all, JUST DO IT.
My mom taught us that *long* before Nike got ahold of it. People tell me how brave I am to move overseas, but I don't see it that way at all. Mother always said I had "one foot at home, and one foot out in the world." I dream of visiting every country there is! I'm determined to be culturally sensitive and flexible. My parents taught us to treat everyone the same and with respect. "People are people are people," they'd say. I've always been a traveler. Now I get to be an expatriate: Best Expat Ever!

All I have to do is say yes to everything, hold my head up high, *and always be brave.*

So, yes: we're off, and I've got this!

I think I've got this.

I've got this, right?

NEW YORK TO PARIS

On the morning of our departure day from New York in June 2000, Patrick and I take one more walk around Central Park, our oasis in this city that never sleeps—through the zoo and around the reservoir, past the majestic Metropolitan Museum and the little pond where kids send toy boats skittering across the green water.

Back at the Pierre hotel, as Patrick says his final goodbyes to his colleagues, I have one last espresso with the general manager's wife in the Rotunda bar, with white-jacketed waiters hovering at a discreet distance. Karin's hair falls in blonde waves onto the shoulders of her softly-tailored blazer. I confide to her, "I'm excited about this move but I'm afraid that—now that Patrick's a GM—people will want to get to him through me."

She smiles, saying, "Oh, they *will* do that. They'll ask you for a discount on a hotel room before they even know your name. They're that shockingly transparent: you'll know right away. Margaret: just be yourself."

Mother always said that, too. *But what does that mean for me, now?*

Karin and I walk to the hotel's marble lobby, where her husband, Didier, is shaking Patrick's hand. He's given us snorkel masks and fins for our farewell gift, as we'll eventually be moving to Sharm el Sheikh, Egypt, one of the world's most celebrated scuba destinations.

Now, Didier gives me a kiss on each cheek, leaving the lingering scent of French *eau de cologne*. I hug Karin once more, and Patrick and I walk out onto Fifth Avenue, to the rush of yellow taxis and the cacophony of car horns. The bellman has loaded our suitcases into a shiny black hotel van. In the back seat between us is our hand luggage with jewelry, diskettes, checkbook, camera, and laptops—plus Nadia and BooBoo, our rescue-cats-in-carry-ons. As the driver steers the van into the flow of traffic, we wave farewell to the hotel—and to a city I've come to love. As Dorothy the Meek and Mild Midwesterner, it took me months to stop being shocked by Manhattan's brash energy. Now I'm finding it hard to leave.

But I've always been a traveler! When I was a baby, my mom carried me to PTA meetings in a woven picnic basket, sliding me under her seat where I'd sleep snuggled under a colorful cotton quilt. My curiosity about the world grew during family road trips as I gazed out the window of our Ford station wagon, wondering, *What are people's lives like in that little town, or on that farm?* I traveled through the books that Dad read to me before bed: Kipling's "The Elephant's Child" in India and my Little Golden Book favorite: *The Sailor Dog* named Scuppers who survived storms and shipwrecks to roam the world over. I had a pen pal from England who sent me crisp blue airmail letters. When my parents took me to London as a ten-year-old, Dad taught me about Henry the Eighth and his unfortunate wives: "Divorced, beheaded, died, divorced, beheaded, survived." In Edinburgh, I danced a clumsy Highland Fling: a chubby girl twirling in the new Black Watch tartan kilt Mother had chosen for me.

My parents said they'd moved to Evanston so my three older brothers and I would be exposed to many kinds of people. While in our neighborhood, those were limited to a professor from India, a Greek diner proprietor, and a family from exotic-to-me Mississippi, I was still fascinated by their cultures. In junior high school Spanish, I glimpsed a world of warmer expression than my Anglo-Saxon heritage. I started collecting stamps (and beaux) from around the world: doing my part for international diplomacy by dating guys from Turkey, Sweden, Germany, France, and Persia.

Indiana University brought even more expanse on the international front. My Brazilian suite mate introduced me to *real* coffee (plus samba and bossa nova: a delightful departure from "The Age of Aquarius as Arranged for High School Marching Band"). Then my South African French teacher introduced me not only to his friends from Iraq, but his American boyfriend, who became my best bud. Don was a multi-lingual word nerd like me. We played Scrabble scrambling every language we even faintly knew.

I graduated with a degree in French (because France makes sexy, smart movies *and* they had what we didn't have in the Midwest in 1980: croissants with dark chocolate melted inside). I also managed to eke out a double major in Arabic. For that one, I blame the movie *The Wind and The Lion*. Sean Connery as a desert chieftain riding across the sand dunes of Morocco on an Arabian horse—who doesn't want some of *that*?

But I struggled to learn Arabic. Many of my classes were in a tiny boardroom with no windows and everyone smoking nonstop except me. I was often the only woman and only non-Arabic-speaker (Arabic 101 is taken by some grad students like English 101 is taken by some athletes: for the proverbial easy A). The written language is the language of the Qur'an, the Islamic holy book, but spoken dialects vary wildly from that—and also country by country (and each of my instructors was from a different country). The State Department declares that it takes over two thousand hours to learn Arabic (while French needs only a paltry six hundred). I told my parents I was considering dropping Arabic. The all-nighters at the library were killing me. I'd still have a degree in French, I reasoned. My normally gentle dad said, "No, Margaret. You will not give up. You have one final semester to go—you're so close. *Illegitimi Non Carborundum*." He told me that was Latin for "Don't let the bastards get you down." As it turns out, it's made-up Latin, but it worked; I earned my degree and gained a conversation starter (as long as the conversation included, "I studied Arabic at Indiana University," or the super-not-useful, "My office is across from the petroleum minister's office"). I did not quit.

Once I graduated, I moved back in with my parents, working at the local bank down the street. Having successfully shepherded four kids through college and into productive adulthood, my mom was a lot more relaxed around me by 1980 than she'd been during my growing-up years. As we sat at our round family table, she smoked and listened intently as I pondered, "Maybe I should get an international MBA? And definitely, *definitely*, I want to *travel*."

After just a few weeks of these dinners, I got it: my mom wanted to know me—as an adult. I wanted to know her, too, but does anyone at twenty-one know her own mother? I started to ask her about things that mattered to her: studying English in college, Studs Terkel, her intellectual mother, and her business-savvy dad. She and I sang folk songs around the piano and chuckled together over the cartoons in the *New Yorker*. I liked this version of my mother; she was *so* different. I could feel her making an effort, so I made an effort, too. We were skittish, still foreign to one another, but trying to learn each other.

After several months at home, she told me, "Missie, get out into the world. It's your dream. You can always come home. Now go!"

She was right. The National Bank of North Evanston could not hold me. I converted my teenage waitressing and recent bank-tellering money into American Express traveler's cheques, and off I flew to Europe in 1981. I intended to stay for a year on a budget I'd set for myself of five dollars a day.

I loved every country I visited on my Eurail train pass, but most of all Italy. I learned Italian. I fell in love with a handsome Roman boy (OK, so that's how I learned Italian).

To save my precious dwindling funds, I spent the summer as

an *au pair* in exchange for free room and board and the Italian lira equivalent of fifty dollars a month. I worked six days a week from before dawn until late at night. I was all right with that, but shocked by how dismissive *la signora* was of her other employees—and how she seldom spoke to her own children unless she was showing them off to her friends once they were dressed in designer baby clothes. When she insisted on my sitting at the dining room table to teach the kids English—while the other staff ate in the basement—I should have said, "No. This doesn't work for me. I'll help you find another girl to take my place," but I didn't. I had made a commitment, and I felt that it was my duty to see that through.

One day, as *la signora* stretched out on a chaise longue on the terrace, sunning her long legs as I mopped the tile floor around her, she said, "Your Roman boy is not right for you."

I bristled. She knew nothing of him, except that he didn't come from what she would have considered "the right class of people." But I knew him and his warm, welcoming, wonderful family. I should have given back the pittance of a salary, leaving her a scathing note that humans should treat humans better. But that wasn't even a possibility in my mind. Even though my heart whimpered, "Quit!" I did not quit.

At summer's end, I stayed on in Rome. After spending Christmas alone, missing everyone back home, I realized that—even though I was crazy about the Roman boy—it wasn't going to work for me to live so far from the States forever. Crying so hard I thought I'd never stop crying, I flew back to Chicago, threw myself into work and into new relationships, playing out the same pattern prescribed by The Handbook: Once committed, I could not be clawed away from keeping my commitment.

What echoed in my head was, *Make it work. Keep it up. Just Do It, Margaret.*

Years went by with me doggedly staying in relationship after relationship, even after it became abundantly clear each time that they weren't leading to happiness—for anyone.

Finally, when I hit thirty, Amy, my friend since junior high, took me aside after too much wine at La Crêperie in Chicago and barked at me, "Marghi! Read this!"

She thrust a slender paperback book at me, *Creative Visualization* by Shakti Gawain, the drawing on the cover depicting women in some sort of tribal attire.

"Thanks, Ame, but that's a little too New Age for me. Besides: I'm good." Some of the least true words I've uttered (often) in my life.

Amy glowered at me. "No, you're not good. And your friends are all sick of watching you being whittled away to a shadow of yourself. I am losing you, and I'm not gonna let that happen. All I ask of you, Marghi, is that you try the Pink Bubble exercise in this book."

I was touched by her ferocity, told her *OK*, and gave her a long hug.

Once home, I read the instructions to place inside a pink bubble of my imagining whatever my heart desired. On a piece of paper, I wrote, "I want a partner who is kind, funny, smart, and affectionate. Someone who loves his family and friends—and will love mine." Shyly, I added, "Someone who will love *me*."

Suddenly, I felt overwhelmingly anxious. Was I asking too much? Then I realized that I hadn't written, "Must own yacht, multiple polo ponies, and at least one helicopter." The things I'd written were true for the people I felt closest to.

Emboldened then, I added, "Ideally, loves classical music and foreign languages." I paused. "Must love the world and *must* love to travel."

I held that book and that piece of paper to my heart. I called Amy to thank her for taking a stand for me—for helping me believe that a man like that was out there for me.

And, on Halloween 1991, I met Patrick. He was transferred from Swissôtel Bangkok to Swissôtel Chicago as its new #2: the hotel manager. On his first day, he made the rounds to meet the hundreds of staff in the hotel, including me. On his second day, I stopped by his office to invite him to lunch. I didn't mention that it was a Pity Lunch—inspired by my knowing how lonely it can be far from home—but I wasn't interested in romance. I was in the throes of separating from a man I'd once loved very much. It was over and we both knew it, but we hadn't yet untangled our life together.

The place I splashed out on for Patrick's Pity Lunch? Four Dollar All You Can Eat Chop Suey in the underground mall next to our hotel. As we ate gravy-sloshed food with splintery wooden chopsticks, Patrick and I shared about our family and friends. When he was listening to me, his big blue eyes never wavered. Then we talked excitedly about classical music. Foreign languages. The world. Travel!

I felt a shiver: *My Pink Bubble*!

Once we'd walked back to the Swissôtel together and parted with a handshake, I called Kimetha, my other oldest friend. We'd known each other since we were sixteen. She'd vetted every boy I'd ever dated—and comforted me through every heartbreak.

"Kimmie, I just had lunch with this guy. He's handsome, and he's the nicest man I've ever met."

Kimetha, my wise owl of a friend just said, "Hmmm."

I called my mom, too, babbling, "I have a new colleague. A Swiss guy. We went to lunch today. He's funny and smart and has lived around the world."

I heard her suppress a chuckle. "Well, your new Swiss *colleague* sounds intriguing, Missie. Keep me posted."

Patrick and I went out a lot in November and December, but always with a gaggle of colleagues around us. At an outing to an ice rink, he skated enthusiastically with every woman. At the holiday party, the slender Swissman line-danced with everyone, grinning the whole time. Around the hotel, he worked nonstop and was kind to every person he encountered.

The only thing that annoyed me about him was his speaking more languages than I did. As foreign language proficiency had always been one of my unique selling points, I felt seriously out-classed by his repertoire: Swiss German, German, French, Italian, some Thai and Spanish, not to mention perfect and slightly UK-accented English. But it was fun to converse and joke with him in Italian and French—and I had the honor of teaching him his first words in Pig Latin.

By January, Patrick was surviving his first winter in Chicago pretty well for a guy who'd just spent years living in the tropics. One day, though, a sniffly cold laid him low. I called my mom.

"You know my Swiss colleague? He wasn't feeling well today, so I took some chicken soup up to him, to his suite inside the hotel."

"Just curious, Missie," my mom said. "Do you take soup to *all* your colleagues?"

"Just this one, smarty pants," I replied. I could almost hear my mom's smile down the telephone wire.

In February 1992, Patrick asked me, "Is there *any* chance that we could ever go out—just the two of us?"

"Yes, please," I said with a smile.

We met after work for drinks. That evening was followed by meals and movies, symphony and opera. We had our first kiss on the dance floor of a smoky piano bar.

The only blow to my growing attraction to Patrick came when we met for a long lakeside walk on an especially bitter-cold Chicago day. When I saw him, I thought, *Oh-oh. Who wears black polyester fake fur ear protectors?* But my next thought was, *Keep those ears warm so I can whisper in them: "I'm falling in love with you."*

I introduced him to my friends over dinners, my parents over coffee in their home in Evanston, my brothers over burgers and tater tots at Meier's Tavern. Patrick charmed them all by listening hard and asking questions, and giving them big hugs when they weren't expecting them. Everyone loved Patrick on sight. And everyone loved seeing me relaxed and happy.

In springtime, he and I took a trip to Florida. We both knew we needed to travel well together in order to make this work. When our travels unfolded differently than we'd imagined—with delays and lost luggage—I was delighted that Patrick was flexible in the face of *Planes, Trains and Automobiles*. He took glitches and snafus on the road in stride—a wonderful change from some past travel partners. We had fun together, and it felt easy being together. *Oh, I thought, so this is what people mean when they say you just know when it's right.*

Patrick's parents visited us in Chicago and met my parents; he took me to Switzerland to meet the rest of his family. He taught me my first words in Swiss German: "*I ha Di gaern, mi Schatz.*" "I love you, my treasure."

Back in Chicago one early summer weekend, we rented a car to drive to the Indiana Dunes, running screaming with laughter down those steep sand hills, then lying in each other's arms on the sand, with the waves of Lake Michigan shushing onto the shore nearby. We talked about the big issues couples talk about before marriage and— by the time we drove back to Chicago—it was clear that something between us had been decided.

Patrick phoned me in my cubicle the next day asking, "May I invite you to the roof of the hotel after work?"

After mumbling a nervous *OK*, I hung up the phone and straight away called Kimetha.

"Kimmie," I gasped, "I think Patrick's going to ask me to marry him!"

She laughed out loud. "Hang up the phone and go say yes! You're in love with him! Bye!"

At five, I took the elevator to the top of the hotel, my heart pounding. I pushed open the door to the roof and walked on a red carpet that Patrick had stretched to the roof's edge. Grant Park was spread out forty-two stories below, and all of Chicago was glowing in early evening light around us. Patrick was standing beside a small table with champagne chilling in a bucket. Handing me a tiny paper box—onto which he'd pasted photos of a Thai Airways plane and purple Thai orchids—he asked, "Would you like to go to Thailand to pick out a ring with me?"

"Yes! Yes! Yes! I wouldn't just like that, Patrick—I'd love that."

We kissed, then he popped open the bubbly, pouring out two flutes' worth. We drank to our luck in having found one another, then dashed downstairs to phone his parents in Switzerland, waking them up with our news.

The next morning at six, I phoned my parents. "We're coming out to Evanston to see you; we'll be there in forty minutes."

Once the taxi dropped us off, my parents met us at the front door and ushered us into the living room, where cups of fresh coffee awaited. My parents sat in the paisley wing chairs; I sat on the velvet love seat next to Patrick, who turned to my parents and said, "Onnie, Dick: I'd like your blessing to marry your daughter."

My mother said, "Of course!" with a smile. She'd known long before I did that this was the man for me.

My father, relishing his last opportunity to play the protective patriarch said, "Not so fast, Patrick. Are you a wealthy man?"

"Um, no, Dick. I'm not."

"Are you going to be a wealthy man, Patrick?"

"Probably not in the hotel business, Dick."

My father sighed, dramatically. "Well, then, Patrick, here's the deal: Margaret's grand, but I think you can do better. Have you considered the Morton Salt Girl? *Everybody* needs salt!" That was my dad's unique way—with a twinkle in his eye—of giving Patrick his blessing to marry me.

I gave an exasperated sigh, "Daaaaad!" and we all hugged and kissed goodbye and Patrick and I headed back to the city in our waiting taxi.

We married at the Swissôtel on a brilliantly cold Chicago day in January 1993, fourteen months after we'd met. Friends and family gathered on the top floor of the hotel, just under the roof where Patrick had proposed. In the "green room" before the service, Kimetha helped me rehearse the vows that Patrick and I had written and memorized. When I panicked that I'd forgotten one, she acted out "I promise to grow alongside you" by spreading her arms wide like a bounteous oak tree. She was wearing the burgundy velvet dress I'd recently worn as her maid of honor; I was in the cream satin-and-lace wedding gown she'd worn as a bride.

As the harpist played "Save the Best for Last," I took Dad's arm to walk up the aisle whispering, "Dad, I'm really nervous!"

He patted my hand. "You should be nervous, honey; this is a big deal. But Patrick is a good man. I'm happy for you both."

Kimetha and my brother Peter were our witnesses. My brother Charlie ushered our guests to their seats, holding his young daughter, our niece Katie, in his arms. His wife, Mary Ellen, was pregnant with our niece-yet-to-arrive, Meghan.

Amy read "Love is patient; love is kind" from Corinthians, and my brother Hal read excerpts from Walt Whitman's "Song of the Open Road."

Allons! whoever you are come travel with me!

I swear to you there are divine things more beautiful than
words can tell...

However shelter'd this port and however calm these waters
we must not anchor here...

Camerado, I give you my hand!

I give you my love more precious than money,

Will you give me yourself? Will you come travel with me?

Shall we stick by each other as long as we live?

The harpist softly strummed Bach's "Jesu, Joy of Man's Desiring" and the folk song "Simple Gifts." Patrick and I remembered our vows after all: not only to grow alongside one another, but also to tenderly care for one another. We said to each other, "Of all the people in the world, I choose you."

Once pronounced husband and wife by the judge, we kissed.

And—to my eternal regret—I rushed away from my beloved to spend most of our wedding reception skittering around, making sure our guests were happy.

It wasn't just the usual whirl of accepting congratulations, smiling ceaselessly for photos, trying desperately to find a moment to eat just a bite of the Swiss food we'd chosen—or more than a mouthful of our wedding-cake tiramisu.

Even at my own wedding, I was "always putting others first."

So, now, in 2000: after seven years of marriage—and five years since Patrick left Swissôtel to join Four Seasons Hotels—it's on to our next adventure: life overseas together!

At JFK airport, the driver unloads our possessions into the middle of the departures lobby. We drag our suitcases and carry-ons and cat carriers to the check-in counter, two-by-two, as though we're booked on Noah's Ark. Once onboard, with the cats in their cases safely under our seats and holding Patrick's hand, I slump with exhaustion. Over the past few weeks, I've handed over my Ritz-Carlton accounts to colleagues, shipped huge boxes of files back to my boss, and donated the cheap office furniture I won't need anymore. I've served on jury duty in Chinatown, walking all the way home to the Upper East Side, trying to memorize each Manhattan neighborhood.

Patrick and I've bought one last bunch of tulips at our corner bodega. We've sat alfresco at Mediterraneo Café to sip cappuccinos; we hardly ever missed a Saturday afternoon there. At the diner up the block from our (tiny, noisy, excruciatingly expensive) apartment, we've devoured one final Sunday morning 2-2-2: two eggs sunny side up, two strips of crispy bacon, two pancakes with too much butter and maple syrup.

Now, New York is behind—and below—us as our plane climbs into the air.

Eight hours, a mediocre movie, and some fitful sleep later, we land at Charles de Gaulle International Airport. A shiny black hotel van awaits us there, too, and we are driven to our home for the summer: Four Seasons Hotel George V, an Art Deco *grande dame* on the Right Bank—between the Champs Elysées and the River Seine. I've stayed in Paris with Patrick, with my parents, with exes, and alone. But I've never stayed here in any place this majestic.

The general manager, another Frenchman, is at the door to greet us. Patrick's here as his temporary assistant, as there are delays with the Egypt project. This is the perfect place for Four Seasons to "park" Patrick for three months. The GM kisses me on each cheek, warmly but formally. "*Bienvenue, Mar-gah-rette.*" He turns to shake Patrick's hand. "Welcome, *Pah-treeck.* I'll see you in my office in one hour," he says, and he strides away.

I'm used to 24/7 in the hotel business; that's the nature of the beast. Plus Patrick was raised by a father who will go into the office of the family business every day until the end of his life, just as his own father did. That being said, I would really have appreciated just one day to be together with Patrick in this new chapter. *But we're here for work, not a holiday, and I'm not here to jeopardize Patrick's career,* I think. So I just smile. A very tight smile.

The front office manager leads us through the lobby, past stunning seven-foot-tall floral arrangements and up in the elevator to an apartment within the hotel. The living room furniture and heavy curtains are upholstered in a satin of pale gold. The bedroom is flooded with sunshine through enormous windows. It's all right out of *Elle Décor* magazine. There's even a kitchenette with a fridge, oven, and stove top, although we can call room service, which is another perk of "living in." "Yes," I've responded to friends when they've asked. "We'll be able to order up a banana split in the middle of the night if we want!"

Our luggage is delivered; we shake the manager's hand, thanking him for his welcome; we release Nadia and BooBoo from their carry cases. The staff has thoughtfully provided ceramic water and food bowls in the kitchenette next to a rubber squeaky toy: a French poodle! There's a fresh, new kitty litter box in the bathroom. The cats don't even sniff their new loot, slinking under the bed to hide instead, but already I'm anxious about what they'll do to these dreamy, creamy furnishings. Once they emerge, I'm sure that they'll gleefully claw the sofa and armchairs into a contemporary art installation. I'll need to find something to cover this furniture, but first I put water and kibble in the bowls then unpack our valuables and place them in the safe.

Patrick, meanwhile, showers and shaves and emerges from the bedroom fresh and bright-eyed in his navy double-breasted suit. He says, "I'm really sorry, but I have to go, *chérie*." (I love it when my Euro-husband calls me that!)

"I know that, Patrick," I say as brightly as I can. I also know that, soon enough, we'll move to Egypt and he'll be a general manager for real. He's not calling the shots, yet, on how he spends his time. "I wish you a great start, *amore mio*. I'll see you tonight. I'll save a place for you in bed."

He protests, "I'll be home well before bedtime, Margaret! I'll see you for dinner!"

I nod, but this is not my first rodeo. I know from seven years married to a hotelier that the GM will want to go over "just one more thing" with Patrick, and then another. I'll save a place for Patrick in bed.

I get it! Work comes first. I don't expect him to say no to his boss. I'm grateful that he's hard-working: I'm hard-working, too! *And, come on, Margaret, it's not a tragedy. You're in an apartment inside one of the most luxurious hotels in the world. You have nothing to complain about! How lucky are you?* I quickly squelch the twinge of resentment I feel at not even getting one afternoon to enjoy this iconic city together before my husband is back at the grindstone.

Once Patrick has kissed me *au revoir* and the door has closed behind him, I take a long shower, too. Then, in a fluffy white hotel bathrobe and slippers, I unpack everything I carefully packed up in New York. To make my hyper-organized Swiss man happy—and because now that I'm not working I have the time—I do what Patrick does first whenever we check into a hotel: I arrange his shirts by color in the tall white-painted wood armoire. In a dresser drawer, I line up cufflinks next to carefully folded neckties. After I've hung up my own dressiest items, I crawl into the king bed, pull the cloud of white duvet over my head, and fall into a jet-lagged nap.

At 8:00 p.m., Patrick does come back to our apartment, gently awakening me and inviting me to dinner. I couldn't be more surprised and delighted as I slip on my little black dress, pull a lacy black shawl over my bare shoulders, and slide on the dangling gold earrings my parents bought me in Italy. After I've brushed out my hair and put on blush and eyeliner, I link my arm through Patrick's for added balance on my heels and because I'm just so happy to be with him. We walk the long, carpeted hallway, lined with prints of pastoral French scenes, and down the grand staircase to the entrance of the hotel's restaurant, *Le Cinq*.

In the foyer, glass vases hold masses of red roses in front of an antique tapestry. Inside the hushed, dark restaurant, candles glow on each table, reflected by tall mirrors framed in burnished gold. After we've been seated by the maître d', I ask Patrick to tell me about his afternoon. He says, "The hotel is magnificent, and I'm excited to be a part of this re-opening." I'm nodding and smiling: my husband lives for this stuff. Then he adds, "There are challenges, though. It's going to mean long hours for me, *chérie*." I flinch. Does he *really* feel the need to remind of this? *I get it, Patrick.*

When he asks me about my afternoon, I describe all I've done to settle him in. He reaches over to take my hand. "Thank you. I really appreciate your help. You're wonderful."

And there it is: ahhh. I can feel relief flood through my veins as surely as the first glass of wine.

See! I tell the voice of self-doubt inside me. I may not be working for a separate paycheck anymore, but Patrick has reassured me that his salary is our salary and I'm already doing something important here in Paris. I can relax now and enjoy this Michelin-worthy meal with my husband, knowing that if I take care of someone I love, they will love me in return, and everything's just fine.

After dinner, we stagger upstairs, full of Camembert and Cabernet, my arm again looped through Patrick's. While we dined, Nadia and BooBoo emerged from hiding but luckily haven't ravaged anything yet. Instead, they've claimed what they consider their rightful place in the middle of our bed. We collapse around them and sleep.

We're up early the next day to breakfast on buttery croissants and espresso together in the lobby café. I'm careful to dress up in one of my new white linen blouses, my darkest jeans, and patent leather flats. When Patrick heads to the office at eight, I return to the apartment upstairs to change into black walking shoes.

Suddenly, I feel shy and unmoored. I'm used to having a pile of work awaiting me every morning: client voice mails to return, emails to answer, and faxed contracts to review. There was always business to book and a sales quota to surpass. Now I've got total freedom and no direction, and I feel like I'm floating, untethered. I take a deep breath and say to myself, "Margaret, it's Day One of your time in Paris and your new life as a writer. Let's get out there!"

I stride down the hallway and the marble stairs, past the doormen, and out onto Avenue George V. I'm carrying the brand-new turquoise-blue journal I bought in Manhattan once we knew we were moving. My goal today is to find and claim a café near the hotel to be my home-away-from-home for the summer. I'm going to drink *café au lait* and write and write, and—before you know it—my book will be published by Scribner's, the publisher of both Hemingway and Fitzgerald! Well, the publisher doesn't matter. My book does.

I have a vivid picture of the cover in my mind: a map, a journal, and Margaret Davis Ghielmetti in a bold yet elegant typeface. As for the plot, that's a little fuzzy. I don't have a clear idea of the characters, either. Yet. But I'm confident I can churn out a novel in three months in Paris. My teachers always told me I was a skillful writer. And I've always loved to write; I'd written that whole "novel" by the time I was ten! This is my chance to do what I've always dreamt of—and to get it right.

I walk towards the Seine River and stop at the first café I see, sitting outside at a small wicker table under a poplar tree, tucking my sensible walking shoes under my wicker chair. The server approaches and I order, "*Un café crème, s'il vous plaît.*"

He repeats my order in English, "Coffee wiz cream."

The color rises in my cheeks. I didn't expect to be taken for a *Parisienne*, but I was hoping to seem as little *Americaine* as possible. I have a degree in French! But I just say, "*Oui, merci,*" and he walks away.

While I'm waiting for my coffee, I place my journal on the table in front of me, open it to page one and write Paris 2000 with a flourish. *Voilà!*

Then I sit, back straight but not rigid, hoping to look as if I'm simply relaxing in the sunshine filtering through the leaves, while actually I'm feeling flustered and self-conscious. I'm sure that every other woman in the café—each one chic and lean and high-heeled—has noticed my shoes and is appalled and offended on behalf of the very essence of French style. There's no way I can write, imagining their tut-tutting. I gulp down the coffee when it arrives and fumble to pay my bill, agonizing over what to tip. Too much signals tourist but stingy feels wrong, so I leave a few coins, even though the server's done nothing to endear himself to me. I stand and walk away toward the Champs-Elysées, hearing my mother's regal voice, "When in doubt, hold your head up high." I lift up my chin with what I hope looks like confident nonchalance.

I'll write tomorrow.

For now, it's off to Le Bon Marché department store to find something to protect the hotel's furniture from kitty claws. I buy four inexpensive cotton tablecloths in a blue and white Provençal pattern and I feel happy, just looking at the cheerful fabric. Then I buy a picnic lunch for myself at the Monoprix grocery store—cheese, olives, a baby baguette, and some unsalted butter—and return to the hotel by noon. I wrap the tablecloths around the furniture then listen to the voicemail Patrick has left me: "*Ciao, chérie,* how's it going?"

He's not in his office when I call back, so I leave him a voicemail saying, "*Ciao, amore mio.* I'm fine!" I do feel fine: I've done the right thing by the hotel's furniture and I've already found a café to make my own, whether that server likes it or not.

After my picnic, I sit at the antique desk in the living room and compose a chatty email home to family and friends. They've begged me to keep them posted on this new venture, so I describe the hotel, our neighborhood, and Paris's perfect balance of masculine and feminine: linear façades in warm beige limestone; black wrought iron railings in curlicues; countless flower boxes. I christen this my inaugural "Trip Report." That's something written! This is just the latest in a string of words that started with childhood poems in a little white diary with a tiny gold key.

After I've sent my Trip Report, I curl up in an ample armchair—the afternoon sun streaming in through the windows—and page through Proust with a snoozing cat on either side of me. The summer sky stays bright until after eight, when it softens to lavender at "*l'heure bleue.*" Patrick's already told me he won't be home for dinner tonight so, in this blue hour, I order soup and salad from room service. I eat while trying to decipher the French news on the television until Patrick gets home to regale me with details of another busy day and we snuggle to sleep.

When I check my email the next day after breakfast, there are already responses in my inbox. "You have room to spare inside your Four Seasons apartment? Sweeeet! When can I come visit?"

I type back, "Any time! Patrick and I would *love* to have you." And, with that invitation extended, our first house guests start booking their flights to Paris.

I decide to skip Mon Café. I'm too excited about friends coming. It'll be fun showing them around my Paris. It's back to the Bon Marché department store, this time to buy blue ceramic espresso cups to match my new tablecloths. When I phone Patrick in his office, telling him about the impending visits, he's pleased. When I tell him about my purchases he says, "That's great, Margaret, but keep in mind that you can just phone housekeeping, and they'll happily bring you anything you need."

"I know, Patrick," I say. "But I'm feathering our nest!"

I do realize that I could have borrowed tablecloths, and that our kitchenette does already have cups, but they're not the perfect blue. Our luxury nest is already *bee-yoo-tifully* feathered. It does *not* need my feathering, but I can't help myself. My surroundings are important to me. I learned from my mother's example: she always chose the perfect frame for every picture and was a master at assembling pleasing-to-the-eye placements of objets d'art. I'm creating beauty. I love to do that and I'm good at that, too.

I have a right to be good at something while Patrick is soaring in his career.

That evening, after another long working day for Patrick, room service brings us dinner: grilled chicken, steamed asparagus, and an apple *galette* tart for dessert. I tell Patrick, "I went to the market after we talked. I bought little plants in terracotta pots and put them out on the windowsill. You know I love to make an elegant home for us."

He says, "I do know that, *chérie*, and you do a fantastic job at it and—again—I thank you. Just don't forget: your journal? Your book?"

I feel my face flush. "Yes!" I say. "I'll start writing. Soon!"

"I'm glad," he says, and I know that he *is* glad. But he's not going to *force* me to choose my writing over making his life easier and his surroundings more pleasant. *Who would choose that?*

He's worked hard to get us to this place. It's my pleasure to let him shine for now.

I'll bask in his reflected glory, and then I'll create my own glorious story. Just not yet.

In the days following in Paris, I make us breakfast in our little kitchenette. I water and tend the plants, hoping to coax buds into blossoms. Afterwards, I get out to Mon Café, where the server still insists on speaking English to me, but gets a little less frosty with each visit. Mostly I go in the mornings, but if I'm busy with my Trip Reports or responding to emails and only get there by midday, I order a *Salade Niçoise* with a glass (or two) of rosé wine.

Each day I've arrived at the café determined to work on my novel, but I've ended up writing postcards to my family and Patrick's family and our friends around the world. I carefully choose a different image for each recipient, specific to them, showing everyone that I haven't forgotten them. Really, I don't want them to forget *me*. I'm the Perfect Correspondent to stave off the dreaded "out of sight; out of mind."

After two weeks of postcards—and only sporadically jotting down bare bones ideas for my novel—I am overjoyed when our first house guest arrives: my fellow bookworm and history geek—my dad! I meet him at the Paris airport, running up to hug him, even though he's not much of a hugger. "*Bienvenu, Papà!* Welcome!" I'm suddenly aware that he looks his age—seventy-seven—and tired from the flight from Chicago. I wrestle his small brown suitcase out of his hand, saying, "I'm so happy that you're here!"

He smiles his gentle smile and says, "I'm happy to be here, too, Mouse."

Dad has called me that since I was a little girl, when he would read to me at bedtime from the book *The Rescuers*. All the characters are mice, and I loved both Miss Bianca—plump with shining white fur, wearing a silver chain necklace (gold on Sundays)—and swash-buckling Nils in boots and a striped stocking cap.

I still love being my Dad's Mouse. Even at forty years old.

Dad looks at me, his brown eyes magnified behind thick tor-toise-shell glasses. "Now, Mouse, let me say this: I know Patrick's busy with his work, and you have your writing to do. I'm comfortable exploring Paris on my own and meeting you two for dinner."

"I know that, Dad," I say, "but I'm spending this week with you! Of course I am. You're my darling *Papà!*"

"OK," he says, smiling, his obligatory parental lecture-duty done. He does add, "I wish your mother were feeling well enough to be here with us."

"Me, too, *Papà*." And I *am* crushed that Mother wasn't up to the trip. My parents had visited me in Italy on my year abroad in 1981 and had surprised us all by falling as deeply in love with that coun-try as I had. We took several trips there together over several years during my twenties—and their fifties—leaving chores and WASPy roles and rules behind. The photos from those trips are all smiles. Dad—in his tweed blazer and khakis, his camera bag slung across his chest—took pictures of architecture and scenery and was the driver and historian. I was the translator and navigator. Mother—in her tan trench coat, her brown leather Coach bag around her wrist—marveled at everything and made friends with everyone we met, in her quiet, ladylike way.

Italy gave my parents and me the gift of time over endless meals and long country drives to learn each other better. Plus we gained first words for them in Italian (*ciao* and *arrivederci*) and new terms of endearment for me (mostly now I call them *Mammà* and *Papà*—the accent gently on the second syllable).

Then, almost a decade ago, at the end of one more Italian sojourn together, my mother stumbled on a cobblestone in Pisa, falling hard to the ground, sprawling in front of a crowd of tourists, struggling to smooth her navy wool skirt back over her stockinged legs. For one moment, time stood still as I stood over her. In her big brown eyes, I saw pain and fear. And, suddenly, it was so clear: *She'll always be my mother. I'll always be her daughter. But I'm not just her child any more.* Everything changed in that moment. I saw that she was just a mortal, like me.

I bent close to her face. "*Mammà!* Are you OK?"

An older Italian man rushed over to help us.

"Tell him not to move me, Missie!"

"I'll tell him."

"And then, Margaret, don't forget to thank him for his kindness."

I took a deep breath. "Mother, please! For God's sake, of course I'll thank him! You raised me to be a lady and a Davis!"

My mom never recovered her strength after that accident. Once tall and slender, she's now shrunken from osteoporosis and the pain of vertebrae probably broken in that fall. Her bright sense of wonder is not extinguished, but dimmed. I'm grateful for what we shared on all those trips, but I'm heartbroken, too, that Mother can no longer join Dad and me on these adventures.

I know she's sad, too, but I'm sure she's told my dad, "Go!" She's been sending me off into the world with that word forever: when I went to college, to Europe, to life overseas. She's never once held me back.

She knows that travelers need to travel.

Like painters need to paint.

And writers . . . need to . . . writers should be . . . writers . . .

Oh, shit, I think, panicky. *I'm not writing my book. At all.* I rush to say, "*Papà*, let's just have fun while you're here. I'll get back to my work soon. Patrick and I have a couple of months in Paris. For now, let's enjoy, OK?"

"OK," Dad says, because we do love being together. Being with him is like being with a super-smart Dr. Seuss. We make up limericks—and sing songs from *Winnie the Pooh*. When inspired, he's given to quoting epic literature, raising one index finger to quiet the clamoring crowd (me). "From Shelley's 'Ozymandias,'" he begins. "'I met a traveler from an ancient land.'" Dad should've been a college professor, imparting his knowledge to students. Instead, he suited up and showed up to work Monday through Friday in an office in downtown Chicago, making a living as a salesman for his wife and four hungry kids, taking the train home at six for a Scotch (or two) followed by dinner at six-thirty.

Dad spent Saturday mornings in a faded olive-green sweatshirt and tan corduroys. He dragged soggy oak leaves from the gutters with his cracked suede work gloves while I held the ladder for him. I helped him rake leaves, piling them up and burning them in a fragrant bonfire. I can still smell that smoke and feel the pleasure of just hanging out with Dad. I always loved being with him, but—even as a kid—I could feel the weight of his disappointment in never having

been promoted to top dog in his office. When he felt blue, I jumped
to brighten his day.

He was tops to me, especially because he let me be who I was: a
little girl who wanted to be *Harriet the Spy* with her journal, and to
do what her big brothers did as Boy Scouts—climb monkey bridges
between trees or compete in Pinewood Derby car races.

And I wanted to play football! In my mind, I was Bart Starr, famed
quarterback for our family's team—the Green Bay Packers. Saturday
afternoons, after chores, Dad and my brothers and I would head to
the schoolyard next to our house. When our team was huddled up,
Dad would draw the play on the palm of his hand. My heart would
leap when he'd turn to me. "Mouse, you're the receiver this time. Run
out five feet then turn around. It's the classic Button Hook Play. I'll
get you the ball." Once I'd caught his gentle pass, I clutched the football with both arms and ran as fast as I could toward the end zone.
Sometimes I even scored a touchdown and glowed with pleasure.

Dad let me be a tomboy. And he let me be a kid—which was very
welcome in a household where Mother expected my brothers and me
to act like adults even as children. Every weekday afternoon when
I got home from school and walked in the back door to our house,
Mother was at the Formica kitchen counter, getting meat, potatoes,
and a vegetable ready for dinner for the six of us. She had a little
streak of silver in her dark brown hair, and a cigarette always close
at hand.

"How was school, Missie?"

"Good. I got a star on my spelling test."

She'd turn to me to nod, then turn back to preparing pork chops
or chicken livers, saying, "Don't forget your homework." It was full
steam ahead for my mother every day: running a household, raising
four kids, volunteering, working part-time.

Dinner at our round family table was lively with adult conversation, even when I was seven, and my brothers eleven, fifteen, and

seventeen. The expectation was for each of us kids to participate; to be smart, but not a smart-ass; to be clever, but not too clever; to hold our own, but to never, ever disagree with Mother, who—when contradicted—would state, simply, "You're wrong."

If I wasn't as appropriate and genteel as she expected a young lady (and a Davis) to be, she'd say, "I'm disappointed in you, Margaret." Oooh, that was her big gun. I knew on some level that she was in fact angry. But a lady (and a Davis) doesn't show anger. Instead, the temperature in the room would drop below zero in the time it took her to raise and lower one dark eyebrow. I felt, then, like the Cowardly Lion running down the Wizard of Oz's hallway to jump out the window—anything to get away.

At dinner one night, when my brother Charlie tickled me under the table, I laughed so hard that Borden's milk spurted from my nose. For my friends, the punishment from their parents would have been, "Go to your room." For me, the punishment was not being allowed to help with the washing up after dinner. I had to sit in the corner of the dining room as my brothers joked in the kitchen and whipped each other's butts with rolled up dish towels. I was frozen out.

Even hints of laziness or self-pity were not acceptable from my brothers and me, nor from our dad. The romantic love that's so clear in my parents' wedding photos was long behind them. I watched my mom turn away from my dad's increasing sadness, abdicating that part of the role of supportive spouse. When Mother would bark at Dad for reading the paper on Sunday morning—instead of always-more-chores—I felt my heart straining toward his. "We'll do the chores together, Dad. It'll be fun." That cheered him up a little, and, as long as I could cheer him up, he stayed present. Very young, I perfected the art of peacemaker and people-pleaser. I learned to calibrate precisely, pivoting between them, changing like a genius chameleon to keep Mother not-cold and Dad not-sad. I was always ready to abandon myself so that no one else could abandon me first. Busy and productive. Appropriate and genteel. Cheerful and engaging. All of these kept me safe.

So now, in Paris, in 2000, I want to make Dad happy as I always have, but—also—being with him is so fun for me. We check out more esoteric sights than the usual tourist fare: the tomb of Napoléon, the Canal Saint-Martin on a leisurely barge trip, the Basilica of Saint-Denis, final resting place of sixty-six French kings and queens.

Our Father-Daughter Geek Week feels over in a flash. It's time for Dad to head back to Evanston. He puts his hands on my shoulders and fixes me again with his brown eyes. "Get to your writing now, Mouse. Your mother and I are expecting a copy of your book very soon, inscribed 'To My Marvelous Parents, without whom none of this would be possible.'"

I laugh and hug him one more time. "I promise, *Papà*. I'll get to Mon Café and to my book soon. I'll go this afternoon!" I help him into a taxi on Avenue George V and lean in to say, "Bye bye, *Papà*. Give my love to Mother."

My parents had often said they were sure I knew they loved me, adding, "We don't need to say it." But now, when my dad pats me on the head, saying, *"Au revoir, ma petite* Mouse," I know that's his way of saying it.

Once the taxi pulls away, I suddenly feel terribly alone. Dad's leaving means that I have truly cast off from shore, from home. I remind myself fiercely of the Mark Twain quote I've had taped on my computer forever: "Twenty years from now you will be more disappointed by the things that you didn't do than by the ones you did do. So throw off the bowlines. Sail away from the safe harbor. Catch the trade winds in your sails. Explore. Dream. Discover."

When I feel tears hot on my cheeks, I hiss to myself, "Set sail, Margaret!"

I wipe my face, run up to our apartment in the hotel and grab my journal. I'm snarling "Just Do It!" to myself as I stomp down the street to Mon Café. I get in a full afternoon of writing. Or at least it was scribbling a few pages of passionate commitment to my novel. But what's my novel about? I still don't know. I'm just writing "The journey of a thousand miles begins with the first page"—buying myself a little more time by honoring the ancient philosophers—when it hits me: *I have to go! Our next house guest arrives tomorrow, and I forgot to buy flowers for her!*

Brenda and I spend the first hour after her arrival laughing and catching up. Then we have dinner with Patrick, who treats us to *foie gras* and champagne. Brenda sighs, "I have died and gone to heaven!"

But, after that evening, each morning of her week with us, she spends what seems—to me—like an inordinately long time getting ready. As I'm chomping at the bit to get out and show her Paris, Brenda drawls, "Honey, I gotta fix my hair. Otherwise, I just don't feel dressed for the day." I've never in my life done anything except tuck freshly-shampooed hair behind my ears to dry, but I have to admit that Brenda looks stunning. And, once we're out and exploring, she's enthusiastic about the Louvre's tiny "Mona Lisa," our *Bateaux Mouches* river cruise, Notre-Dame's fierce gargoyles of Hunchback fame—and we both enjoy admiring handsome Frenchmen in well-cut suits.

Mid-way through her week with us, we rent a car and drive three hours northwest of Paris to Normandy. We stand on the cliff overlooking Omaha Beach, where our troops landed during World War II. At the American Cemetery, we gawk and walk between nine thousand graves in perfectly straight rows across perfectly green grass. Visitors are bent over white crosses and Stars of David to read the inscriptions to loved ones lost. I'm feeling very moved—and I can see that my friend is, too.

I'm also very anxious to see one more national treasure while we're in this corner of France. I whisper, "Hey, Brenda, remember how I mentioned that we'd be just twenty minutes from the famous Bayeux Tapestry here? It's nine hundred years old and 230 feet long! OK with you if we leave now to swing by? I want to get there before the museum closes."

"Oh, girl!" she says. "I'm sorry, but I'm ready to check in at that petite country inn you booked for us. I need a glass of wine. This has been a *day*."

It takes me a minute to ask again, "Brenda, please? The museum is so close. How about this? I'll just run in, if you'd rather wait in a café. Drinks are on me!" It occurs to me that I'd really love some wine myself, but I don't feel I can stop for even one second.

Brenda says, "Oh, no, darlin'. I'm all done in. I need a bath before dinner! Then my hair . . ."

Again with the hair? I think. *We're just minutes away from one of the supreme achievements of French art. I'm fairly sure she's not gonna die from not having a bath and a refreshed coif within the next sixty minutes.*

But instead of insisting on visiting this artistic miracle, I say, "I understand, Brenda. This day took a lot out of both of us. You know I want this to be the best possible trip you could ever have."

She thanks me as we head towards our country inn. And—even though I'm the one driving the rental car and could just turn the steering wheel to the museum—I'd never do that. I feel a *whoosh* of relief from avoiding conflict, and a *ping* of happiness from doing everything in my power to make someone else happy. It's not a choice. It feels inevitable. Irresistible.

The next morning, Brenda kindly suggests that we could stop by the museum on the way out of town, and—even though that would be an easy solution—I'm determined. "No," I say. "Must get back to Paris." As the Perfect Guide, I have activities planned for us, so that's what we're doing. *No gray areas for me.*

Brenda leaves on a Sunday. On Monday, I spend the afternoon at Mon Café, scrambling for inspiration, scribbling down dialogue I hear from the table next to mine, which I translate from French. "Oh, La Boss is a bitch. And—get this! She's sleeping with her assistant." Is *that* the inspiration I've been waiting for? Should I build my novel around a corporate bigwig and her sexy male assistant, Jean-Louis? *Confound it, Margaret! A bodice-ripper isn't what we're aspiring to here. Come on, think!* I try to brainstorm brainier ideas. Nothing sticks, but at least at last I'm a little bit in the process and I still have almost two months in Paris.

This is a relief, because I have no time to write the next day. There are more flowers to buy for new guests arriving: *Bonjour!* After we spend a few days or a week together: *Au revoir!*

Yes, each visitor suggests that I take time to write, which I decline with a rigid smile, saying, "I *promise* you I will get back to that. Now, *please*, let me show you my Paris. Don't worry about me!" I feel my brain scrolling through The Davis Family Handbook for guidance to land with a sigh on "Always Put Others First."

So: after almost three months in the City of Light, what do I have to show for it? Delightful memories of time with Patrick in the rare moments when he wasn't working, doing simple things we love: strolling boulevards and back streets; buying fragrant fruit and stinky cheese at markets so picturesque they make me want to learn to cook just so I have an excuse to come by every day; picnicking and people-watching in parks; the pleasure of sharing with our visitors, and pride in being the Perfect Hostess.

Also, though: guilt for "the opportunity of a lifetime" squandered. Writing a book is much harder work than I realized, and it actually needs my sitting down to do it. Instead of writing like Virginia Woolf, I have distracted myself like her Mrs. Dalloway, always buying the flowers.

Then, when there are just ten days to go—before we depart from

Paris to Patrick's new assignment in Egypt—we get one more call. It's not a close friend or a relative, but an acquaintance in the US. She chirps, "Hi, Margaret! OK with Patrick and you if I pop over for a quick visit? I could be there this weekend! It's always been my biggest wish to visit Paris just once in my life. Your being there makes that possible for me."

I get this call late in the evening. I'm alone in the apartment, a cat on either side of me in the bed. Patrick's still in the office, or maybe he's entertaining clients? I've lost track after almost a bottle of Cabernet. I clench my teeth, saying, "We're just about to *leave* Paris. I wish you'd called earlier this summer; there was a whole *week* when we didn't have houseguests. If you'd asked to come then, *of course* I would've said yes! I would've loved to make your wish come true!" I'm just saying "I'm sorry" when she hangs up without another word.

Instead of feeling anger at her abruptness, I feel awful. I should've told her that this is my final chance: ten days to make up for lost time as a writer. I swear to God, I will fill up my journal!

Which I don't do. I can't. Because, as of the next day, I'm spending hours getting the cats to the vet for their shots and their feline passports; packing up my new espresso cups; giving away those terra cotta pots and the plants, which never did bloom.

Now we're leaving Paris with only twenty pages scribbled in my turquoise-blue journal—nothing Scribner's is going to publish.

I've tried my best to put everyone else first. I want to make their dreams come true.

But what about my life? My dreams? What about me?

CAIRO

I feel hopeful of a new start in Egypt.

Patrick and I visited Cairo in spring 2000 for his final job interview. I waited for him in our room in the Semiramis Hotel, wearing a modest gray knee-length dress, in case Patrick had phoned to say the owner wanted to meet me, too.

After an hour of me fidgeting and no call from Patrick, he returned to our room with a huge smile on his face. "It's done, *chérie*! It's happening. I'm going to be the opening general manager for Four Seasons Resort Sharm el Sheikh. We'll get to live in a new place together again!"

One of the first things I'd fallen in love with in Patrick was that his desire to see the world matched mine. I'd read about a "wanderlust gene," and I'm quite sure we were both born with that. We already had a travel bucket list a mile long. I would've been happy just ticking off a vacation destination a year for the rest of our lives.

Patrick, though, has been an expatriate since his mid-twenties and he loves "living inside another culture."

Well, I'd vowed to "grow alongside" Patrick at our wedding, so I'd moved to New York and Paris with him, and now our move to Egypt was becoming a reality. After hugs and kisses, I looked into his blue eyes and said, "Congratulations, *amore mio*, on making this dream a reality."

He beamed and said, "Let's go explore!"

We'd changed out of our business clothes to hop on the American Express tour, "Highlights of Cairo," topped off with us grinning from ear to ear as we rode camels in front of the Pyramids and the Sphinx. Everywhere we went, Egyptians of all ages called out, "Hellooo!" and we called back, "*Salaam Aleikum!*" "Peace be upon you!" We felt very welcome as travelers.

Now, in autumn 2000, arriving at Cairo International Airport with bags and cats, it feels different than when we'd visited in spring. In the excitement of our previous visit, I hadn't noticed the crunch of dust under my shoes even inside the terminal, or the crush of people waiting at passport control—some in suits and some in long gray, blue or black robes. Once we find a rickety metal cart for our luggage, I stop for a moment to catch my breath before we head outside the airport into the blinding Cairo sunlight.

A driver is waiting for us from the Hilton Residence, which will be our temporary home while we search for a rental apartment for ourselves in this city of eighteen million people. The driver loads our bags into the back of the hotel van, then drives us into the city, which is choked with the traffic of diesel-fume-spewing buses, the occasional donkey cart, and pedestrians weaving in and out of traffic—as any sidewalk is cracked and crumbling. The Hilton Residence is along the Nile, but far downriver from the major sites and not within walking distance of anything but endless concrete buildings. The front desk clerk checks us in and helps us take our luggage upstairs.

Once inside the apartment, Patrick and I let the cats out of their carry cases and walk out onto the balcony, overlooking the muddy brown Nile. He puts his arm around me, saying, "We're here, *chérie*. We made it."

I give him a smile, but I'm quite sure the next thing out of his mouth is going to be that he needs to get to work, so I beat him to the punch. "I'll get things organized so you're ready for your first day on the job, Patrick."

He squirms, saying, "Just a reminder, Margaret: I'm not going into the office tomorrow. I have to go on a sales trip to Europe to promote the resort. I fly out first thing in the morning. I'm pretty sure I told you about that, right?"

"Yes, Patrick, you told me." But I'm thinking, *Jesus. Once again, we don't even get twenty-four hours together in a new place.*

"I'm sorry," he adds, "I know that it's rather soon after our arrival."

"Really, Patrick? Rather soon? I don't think it could be any sooner." My tone is brittle and Patrick looks at me, hurt.

"Margaret, you know I couldn't have gotten to this place without your support, right?"

Ahhh, that feels good. But not good enough to hold me in the moment. I disengage from his arm around me and stomp off the balcony back into the apartment to unpack.

First out of my bag are cat dishes and food. Just like in Paris, I pour out kibble and open a sealed bottle of water for Nadia and BooBoo. Then I carefully unwrap my Parisian demitasse cups and place them on a chipped wooden shelf in the basic kitchen. *There: that's already better.* What will help me feel *even* better is smoothing things over with Patrick. I can't bear the thought of being in conflict with anyone, and certainly not with him.

I walk into the bedroom, where he's laying suits, shirts, and ties in a garment bag for his trip.

"*Amore*," I say. "I'm sorry that I snapped at you. I'm just tired from the trip. How about if we stop unpacking and go find groceries?"

Patrick is visibly grateful for the olive branch I'm extending—and anxious to do anything to help me feel at home. So, even though I'm sure he'd love to finish what he's doing, he agrees. "Would you make me your world-famous pasta, *chérie*?" he asks, smiling.

"I'll be happy to, *amore mio*," I say, smiling back.

On the ground floor, we ask the front desk clerk to direct us to the nearest supermarket. "Sir, *Madaam*," he says, "I am proud to tell you a mini-market has just opened in the shopping mall next door."

That sounds encouraging, but when Patrick and I pick our way through honking traffic across the dusty street and enter the mall, it's nothing like I'm expecting. There are empty glass store fronts alternating with shops selling cheap souvenir camels and miniature plastic pyramids. When we finally find the mini-mart, it has no cheese, no fruit, and exactly three tomatoes as the full selection of vegetables. I pounce on those, plus a box of spaghetti and a tin of olive oil. At least I hope it's olive oil. My college Arabic is long-faded. "My office is across from the petroleum minister's office" is no help here.

I grab a box of corn flakes and a carton of milk, plus coffee, as I've seen an old-fashioned espresso maker on the shelves of the kitchen.

The Egypt guidebook I've been reading advises that produce should be sanitized in a solution of water and bleach, so I also buy bleach.

Back in the Hilton Residence lobby, Patrick spies a solitary book wedged between the bent-edged postcards on the front desk. It's *Gone with the Wind*, which he buys for me saying, "To keep you company while I'm gone." The cover depicts the movie poster with Clark Gable hungrily bending over Vivien Leigh's porcelain face and I feel a pang of homesickness. We just got here: I didn't think I'd want the familiar so soon.

As Patrick continues his unpacking and re-packing, I wash the three tomatoes in a solution of bleach-and-water, then set them in a pan of boiling water for good measure: I'm taking no chances on us getting sick. In my mind, I imagine blanching them so their skins will simply slip off, like my mother used to do for ladies luncheon salads (served with chicken salad and placed on an iceberg lettuce leaf). Instead, when I ladle the tomatoes out, their skins are blistered off and the resulting flesh is a soupy, bleach-skunked mush. I put my hands on the kitchen counter and cry silently for a minute, frustrated that I can't even seem to prepare such a simple dish. I'm frustrated that Patrick's leaving me so soon and especially frustrated that it doesn't seem fair of me to feel frustrated: *I knew what I was saying yes to in coming here. Didn't I?*

I wipe my tears, call out, "Dinner's ready!" and serve the tomato remains to Patrick on top of olive oil and spaghetti. At least I've managed to cook that al dente. Patrick diplomatically pronounces the whole thing delicious, and I burst into tears again. He stands, comes behind me, and puts his arms around me.

I whimper, "We have no fruit, no cheese, and who knows what vegetables might be available tomorrow." What I'm really thinking but don't say is, *And my husband is leaving me alone in this remote residence hotel after what—a day?*

Patrick squeezes me and I let him, but when I don't squeeze back, he sits down again and we eat in silence. After we've finished, he ventures, tentatively, "Are you OK, *chérie?*" I assure him that I'm fine.

I'm not fine and he knows it, but I can hear my mother's voice, "You chose this together, now see it through," and the Davis Family Handbook is wide open with "Don't air your dirty laundry in public" having become twisted into not even sharing myself fully with my husband, a man who loves me and whom I've loved for seven years. Instead, we wash up the few dishes, brush our teeth with bottled water, and climb into bed. Patrick puts his arms around me and I sleep, a little.

I wake up the next morning resolved to re-group. Over corn flakes, I say in as bright a voice as I can muster, "I wish you a successful trip, my brand-new general manager husband! I'm so proud of you." It's a new day and I won't question his leaving; he has a job to do. That's why we moved to Egypt. I walk Patrick to the elevator on our floor, handing him his computer bag. "Bon voyage, *amore mio.* I love you."

He kisses me and says, "I love you, too, *chérie*, very much. I'll call you once I arrive in Europe." He rolls his garment bag into the elevator, and he's gone.

When I close the front door behind me, I suddenly feel exhausted from the move and too tired to even imagine looking for my turquoise journal. Instead, I flop onto the sofa with my thousand pages of Scarlett O'Hara and Rhett Butler. At noon, I call room service and they bring up a plate of hummus and falafel. I read again after lunch, stopping only to order a bottle of wine midafternoon: a local red called Omar Khayyam, its poetic name masking its nasty sourness. I drink that while I finish off the pile of pita bread that came with lunch, slowly sinking into a dull sleep.

For dinner, I force myself to leave our apartment, walking timidly onto the Hilton's Nile-side terrace restaurant and ordering mixed vegetables ("boiled") rice ("plain") kebab ("well done") and another bottle of wine, another local red called Obelisk. It's as unpleasant as the Omar Khayyam, but also as effective at quieting my buzzing brain—and my guilty missing of the luxury of Paris and the George V. I stare out at the spectacular orange evening sky and think, *Well, at least the dust and pollution make for a spectacular sunset.*

Patrick phones after dinner to check in, telling me his trip was easy, and he has good news: "The company has assigned us a car and driver as of tomorrow. You can ask to go anywhere you want!" It is good news, as I'll be finished with Tara and the Civil War sooner rather than later, and I am determined to continue rebooting my brave spirit and exploring more of Cairo as the Perfect Expat. I am committed to being completely settled in within one week maximum.

When I go downstairs the next morning, a battered four-door Peugeot is parked in front of the Hilton. The driver at the wheel is a hulking middle-aged man in a rumpled white shirt and gray slacks who only looks up when I open the front passenger-side door. When I slide shyly into the seat next to his, he looks appalled and points to the back seat. I stay in the front seat: I don't want to appear rude—having him drive me around as though he were the, um, driver. I murmur, "*Salaam Aleikum.*" Peace be upon you.

He responds with glaring greetings in return, "*Wa Aleikum as-Salaam.*"

I add, "Egyptian Museum, please."

After these few words between us, he lights up a cigarette, I cough politely, and it's a drive of smoke-filled silence to the center of Cairo.

Inside the museum, though, I'm thrilled as I gape at mummies, scarabs, and statues of slim, muscular pharaohs. I'm transported to childhood visits to the University of Chicago's Oriental Institute and the book on mummies my parents bought me. My inner culture vulture trembles with pleasure, and I forget my frustrations. *The world is an amazing place,* I think. *Behold its treasures!* I am restored to my explorer's delight.

When I exit the museum, the driver is leaning on the car, smoking, with cigarette butts on the ground around him. He pointedly opens the back door for me. It's clear that *Madaam* will no longer ride next to the driver in the front. Back at the Hilton, I mumble, "*Ma'ah salaama,*" to him: goodbye; go in peace. His cigarette is clenched between his smoke-stained teeth, but he manages to say the same to me, gruffly. I get out of the car and walk into the Hilton, go up to our apartment, and collapse onto the sofa between the sleeping cats for a long afternoon nap.

After I repeat last night's dinner on the terrace, Patrick phones, complaining, "Making sales calls all day is hard!"

My tongue is slow with the wine, which keeps me from barking at him that I'm well aware of that . . . I used to do that for a living . . . and count yourself lucky that you're not making calls in high heels.

Instead, I mumble, "OK, best of luck tomorrow, *amore mio*, g'night," before falling into a boozy sleep.

After cereal, coffee, and two aspirin the next morning, I shower, dress, and take the elevator downstairs. The driver is there, and today, I head directly to the back seat of the Peugeot. He doesn't smile at my choice, but appears less agitated than the day before. I ask him to take me to a museum I've read about in my guidebook. There, I pore over illustrated manuscripts with pages adorned with falconers and horses and sigh over a collection of painted tiles in every shade of blue. The tiles in turquoise remind me uneasily of my journal, languishing still in my carry-on.

On our nightly phone call, Patrick describes his business day, then asks, "How are you, *chérie*?"

In a tipsy voice, I reply, "Fine, *amore mio*." I describe my day, but I'm stumbling over the words.

Patrick asks me, "Are you really all right?"

I force my brain to focus. "Yes. Really. Patrick. Thanks for calling. Good night." And I fall into bed.

On the third morning with the driver, I ask him to take me to a hotel I've read about in my guidebook: the nineteenth-century Marriott Gezirah, with lush gardens and a shady terrace where tourists and expatriates sit hiding from the hundred-degree heat. Once I'm seated, I feel ambushed by how seductive this peaceful oasis feels: I'm away from the driver's cigarette smoke and his attitude and the feeling that I don't know what I'm doing—even though I was sure I knew what I was doing just days ago when we got on the plane to come here.

How have I slumped already from courageous sailor dog Scuppers into just a limp Trailing Spouse? I'd used that term in a joking way before our move, but already I feel like I'm trailing behind Patrick. And now even my trusted guidebook turns against me as I read "Try not to spend every minute at the Marriott with all the other expats."

I feel a surge of shame for lollygagging around. *For heaven's sake,* I remind myself sharply, *I am multi-lingual, multi-cultural, optimistic, open-minded. I am brave and have been my whole life.*

I'm the girl who punched out the grade school bully when he backed me into a corner (my brother Charlie had taught me how to jab with my right).

I started the girls' soccer team in high school when girls didn't yet play soccer in Evanston—and defended my teammates from too-rough opponents with a Mafia Enforcer growl, "Back the hell off, or I'll take care of you."

When my makeup bag got stolen out of the youth hostel in Paris on one of my first backpacker nights in Europe, I phoned my mom long-distance, spending ten dollars (a fortune to a backpacker) just to hear her voice. "Mother! They stole my kit bag, with my makeup and everything. They stole my *tweezers!*"

"Well, Missie, think of it this way," she'd responded after a pause. "You're traveling lighter now."

Our family had perfected the stoic art of enduring hardship without complaint over generations. I assumed what she'd say next was, "Crying never helps"—a perennial favorite of hers and a subsidiary clause from The Handbook's "Don't air your dirty laundry in public."

Instead, she'd added, gently, "You're going to be just fine, Missie. I know you: you're strong. I don't want you giving up on your dream. I don't want to clip your wings, and I don't want you to clip your own wings, either."

After we'd hung up, I'd marched over to Paris's biggest department store, bought blush, eyeliner, a shiny new pair of *French* tweezers, and I'd stayed in Europe, traveling for months—more confident with every new country. I'd slept on the beach on Corfu and on a train station bench when the youth hostel was full. In cheap hotels, I'd tied up my waist-length brown hair at night so that any critters lurking under the beds wouldn't mistake me for their Rapunzel.

I did not run away then; I will not run away now.

I pay my bill at the Marriott Gezirah, find the driver, and tell him I'm going to wander the neighborhood a bit. There's a boutique selling locally handmade scarves, and I buy one in olive green to match my eyes. Tomorrow I'll visit a mosque or another museum or I don't know what. Something. Anything. I'm strong and I'm brave. I just need to buck up.

Once the driver takes me back to the Hilton Residence, I open my email. Our closest family and friends have been writing to tell me they're thrilled for me that I'm fulfilling my lifelong travel dream.

A former colleague, though, snarks, "You *still* don't have to work? Patrick's a dreamboat, and you are living the dream. Bet you can't wait to write—when you're not climbing the Pyramids. How lucky are you!"

There it is: "How lucky am I?" I repeat it to myself. This *is* a dream come true. And I'm certain I'll start writing for real—real soon. On our drives through downtown, I've glimpsed Cairo's historic cafés: crumbling old buildings with faded awnings shading terraces from the constant sun. I'm determined to add my volume to the rich literary history here. Lawrence Durrell had set his *Alexandria Quartet* in Egypt, and sometimes I just whisper the lyrical titles—*Justine, Balthazar, Mountolive, Clea*—as I dream of my own.

I find my turquoise journal and scribble some titles. I like the idea of "Voyager" but maybe I should honor Mark Twain with "Throw off the Bowlines" or "Sail Away." I think, *Until I've nailed down my title, it really doesn't make sense to write my book.* I set my journal aside once again.

When Patrick gets back from his first business trip, he bursts through our front door at the Hilton Residence saying, "A colleague tipped me off about an apartment for us, *chérie*. It's just twenty minutes from downtown in a suburb called Ma'adi. Want to come to see?"

Of course I want to come to see! We aren't going to be housed in this residence hotel for very long and I have no idea how to find a rental here, with no classifieds section in the newspaper—or at least not one I can read.

The driver is downstairs. He is overly polite to Patrick while barely managing a greeting to me. Further reading in my guidebook has revealed that traditional Egyptian men may—out of respect—address the man and not the woman, so I determine not to take that personally. He drives us along the Nile, then circles roundabouts with scraggly bushes as their centerpieces, past "faded elegance" mansions, stopping at last next to a Coptic church in front of an Art Deco six-flat painted the soft color of a sand dune.

We're met at the door by a silver-haired man who shakes our hands, introducing himself in British-accented English as a neighbor who's been deputized by the landlady to give us the tour. He shows us around the apartment: the tall windows have dark wooden shutters to shade against the heat, and narrow balconies with wrought-iron railings where I can already picture our cats languidly sleeping in the sun. A master bedroom plus a guest room are just what we need, plus a dining room, a living room, and a vast central "piazza," all floored with cool tiles. The kitchen, hidden in the back, is very simple: intended for a housekeeper, which we won't be hiring.

The neighbor then invites us to his nearby apartment and offers us a glass of local Obelisk red wine. As he pours, he mentions that there's a hardware store on Road Nine, just blocks away, "For you, *Monsieur*." For *Madame*, he mentions the Community Services Association, also just blocks away. "That's where all the foreign ladies gather." Unless, he wonders, we'd like to join the Sporting and Yacht Club, "founded in the 1920s for our British citizens living here." He shows us old black and white photos of this neighborhood when it was in its glory, decades ago. There's one picture of him in bathing trunks at the club's swimming pool, his hair then thick and black.

He leans back in his chair and says that he's sure the landlady would be happy to have "such quality tenants," which I'm squirmingly aware is code for light-skinned people like us. He brandishes the bottle of wine adding with a laugh, "I'll put in a word for you if you promise to share a bottle every once in a while."

Patrick and I look at each other and smile. "Please tell the landlady we'll take the apartment," Patrick says.

In the coming days, Patrick's colleagues help us to jump through complicated banking hoops, decipher the lease, and order some furniture fit for a Four Seasons general manager.

Once we've moved out of the Hilton Residence and into our new apartment, the chain-smoking driver is outside each morning to take Patrick to his "pre-opening" office in downtown Cairo. I can request that the driver come back to Ma'adi to take me to the supermarket along the Nile, which I do every other day. It's comforting to me to keep our fridge stocked, and I'm thrilled that I no longer need to boil three pathetic tomatoes into oblivion. Alfa Market sells many of the foods we like, along with colorful Caspari paper napkins and Italian ceramic dishes—cream with a sage-green border—which I snap up in a delighted frenzy. This store definitely has a finger on the pulse of Trailing Expat Spouses.

On weekdays when I don't feel like asking for the driver, I walk to Road Nine where—next to the hardware store for *Monsieur*—there's Café Greco, with Italy-worthy cappuccino. On weekends, the Coptic church next door to our apartment building erupts with the joyous ululation of women celebrating a wedding. On these days, I'm excited to be here. Early each morning, I read the emails from home that have arrived while we slept. When asked how I'm doing, I write back, "All good!" Every single time.

And I am good. It's just that I'm feeling a little lonely with no one to talk with all day.

The wives of Patrick's expat colleagues in the pre-opening office have children and a focus on family. Patrick's hiring local staff, too, but they have their own lives: family and faith first for them.

Should I talk with the man in a long dirty-white robe who comes to the back door of the apartment looking for payment for having collected our garbage? He writes a number on a scrap of paper: the equivalent of a dollar, which I give him in crumpled Egyptian pound banknotes. When I ask, "Receipt?" he throws back his head, laughing at me, then walks away, muttering. I'm sure he's saying, "Idiotic foreign woman" or some nastier version under his breath. I feel afraid of this looming presence and embarrassed for feeling afraid.

Should I chat with the landlady's housekeeper—who regularly shows up unannounced in our kitchen, having let herself in the back door? And who, one day, walks straight up to me to kiss me on the mouth for no apparent reason. She speaks no English and my Arabic does not extend to, "Is this a local custom I haven't yet uncovered in my reading?" I feel shocked and bewildered.

I try greeting the armed security guards leaning against the front door of the empty villa across the street. Everyone jokes, "Don't worry: they have guns, but no bullets," and they're so young they look like babies to me. But my cheery *"Salaam Aleikum"* gets no response, just stares. I turn my eyes downward after that. I'm reminded of when I was studying Arabic and my fellow students—almost all from the Arab World—teased me that I'd never get my degree. I turned my eyes downward after that, too, studying harder than ever and walking away with a bachelor's degree in Near Eastern languages and literature.

I can't possibly talk with the little boy who drives his donkey cart down our street, laden with the junk he's collected. When I hear the clopping of hooves one afternoon and run to our window to wave at him, he's relieving himself in the street and I don't want to embarrass him by calling out. I feel shame for my life of ease.

Worst of all, as it turns out, is our dash-of-debonair neighbor. One morning, after Patrick's been driven away to work, I hear a knock on our front door. The neighbor's there in tailored wool trousers, a maroon smoking jacket, and a paisley silk ascot. He extends a bottle of the inevitable Obelisk wine toward me, saying, "I thought you might be thirsty in our desert heat. May I come in?" My upbringing compels me to invite him in and I bring out two glasses from the kitchen. Even though it's only midmorning, he pours us each a generous portion of wine then tells me, with a Cheshire Cat grin, "I'm happy for your company."

Suddenly, I feel not just surprised but uncomfortable. I jump up, bumbling something about having to email my parents urgently. "Oh, and I have to get to Alfa Market for groceries, and I'm certain that Patrick will be home early today!" He chuckles: he knows that Patrick's *never* home early. With a slight bow, he leaves.

How is it that I feel resignation—when I know I should feel indignation? Too many times I've felt this in the past. In the 1980s, when the Parisian youth hostel manager asked, "*Voulez-vous coucher avec moi ce soir?*" as I was handing over my passport to him at check-in. I thought, *No, I would not like to sleep with you tonight,* but just shook my head. He switched to English, "You are being an American prude." As though there was something wrong with me.

In the '90s, when men told me during job interviews, "Maybe I'll hire you if you come away with me for the weekend." Or "I'll give you the job in exchange for a kiss." And one interview with an old creep who had a porn magazine open on the coffee table between us. He even had the nerve to say, leering, "I think I can find a position for you."

I didn't know to yell, "Piss off, you slimy bastard!" and walk out.

Not any of these times. I actually just smiled politely: an intelligent young woman being treated like a call girl.

Now, in 2000, in our own Egyptian apartment, once again I feel vulnerable but I don't want to admit it. I think, *Women have endured this forever. This is nothing new. And I won't allow any of this to defeat me as the Perfect Expat.*

When I tell Patrick about the neighbor over dinner that evening, I keep my tone light. He's got enough on his mind with opening a hotel. Patrick responds in a similarly light tone, "I'm glad you're OK, *chérie.*"

I tell myself that I don't want him to worry. Nothing did happen. I can handle myself. But I do feel a prick of anger that he seems not at *all* concerned about his wife alone most days and many nights and he seems awfully ready to accept my nonchalance. I know it's *me* who keeps telling him, "I'm fine," but shouldn't he at least *try* to read my mind? Shouldn't he push past the police tape I use to rope off my feelings—and disbelieve my tired, "Nothin' to see here, folks"?

When I email Amy in Chicago to tell her about the neighbor, she emails back, "Hold on, Marghi: you thought it was a smart idea to invite the wine guy into your apartment?"

"Maybe he's just being neighborly," I respond. "He said he's happy for my company." I'm already reframing my own experience and second-guessing my gut.

With what I know is a sigh, Amy writes back, "Marghi! *Seriously?*" I know she wants to be supportive, but she doesn't get how badly I want—I need—to stay open-minded and culturally sensitive even if that means I have to completely disregard my own instincts. Now I feel foolish—and even more alone.

To be thrown back into extreme loneliness feels like a threatening move backwards in time. As a kid, I'd walked home from school by myself every day, kicking leaves in autumn . . . cloud-gazing in spring . . . ice skating alone on winter afternoons, the pale yellow sun low-slung in the gray Illinois sky. I made up songs to sing quietly—keeping myself company in a minor key: "No real friends. No real anything. La-La-Ru."

I figured out young how to be extra nice to everyone in order to earn affection. As I got older, I stayed in touch with former classmates and boyfriends and colleagues when a more self-assured person would have moved on.

It's all part of an old, old story for me. In fact, when I phone my mom from Ma'adi, confiding in her that I feel blindsided by Patrick working all the time, I'm hoping for understanding. Instead, she says, "Hmm," followed by her trademark pause. "Now what is it that you didn't know about Patrick when you married him?" She has just set the needle down on a well-worn record: the hit song is "Chin Up" and the flip side is "Stiff Upper Lip."

Before we hang up, I revert to my Handbook-scripted lines, telling my mother "I'm grateful for Patrick. I appreciate and respect that his working so hard is supporting both of us."

And I get it, I really do: while he and I are from different countries, we are cut from the same productivity cloth. For now, I understand that he's putting work first.

I just wish—silently—that he wouldn't put me *last*.

I hadn't really minded Patrick's working nonstop when I was working nonstop, too. I knew what it was like to have jobs I'd loved. In my twenties, at the Chicago branch of Italy's government travel office, I'd helped skittish travelers feel confident and excited about a trip they may have saved for their whole lives. "How much does a gondola ride cost in Venice?" "How much should I tip in Florence?" "How do I request an audience with the Pope?" Nothing pleased me more than hearing, "Thanks to you, now I can't wait to travel."

As the only native-English speaker in the office, I was tapped by my bosses to do presentations on tourism. My favorite was speaking in front of a hundred guests at the Chicago Council on Foreign Relations. I flipped through index cards with salient points and ran through carousels of slides. At the end of my talk, I was elated to receive a standing ovation, except for one man, sitting in the first row, who was snoring away. That taught me that you can't please all the people all the time. I loved that job for years, but finally could no longer bear my colleagues berating me, "Don't work so hard! Slow down! You're ruining it for the rest of us!" I was being paid to do a job; they were not following the rules so clearly laid out in The Handbook. *Hadn't they received the same Handbook I had?*

My next job as a sales assistant at Inter-Continental Hotels was a perfect fit: my boss there told me on my first day, "I travel all the time. I'll teach you what I can this week, and then I fly out. Call me if you have questions, but I'm throwing you in the deep end because you're smart and I'm sure you can swim." Boy, did I love that: I got to be efficient and organized, making sure his clients were happy and getting the deals ready for him to close. I used my language and cultural skills with hotels around the world and took advantage of the employee perk to take my parents to Paris. Walking out onto our balcony and seeing their joy at the sight of the Eiffel Tower was one of the most satisfying rewards of that lightly compensated dead-end job. But there was the rub: I needed more money if I was ever going to put aside any savings after paying the rent on my studio apartment.

When jobs that paid more opened up, I took them: sales manager at Swissôtel Chicago, where I'd met Patrick—then national sales manager with the Ritz-Carlton Hotel Company. I loved the slogan, "Ladies and Gentlemen serving Ladies and Gentlemen"—it was exactly in line with how my mother had raised me.

I'd met the boss on the Division Street dance floor after a trade show in Chicago. I definitely knew how to let loose once I had a few shots under my belt, so I imagine she thought she was hiring a fun, outgoing salesperson. What a shock, then, when the company administered the Myers-Briggs assessment to my sales colleagues and me. The facilitator announced the results, saying that almost every salesperson present was an extrovert, recharging their batteries by being with others. Then the facilitator had turned to me. "Only one person on the team is what Myers-Briggs considers an introvert. That's you, Margaret: you re-charge your batteries by being alone."

My colleagues had hooted with laughter, the one next to me saying, "That explains a lot, Margaret. You know we love ya, but you're a freak." Another guy yelled out, "No wonder she's always so *quiet!*" as though quiet were somehow *wrong*. I sat stunned, mute, feebly smiling, feeling once again like the chubby nerd I'd been as a little girl, but also taking in this new information and finally understanding why I felt like such a fish out of water. I felt irritated at how adolescent they were, but I also felt a rush of relief: *So that's why my skin crawls whenever I'm surrounded by caffeine-crazed alphas for too long.*

It helped when my boss's boss advised me, "Since you're different from the other salespeople, do things differently. You don't need to stay at a client cocktail party until the very end. Know that it's enough to make one solid contact and then leave. Save your energy. Re-group. Show up fresh the next day. Be yourself." I almost cried with joy at feeling understood.

It also helped when Four Seasons transferred Patrick from Chicago to New York and Ritz-Carlton allowed me to work "satellite," which was pioneering in the '90s. My desk was wedged into our minuscule bedroom, with faxes churning out at all hours, cluttering my desk by day and dropping onto the floor while we slept. I loved walking Patrick to work each morning, kissing him, then speed-walking in silence around the lagoon in Central Park and back home in time to start my day on Chicago time. I loved not having to interact with people—in person—all the time.

But what had made me a perfect sales assistant did not make me anywhere near to a perfect sales manager. Scrambling like a hamster in a wheel for dribs and drabs of business exhausted me. My bosses tried to help, coaching me on the 80/20 rule: "80 percent of your sales come from the top 20 percent of your clients." But I felt disloyal neglecting my smaller clients, and these little fish told me they booked with me because they trusted me. I was some sort of Honest Abe Lincoln, juggling hundreds of clients and barely making my sales quota each quarter. I overheard someone from the corporate office quote an old adage about motivating sales managers: "Feed the tigers; ride the horses; shoot the dogs." I knew I was no tiger, and I was terrified of being put out to pasture or put out of my misery. But—instead of looking for work that suited me better—I dug in my heels. I'd written inside my copy of *What Color Is Your Parachute,* "I fear that if I don't put myself out there and work hard, I won't be lovable." Instead of leaving, I worked harder.

Mother had always said, "If you want to be a ditch-digger, be the best ditch-digger there is." I always found that confusing: was that job choice actually on offer? But I knew what she meant and—anyway—by the time we'd moved to New York, Patrick was so close to achieving his dream of becoming a GM that I would not quit.

On work evenings, to keep my undesirable introvert hidden, I hit the bars with clients and colleagues, whooping it up. I was the last one to leave any party, which guaranteed me a place on the team. *Alcohol to the rescue!*

On evenings without client functions, I opened a bottle of wine at home, instantly bringing me the quiet I craved. I banished the sadness of no longer doing something I loved. *Alcohol to the rescue—again.*

After a month in Ma'adi in 2001, I can see on Patrick's face that he's anxious about me, but doesn't know what to do. I know my state of mind is not his fault; he doesn't have a gun to my head to keep me from doing what I said I'd do abroad—write the book I've been yammering on about forever.

So when he's home between trips, I can see how grateful he is to say, "The company's offering us a cultural orientation session. It's right nearby at the Community Services Association. Will you come with me, *chérie?*"

This last question is said with a smile. He knows how much I love to be with him—and how much I love to learn. I'm as eager as I was on every first day of school: sharpened No. 2 pencils in hand, hopeful that I'll like the kids in my class. *Maybe one will even like me?*

Patrick takes a day off work, which feels like a miracle. When we step outside the front door of our building, the security guards across the street rouse themselves from their slouch to salute him. This preferential treatment would normally irritate me, but I'm too happy holding my husband's hand as we walk the few blocks to the Community Services Association, the morning sun warming our shoulders.

Inside, we find the meeting room and seat ourselves among the twenty other participants, most with name badges listing oil company affiliations. The smiling tweed-jacketed Egyptian facilitator asks the attendees, "Before we get started, do you have any questions?" Patrick raises his hand, eager to ask how best to successfully do business in Cairo, but the facilitator asks him first, "Sir: may I enquire what country you're from originally?" Patrick responds "Switzerland" and the facilitator shakes his head in mock sorrow. "I'm so sorry for you," he chuckles. "You're going to have a rough time adjusting to our—shall we say—relaxed attitude towards time and getting things done. In fact, sir, you may want to throw your Swiss watch right out the window." The other attendees chuckle.

"Sir," the facilitator continues, "I suggest you start practicing IBM: I for *insha'Allah* meaning if God wills it. B is for *bokra:* tomorrow. M is for *maalesh*, which is essentially never mind. So," he continues, "it will happen maybe tomorrow if God wills it. And—if not—no worries, mate."

Now everyone laughs out loud, including Patrick, but I see a little bit of panic in his eyes. I feel it myself. This will be challenging. I'm used to getting everything done on my own, yesterday, without any help, perfectly, thank you very much. The Family Handbook is shuddering.

The facilitator adds, "Oh, and all of you please keep the following in mind when you ask your taxi driver to turn left and he responds with *insha'Allah*: God willing, I will be able to turn left. As a Westerner, you're thinking, 'Why doesn't the taxi driver just turn the steering wheel?' But for him, this surrender to God's will is an act of faith. Or at least a very strong cultural habit."

The next question the facilitator asks is, "Why did you move to Egypt?"

My hand shoots into the air as it's done since first grade. "My husband and I are here for the experience," I say. "We love travel and languages and learning about new cultures. Expanding our horizons. I have a degree in Arabic, so this is something I've wanted for a long time."

This impassioned teacher's pet speech of mine is met with blank stares from the other couples there. One pot-bellied guy growls, "Yeah, not so much for us. We moved here for the money. Can't wait to get back to God-Bless-America once our contract's up."

Yes, he actually says God-Bless-America just like that. I am shocked and feel a prissy shiver of disdain. But I also think, *Is that what it means to just say what you're feeling?* It's a glimmer of what it would feel like to speak uncensored: dangerous and tempting. *Is that what it means to be not Perfectly Culturally Sensitive?* Is that acceptable? It just feels *wrong.*

When Patrick and I are walking home afterwards, I say, "I'm glad we went, *amore mio*. I'm not sure that I'll be best buds with any of those folks, though."

"No shit, Sherlock," he says, and we both laugh.

"But I did pick up a brochure for classes the center offers. I loved my Gotham Writers courses in New York."

"I remember that, *chérie*," he says and I can see the relief on his face that I may have found something that will interest me—besides sporadic visits to museums and endless emailing home. He adds, "I want you to be happy here, you know?" I know. Maybe taking a class is just what I need.

At home, I page through the course listings. Nothing on writing as it turns out, but—hey, I like anything creative. The next morning, I march back over and sign up for a class in *Bauernmalerei*: rustic German folk art painting. It's fun for the first few classes: learning to paint stylized flowers and birds inspired by wooden chests from the Old Country. When those grow repetitive, I paint a Green Bay Packers plaque in green and gold for my parents. I'm grateful to go once a week: it gets me out of the apartment; I like the walk; I like artists (and would-be artists). Being inside the Community Services Association is like being inside a shelter: not for unwanted pets, but for edgy expatriate women. I'm ashamed to want shelter, but I'm grateful to have it.

One day, I'm just putting my paints away when—out of the corner of my eye—I see a slender brunette in the corridor outside our classroom: someone I know from when we both lived in New York City. She's the Greek-American wife of a colleague of Patrick's. How could I have forgotten that they'd moved to Cairo before us? I call out, "Vivian! Vee!"

She turns on long legs, smiles, strides into the classroom, gives me a hug and says, "Margaret! What a treat to see you! I'm sorry I've been away and haven't phoned to welcome you to Cairo, but I just got back from visiting my parents. Show me what you're doing!"

I hold up the wooden tray I've painted. I've pulled out all the stops with this one: there are pink roses, yellow birds, *and* women in blue peasant dresses.

Vee takes one look at it and says, "Um, pretty, Margaret. Though this is perhaps not the real you, my dear. Let's go talk."

I grab my brushes and tubes of bright paints and wave goodbye to my teacher, who's bent over her own colorful wooden tray.

Vee links her arm in mine, walks me outside and to her apartment nearby, gestures for me to sit on the white sofa in her cool white living room. Sparky, her teacup poodle, jumps up on the sofa next to me. Vee places a glass of white wine and a plate of Hobnob oatmeal cookies in front of me on her glass coffee table. She says, "So, Margaret. Tell me: how're you doing?"

"Thanks, Vee. I'm OK." I take a sip of wine, cool on my tongue, and words start tumbling out of me. "Patrick tells me I'm a big part of his success: that feels satisfying. I'm excited to be learning new things about Egypt—and about painting. I can paint you a tray if you like, Vee. I'd be happy to. I could do something in all white. White roses?" I take a gulp of wine. "I think I'm OK. I'm supposed to be OK. Aren't I supposed to have it all together? My husband's made it to general manager with Four Seasons, and we're in the lap of luxury here, Vivian!"

She moves next to me on the sofa.

"But, Vee, I mean, my old colleague emailed, telling me I'm living the dream. This is the dream, right?"

Vivian flashes her shining brown eyes at me saying, "Sounds like the folks back home have been giving you the old Lady of Leisure nonsense." My eyes sting. "Sure," she continues, "We're proud of our husbands, and we love the company and yes, we live in posh apartments, etc., etc. Don't forget, though, that you've moved around the world. You're thousands of miles from home, friends, and family. Our husbands are away a lot, and they work nonstop. When they're here, they're surrounded by colleague-buddies. But for you and me, Margaret, this life can feel lonely."

And, suddenly, it just bursts out of me, "Vee, I *am* lonely. I thought I would be the Perfect Expat but I don't know what I'm doing. I keep telling everyone back home how much I love the Egyptians and Egypt, and I do—honestly—and I don't want anyone to think less of any other culture in the world, but . . ." and I blurt out about the neighbor and the kissy housekeeper, the garbage man and the security guards, the little boy. "I keep saying, 'These are cultural differences and the world is an amazing place, isn't it?' *But what the hell?*"

She grimaces.

"And, Vee," I yelp. "All the freakin' sand? Our apartment's covered in the stuff. Our cats are *coated* with sand."

Vee places her hand on my shoulder, gently. "Easy there, Margaret."

But I'm just getting *started*. "We went to get our Egyptian driver's licenses last week. The whole time the test-giving guys are only talking to Patrick because, yeah, I know: it's a sign of respect for a man to talk to the husband blah blah blah . . . and then we take the test and they show us traffic signs to identify. Patrick gets a big, red octagon. Duh! They show me, the woman, something like Camels Cross on Thursdays or Oil Drilling Ahead or *whatever* and I could just *tell* that they didn't want a woman to get a license."

Vee's about to say something, but my rant pours out of me.

"And then the parallel parking test? There are a hundred guys hanging around, watching, and Patrick parks well, as he always does. Then they move the traffic cones in *closer* so that I have to parallel park in a *much* smaller space. Can you *believe* that?"

Poor Vee, by now, it's just earful after earful.

"So I think to myself: I'll show you. And I park that fucker like an otter easing into a river. I have never parallel parked so perfectly in such a small space and then what could they say? They *had* to give me my license." I take a breath and add, "Ha!"

Vee laughs and says, "Ha, indeed, Margaret: well done. But, you know what you need? A break from trying to prove yourself. To yourself."

My shoulders slump. I take a bite of cookie. *She's right*, I think. *I'm working so hard to show that I'm brave. To whom?*

Vee adds, "Let's get some fresh air tomorrow morning. I'll drive us out to an oasis in the desert. An artist who works in glass has a studio there with a café. It's peaceful. We'll drink coffee. We'll talk. Maybe we'll buy something pretty for you. I'll pick you up at eight."

It's my turn to nod at Vee.

"And Margaret, answer the door only for me tomorrow. Not for your neighbor and not for the amorous housekeeper, OK?"

I snort with laughter, then bend my head over Sparky, noisily kissing his soft fur and grateful to have a place to hide my tears.

"Margaret, it's all right to cry. Expatriate life ain't for sissies, no matter what people tell you."

I look up at her warm smile. In that moment, I know that I will never, ever forget her kindness. "Thanks, Vee. See you tomorrow." I stand up, setting Sparky down gently on the white tile floor and brushing my tears with the back of my hand. Vee and I kiss on each cheek, and I walk out her door. It feels so comforting to be enfolded in her elegant wings.

When Vee drives us out to the oasis the next morning, the bucolic palm tree setting seems right out of a black-and-white photo of Old Egypt. Over strong coffee, we reminisce about New York. She catches me up on her daughters, and we share about being so far from our aging parents. The glassblower emerges from his studio, and we talk about art with him before I buy turquoise, emerald-green, and sapphire-blue glass vases from his gallery. I am feeling much, much better.

On other days, once Vee has dropped her daughters at school, we hang out, sometimes at Café Greco for their frothy cappuccino, sometimes for excursions. At a sprawling outdoor flea market, she helps me bargain for an Art Deco wall hanging: tendrils of time-burnished metal to enliven our apartment entryway. At the medieval Khan el Khalili bazaar, we turn a corner and come face-to-face with beef carcasses hanging on hooks outside a butcher's shop, untouched by plastic wrap, definitely a first for me. Down the neighboring lane, in a tiny, dark shop, I buy fezzes in burgundy felt to delight my dad and brothers. The old man making the fezzes offers us a place to sit and tiny glasses of sugary mint tea—the epitome of Egyptian hospitality.

With Vee, I discover Cairo's charm and quirk beyond the chaos and decay. I'm happy and relaxed, and I think, *Wait, I don't need to do it all alone?*

All our visits to Cairo's historic center remind me of why I wanted to come to the Middle East in the first place: mosques with arabesques and Arabic script carved into honey-colored stone; the sound of muezzins calling the faithful to prayer five times a day from slender minarets piercing the blue sky across the city.

Back in our cool apartment, I open emails from family and friends: "Cairo sounds fascinating! When can we come visit?"

Exclamation points pepper my responses. "Oh, any time! Patrick and I have a guest room, and we'd love to have you!" I'm excited all over again at the prospect of visitors, of sharing our world with them as the Perfect Tourist Guide. I'd stayed too long in jobs where I couldn't use my talents. Now, I feel re-connected to the passion of work I'd loved. I'll be using my languages and helping others feel confident and excited about traveling.

So, when a stream of family and friends start to arrive in 2001, I scoop them up out of the bustle of the airport, hustling them past the guards in rumpled khaki uniforms. I may still be unnerved by their armed presence, but I don't show that. My energy is dedicated to making sure our guests feel 100 percent comfortable and happy in our new country. They may be overwhelmed at first, but I make sure they are also filled with wonder. I'm back to feeling, *I've got this!* I love these days with people I love.

Before guests arrive, I send them an email outlining suggested itineraries, inoculations, and over-the-counter medications: Pepto-Bismol for a rumbling stomach and Imodium for the next step worse. I tell them to bring lots of tissue packets for the public toilet facilities. I ask them to please buy us the maximum amount of alcohol at the duty-free upon arrival, and I'll pay them back in Egyptian currency they can spend while they're here.

Day One: I settle visitors into our home in Ma'adi in the guest room. I've placed a huge supply of bottled water in their bathroom and woven cotton blankets in sunset hues on their twin beds.

Day Two: I shepherd our guests onto the American Express "Highlights of Cairo" tour. At the Pyramids of Giza, I'm the one negotiating their camel rides, barking *"Ana mish hawaghayya!"* to the camel drivers. "I am not a tourist!" the code for "Don't even try to cheat me," which some of them still do, but not as much as if I didn't know one word of Arabic and the going rate for that bumpy ride. I guide them through the bazaar to buy souvenirs, taking care to avoid the butcher's stall. To counter the shopkeepers' incessant "Where you from, lady?" in multiple languages, I respond with a cool, "Reykjavik" (as no one there can pursue a conversation in Icelandic). Our day is topped off by a cocktail on the terrace of my beloved Marriott Gezirah. I feel like a local, introducing them to this oasis, and—since I'm taking care of our guests and not hiding behind my guidebook alone—I don't feel guilty for being there.

Patrick's parents, Monique and Freddy, arrive, proud of their son and affectionate with me. My brother Pete and his wife Rita manage to tour the whole Egyptian Museum, one gleaming stone statue of

Which-Pharaoh-Is-This at a time, despite Pete's suffering from a rumbling case of Mummy's Tummy. Toronto friends visit the remnants of Jewish Cairo; there's a synagogue just blocks from our home, although it's padlocked shut. Patrick's cousin visits, and it's fun to get to know him better. Kimetha and I attend a Gala Soirée at the American Embassy together, giggling at the men in uniform—just like we giggled our way through high school dances.

When our guests take their jet lag siestas, I transfer notes I've jotted during the day into Trip Reports home to my parents. They won't be able to travel this far. When our guests depart, I feel lonely all over again. That's usually when Patrick suggests a trip to Sharm el Sheikh, six hours' drive south in the Sinai Peninsula. These visits give him the chance to check on the progress of the upcoming Four Seasons there. These visits also give me a distraction from incessantly fretting, *Now that our visitors have left, what am I doing?*

Patrick's team at the start of the project consisted of exactly one person: the director of engineering, who had bulldozers rumbling across the building site—a sandbox of desert on the edge of the Red Sea, which is actually a deep blue-green with endless sun glinting off it. Next, Four Seasons transferred in Patrick's German resort manager—his "second in command"—followed by Italian colleagues to head up the food and beverage and rooms divisions. Egyptians are hand-picked for finance and human resources. Once construction is well underway, with masons laying bricks and landscapers bringing in dozens of mature palm trees to line the new Four Seasons Boulevard, Patrick and his small but mighty team hold mass interviews. Eventually, they hire hundreds of Egyptians to serve in the resort's restaurants, in-room dining, housekeeping, laundry, front desk, concierge, reservations, IT, accounting, human resources, and executive office. Outside contractors are hired for the dive center, spa, gift shop, and landscaping. Acres of grass and endless fuchsia bougainvillea will be planted once construction is completed.

On some visits from Cairo to Sharm, Patrick and I fly on EgyptAir, sipping a plastic cupful of Nescafé powdered coffee (or black tea so anemic it really should be called gray tea). At the end of the hour-long flight, the pilot descends over the undulating reddish-brown Sinai Mountains to land at Sharm el Sheikh International Airport, with the shimmering Red Sea beyond.

On other visits, Patrick drives us himself in the company Peugeot. He loves the driving, which most expats here don't as no one—repeat no one—ever uses the rearview or side mirrors. Right of way is given to the vehicle who can nose ahead of its neighbor and honks most assertively. Honks range from a single "Howdy, neighbor!" to a multiple-honk "Outta my way!" warning. Lane markers are disregarded, as in why not use a three-lane highway to hold at least five lanes of traffic?

Neighboring drivers are so close that I can see the brand of cigarette dangling from their lips, but I never admit that this makes me nervous. I never want to say no to an adventure. Instead I say, "If this is how I die, at least I die happy." I've often felt this way in my travels with Patrick, like the time we rode horses in Mexico and they galloped like the wind, our efforts to rein in our mustangs useless. Only once we'd dismounted did we see that the horses were wearing only *halters*, not bridles: there was no way we could have controlled them with no bits in their mouths. "Since our life didn't end today, Patrick," I'd said, my legs shaking but a broad smile on my face, "it was one of the best days of my life."

Once we're out of Cairo, the drive is peaceful—under the Suez Canal in a tunnel, and across the desert. A few hours into the drive, mountains start to emerge from the sandy ground and wild camels roam near Bedouin encampments. After six hours, we arrive in Sharm el Sheikh, sometimes only by late afternoon but always before sunset. The only thing Patrick won't do is drive at night; some drivers keep their headlights off "to conserve the battery" and "not to bother oncoming traffic."

On these pre-opening visits, we stay at the Hyatt Regency, arriving on a Friday, the first day of the Egyptian weekend. Once Patrick's finished inspecting the Four Seasons site, we snorkel from the Hyatt beach, floating out over the reef. Rainbow-hued parrotfish chomp on the coral with their beaky mouths. Lionfish seduce with fins fluttering in the water (but don't touch: their quills are venomous). Picasso triggerfish dazzle in colors and designs to make Pablo proud. A mini-barracuda slips by, all tiny pointed teeth. Patrick and I beam at each other, our eyes bright behind our snorkel masks. We are never happier than in the water or on it.

We head back to Ma'adi on Saturday afternoon; Patrick begins work again in his office on Sunday morning. We reconnect and recharge on these trips together, and I get fodder for my Trip Reports. But I long for something more. The void of what am I *doing* looms constantly.

Of course, I could be writing my book.

Instead—because it's a value of Patrick's to keep an "open house" and because it's a value of mine that no one feels left out—I suggest that we invite colleagues and home office bigwigs to our apartment in a whirlwind of entertaining each time Patrick is in town. He's happy—and I'm happy because I'm helping build a team. I love being part of a team. We're in this together.

Before these dinner parties, I spend the day tidying up our apartment, being driven to Alfa Market for groceries, chopping vegetables for *Spaghetti alla Primavera*. (My pasta has improved as I've eased up on the bleach.) By late afternoon, I've chilled the white wine I bought earlier at the special store in Ma'adi where alcohol is sold to expatriates upon presentation of our passports. The bottles are pulled from a back room by a sullen salesman and I dread going in there, but a dinner without wine is unthinkable to me. I pour myself a glass as a reward after a long day of preparation.

I've set our table with our cream and sage-green Italian dishes;

candles glow; flowers sprout artfully from my turquoise, emerald-green, and sapphire-blue vases. Lastly, Nadia and BooBoo have been locked inside the master bath; someone's always allergic to cats. Patrick inevitably rushes in at five minutes to seven, gasping, "Sorry I'm not earlier, *chérie!*"

Not earlier? Our guests are just about to arrive! It's like he's the star who just waltzes onto the stage—and into the limelight—at the last minute while I'm holding up an "Applause Now" card.

Patrick tries to kiss me, but my jaw is clenched. He says, "I got tied up on a call!" Or, sometimes, "Traffic was awful!" And, always, "What could I do?" *What you could do,* I think, *is get home on time for a dinner party I've worked all day to prepare—for your professional success!*

But it doesn't feel right to ask for that. I know the pressure he's under. All I can manage is, "Please don't eat the appetizers before the guests arrive, Patrick." This, as his hand is hovering over the hors d'oeuvres I've so carefully plated for our guests. He shoots me a guilty smile and dashes to our bedroom to change out of his blazer and slacks into khakis and a Four Seasons polo shirt. The doorbell rings as he's still brushing his teeth. I hit play on the CD player—Cirque du Soleil's *Alegria* or *Saltimbanco* for an international smooth jazz vibe—then answer the door. All evening long, I do my best to charm everyone. Once our guests are seated in our living room, chattering, wine in hand, I once again know that I am useful. Indispensable, actually.

At our dinner parties, new acquaintances often ask me if we have kids. "No," I reply, "we were not blessed with children." This is the response Patrick and I have developed over the years—instead of going into detail about the heartbreak of infertility back in Chicago.

I had kissed a lot of frogs before I met Patrick in 1991, so I just wanted to enjoy being with the person I wanted to be with for a couple of years—before we started a family. And why not wait? I was absolutely sure that I'd get pregnant exactly when I planned to. I'd already picked out the zodiac signs I wanted for our kids. I'm the Perfect Planner! Baby Number One would appear in 1995, I calculated.

But when I didn't get pregnant once we'd been trying for several months, people teased, "Keep practicing, wink, wink." Instead, for Patrick and me, it became a grim, "Get in the bed—and in the mood—now." This was followed by injections (endless), surgery (unsuccessful), and ultrasounds (weekly) reminding me that I wasn't looking at images of our future family.

I'd gone to visit my mom in Evanston, sobbing, "*Mammà*, I wanted our kids to bake Christmas cookies with you, run through your sprinkler, sit next to you at the piano bench, singing songs together."

She took my hand. I could never before remember her simply holding my hand.

"And, *Mammà*: I'm so sorry that I'm not giving Dad and you grandchildren."

"Missie," she said. "That doesn't matter to us. All we want is for Patrick and you to be happy." Her tenderness was a balm.

But *happy*? I was nowhere *near* happy. I was sad all the time. When I wasn't sad, I was raw and angry. And I felt so alone because it was me going through all those procedures, and because I kept telling people—including Patrick—"I'm OK," while really I was dying inside. The kicker was when the fertility doctor handed me off to his junior partner. I was furious to be made to feel a statistic and a failure, but I didn't succeed in finding the words to tell him that.

It did succeed in helping me decide with Patrick—enough on the procedures. We accepted the Four Seasons move to New York and dove into our careers—keeping busy to keep from thinking about every month feeling like a little death. There was *no* Baby on Board.

That's when new advice started, from acquaintances and strangers: "Just adopt!" Like we could just pick a baby out of a catalogue. And what if the adoption inspector had seen our tiny Manhattan apartment and found out that we might be moving a lot for Patrick's job and told us, "Yes, I have a baby who needs a loving home. But I won't give a baby to *you*!" I felt I would have killed myself. After I'd done I-don't-know-what to the adoption inspector.

I was out of resilience and—not surprisingly—our marriage was in trouble. In desperation, we found a couples' counselor: a white-haired gentlewoman from the Deep South. Diplomas and tribal masks covered the walls of her office. We sat on her gray sofa; she sat in a leather armchair, facing us. Week after week, in her slow drawl, she helped us to see that we were coming at this pain from opposite directions: Patrick had retreated silently into a shell and I was poking at him inside there, begging, "Come out and talk to me!"

Well, that image of a poor turtle husband under attack from his hysterical wife made Patrick and me laugh: our first laughter together in a *long* time. We started to understand each other better and to talk more honestly with each other. We finally decided to stop trying to get pregnant. And I finally knew that our marriage was going to survive.

On a visit from New York to my parents in Evanston, I shared our turtle story with my mom and we laughed together. She and I had the opposite experience about getting pregnant. My parents had been happy having my three older brothers—then I came along. Surprise! But I didn't need my mother to have lived my life. I needed her to say what she said next. "Missie, I'm just so sorry." These are some of the most soothing words in any language.

My mom, who—for years—had only known to spout platitudes like "Just Do It," and "Keep moving forward," was becoming one of the best friends of my life—as she loosened her grip on the very rules and roles she'd raised us with.

Now—in Egypt and far from home—I want to loosen my grip, too, but I feel like all I have is The Family Handbook to hold onto.

When our guests hear that we "were not blessed with children," the sensitive souls simply say they're sorry. Some expat women, though, just can't resist telling me, "Oh, it's easier for you this way, Margaret."

Patrick shoots me a sympathetic look, watching me bite my tongue. I don't say out loud that this wound is still fresh in my heart, and I certainly don't admit that I'm jealous sometimes of the Mommy and Me crowd and whatever the PTA is called at the American School of Cairo. That's where other expat wives meet and make friends, or at least acquaintances. Instead, I respond, "If you say so," as I guide our guests from the living room to the dining room, helping them find their seats by the place cards I've written out in my best calligraphy.

"Margaret, trust me," these idiots continue, "No kids means you can do whatever you want. How lucky are you!"

I'm baffled because I don't quite get what it means to do whatever I want. There are so many things I *have* to do!

They rattle on, "For starters, Patrick tells us you're writing a book," and suddenly the chatter stops, and everyone turns to look at me. "Tell us what you're writing, Margaret!"

I burn with anger at this tenderest part of me suddenly exposed. "Oh, nothing," I say, which is mostly true and makes me feel nauseated with shame. I'm not going to talk about my Trip Reports: writing home to my parents suddenly seems childish. Instead, I turn a bright smile on our guests and ask, "More wine, everyone?" and the conversation moves on. I regain my tight grip on the dinner party and my role of Perfect Hostess. At least I have that. Even if I feel hollow and shallow with people who don't seem to see me.

∾

What a relief it is, then, to reunite with the closest friends we are truly ourselves with. Patrick's best friend Marc phones to say he's coming to visit and suggests that we take a Nile cruise together to visit the ancient temples of Luxor, Karnak, and of the female pharaoh Hatshepsut.

Patrick is thrilled, also because it's just after Coptic Easter, so he can take a few days off of work. Perfect Travel Planner me announces, "Sorry, guys: it'll be impossible for me to find us space during one of the busiest times of the tourist season." Undeterred, Marc simply contacts a travel agent—who books the trip. I'm dismayed that my over-the-top organizing is not needed at all, but I also wonder, *Can I really just show up and board the ship and let someone else do the planning?* As it turns out: yes.

We plant ourselves on the open-air deck as our boat chugs away from downtown Cairo into the Egyptian countryside. We glide by peasant farmers' houses built of earthen brick near the banks of the Nile. The Sahara is just a few kilometers away but, here, the fields are vibrant green along the river.

It turns out to be the holiday of *Sham el-Nessim,* celebrating the beginning of spring. The riverbanks are dotted with farmer families picnicking. The women are dressed in bright red and pink robes. Entire families wave and call out, "Hellooo!"

Once the sun has set, we luxuriate on deck in the soft spring air. After dinner, Marc and I, after too much Egyptian wine, become so loopily philosophical that Patrick excuses himself, saying, "I'm going to bed. Good luck solving the problems of the world."

The following morning, my head hammering and my tongue parched, I droop off the boat to follow our guide, Mahmoud, a short man in an ill-fitting khaki suit, to the first temple of the day. He flourishes his cigarette-stained hand from top to bottom over the hieroglyphics carved into the ancient stone. "Do you recall who committed suicide by the bite of an asp?" he asks, drawing the word *asp* out into at least three syllables. I picture raven-haired Elizabeth Taylor in the movie role and hear the hiss of a snake. Mahmoud then intones in a deep voice, "Kuh-Lee-Oh-PAH-Tra!" Patrick, Marc, and I glance at each other, trying not to laugh.

At the next temple, Mahmoud launches into a highly dramatic re-telling of Isis and Osiris, the mythical siblings who married. "Their evil brother killed Osiris and had his body cut into fourteen pieces." He pauses for us to take in this awful scenario then continues, "Patient Isis was able to recover thirteen of the pieces of her beloved husband. But the fourteenth piece was nowhere to be found!" *Oh-oh,* I'm thinking. Mahmoud, black eyes ablaze, asks us, "What piece do you think was missing?" Patrick and Marc look at each other with mock horror when Mahmoud confirms our fear, "Yes! His genitals!" Mahmoud's tone is more upbeat, though, when he finishes his tale, "The son of Isis and Osiris, brave Horus in the form of a hawk, forms a model of his father's privates. Osiris was made whole again!" At that point Mahmoud walks away from us—triumphant—to smoke another cigarette. Marc and Patrick and I look at each other and crack up at last. We don't get how a hawk could model *cojones* with his claws, but who cares? This is terrific! I love these stories, and I love this time with my husband and with a dear old friend. This is all Pink Bubble stuff and I couldn't be happier.

Almost a year after we've moved to Egypt, I grant myself another fun trip in September 2001: flying to Amsterdam to meet up with Don, my college buddy, who is working at a book fair there. I traveled through Holland before, on my Eurail adventure two decades ago. From the train, I saw the endless fields of tulips in every color and I felt—even at just twenty-one—that I could die happy having seen that beauty: seven million bulbs a-bloom.

Now, on this sunny autumn afternoon, Don has finished his

official book buyer duties, and we're strolling over arched bridges across tranquil green canals, having exhausted ourselves meandering through museums. Our eyes are peeled for the café serving the most tempting cake and coffee we can find: our daily afternoon treat. We need a place where we can dawdle and play our favorite game, "Which painting would you steal to take home with you?" I feel so happy: a Culture Vulture outing with another dear old friend, my molecules jazzed up with art and conversation and the anticipation of caffeine and sugar.

As Don and I turn down a narrow cobblestoned side street, we glimpse a big TV screen through the open door of a bar. A video shows an airplane that almost seems to be flying into a skyscraper. "Ugh," I snort. "Stupid, violent movies. Who'd want to watch such terrible stuff?"

That's when I notice that it's not a movie—it's a newscast—and that plane really *did* fly into a skyscraper. I ask Don, "My God, how did that happen? Pilot heart attack?"

Then that skyscraper and its twin suddenly become *very* recognizable to Don and me. We stare, shocked, as the newscast cuts to scenes in parts of the Arab World: of celebration in the streets there? I feel shock jolt through my body. I'm a knee-jerk liberal with an Arabic degree, living in Cairo—where I may feel foreign, but I definitely feel safe. Isn't this just a terrible mistake?

Don and I hold each other, watching the nightmare loop over and over. The North Tower. The South Tower. Amsterdammers walk by us, busy with their daily lives. They hadn't seen what we'd seen; for them it was just another Tuesday afternoon. Finally, we stumble back to Don's hotel, where he phones his partner Daniel in DC. "Flights are being cancelled all over," Daniel says, "but I'll get you home, Don."

I reach Patrick in Cairo by phone, too. He has our travel agent there scrambling to book me a flight back, but no luck so far. I tell Don, "I want to fly home to America, to New York, to Washington, to

Chicago, to protect everyone I love somehow." Don nods. "But most of all," I say, "I want to be with Patrick. Patrick's my home." He gets it—Daniel is his home, too.

We sit and cry and watch the news. Only when it gets dark do we realize we need to eat something. In a quiet bistro, our young Dutch server is the only person in Amsterdam that day to say, "I'm so sorry for what happened to your country." One woman offering condolences. Are people too shy to speak? Or are they secretly gloating over a self-proclaimed super power's pain? A part of me is wondering how long the rest of the world has been longing to see the United States wounded. I feel baffled and stunned.

Daniel manages to get Don a seat on a flight out, but only on Sunday. Don and I spend four days wandering Amsterdam in a daze, mourning the death and destruction in America.

I'm relieved for them and kiss my friend goodbye as he gets into a taxi to the airport. My airline, though? Patrick tells me, "I'm sorry, *chérie*, we're really trying, but I have no idea when you'll get out." So, I'm stuck in Amsterdam, filling hours in cafés in a numb sort of limbo, waiting to get a flight. I'm desperate for emotional release and—while it feels selfish to do anything even remotely lighthearted—I go to a stand-up comedy club. There are loads of stranded Americans in the audience with me. We drink too much Dutch beer and laugh in high-strung hysteria. It's a relief to be doing anything besides just waiting for the world to end.

After several days, our miracle-working Four Seasons concierge manages to get me a flight back to Patrick. When I arrive at Cairo's airport and am handing over my passport at arrivals, I feel a hostile heat towards me. *Wait, weren't we the ones attacked?* I am face-to-face with the capital-H History of the Middle East and the United States; I'm no longer at a safe distance back in my college Arabic classes or in the suburban bubble where I grew up.

Patrick is waiting for me after baggage claim. "Welcome home, *chérie*. Or welcome back to Egypt, at least." I collapse into his arms, and he holds me for a long time before driving us back to our cool, quiet apartment in Ma'adi. He pours me a tall glass of wine, and we sit together holding hands, not speaking. Neither of us knows what to say or what to do—except get back to the life we're living and the work at hand.

Acquaintances back in the States email, "Pretend you're Canadian!" which I've heard ever since I backpacked across Europe in the 1980s and the US was already out of favor in some countries. Instead, as I return to my daily routine over the coming days, I greet shopkeepers, "*Salaam Aleikum*"—peace be upon you—with as much serenity as I can muster.

They respond with, "*Wa aleikum as-Salaam*."

"*Keif el hal?*" I ask next. How are you? This surprises them, as most tourists never get past the simplest hello.

"*Alhamduli'Allah*," they answer: praise be to God. Then ask me, "*Enti mineen?*" You are from where? "*Europa?*"

"*Amreeka*," I respond, feeling that I may be the only American an Egyptian might meet—that day at least— who can say a few words in their language. It feels so urgent to me to connect.

We receive a bulletin from the US Embassy: Don't make yourself a target: avoid gatherings of US citizens. Followed by: Meet tonight for a safety briefing at the American School. *Don't gather, folks, but come on over to the biggest symbol of the Red, White and Blue for miles around?* At the meeting, a burly middle-aged military man strides up to a podium with swaying palm trees behind him. He Bruce Willis–growls to the hundreds of Americans there, "If we need to evacuate, I will personally find each and every citizen and I will get you out!" I'm sure he means well, but that would be impossible; there are thousands of American expatriates living in Cairo.

One warning from the embassy that I do take to heart is to prepare emergency suitcases so we'll be ready if we actually do need to leave quickly. Into Patrick's and my carry-on bags I stuff our down jackets (in case we're sent to a refugee camp; it's cold in the desert at night); tennis shoes (in case we need to walk long distances, like south across the border to the Sudan); swimsuits (although I'm not certain I can breaststroke to safety all the way across the Mediterranean, and I doubt we'll be swimming to Saudi Arabia).

On a call back to my parents, my dad picks up the phone and says, "Mouse, we're so glad you're reunited with Patrick," then passes the phone to my mom.

"How are you, Missie?" she asks.

With everything that's going on, I need a link to some semblance of normal, so I tell her OK then describe the contents of our emergency suitcases to her, adding, "You know my little black dress, the one that's curvy but not too tight? The one I can sit down in and eat in comfortably? I put that in my emergency suitcase, too. I think I'm losing touch, *Mammà*. I don't know what I'm doing."

My famously calm mother says, "First of all, you keep that dress in your suitcase—you love that dress." Then she adds, gently, "And just keep going, Missie. The world may have gone haywire, but you haven't."

Over the coming weeks, I keep reassuring myself—believing it, too—that the world has always been a dangerous and uncertain place. I just don't know what *my* place is. I never imagined I'd find myself so much a stranger in a strange land, tension crackling around me daily, worrying that my parents were wrong about "People are People are People." What would that mean for everything else I was raised to believe?

What else could The Handbook be wrong about?

Once Patrick and I were finally reunited after 9/11—and it was soon enough "back to business as usual" for him—it hit me how much I hated being separated from him so often. Now, the air around me sizzles with resentment, even though I understand how important his sales trips are with the resort opening approaching. I still don't tell Patrick what I'm feeling: I'm afraid that anything that erupts from me will feel like an ultimatum, "Either you spend more time with me, or I'll . . ."

I'll what? Leave? I don't want that. I want to be with Patrick. *Doesn't he want to be with me?* He tells me yes, but then he takes off again. I turn increasingly to a familiar confidante to soothe me: my ole pal alcohol.

At least it used to be my pal. In my twenties, I did aerobics after work every weekday then sipped exactly one beer with dinner afterwards (plus red plastic glassfuls at raucous parties on the weekend). By thirty, my drinking had inched up—as a long, sad relationship wound down. I plowed my way through heavy jugs of cheap Californian wine.

Once Patrick and I started dating seriously in 1992, he mentioned to me once, shyly, "I don't mean to criticize, Margaret, but I feel like, um, sometimes you drink a little too much." I didn't feel criticized; I was genuinely stunned: I thought how I drank was normal. It certainly wasn't unusual in sales to order up cocktails and wine galore at client dinners. A night cap or a few before bed, of course. Show up the next day at the client's as clear-eyed as possible, Altoids rattling around in my desiccated mouth, smiling, joking, hoping I hadn't done anything too shameful the night before.

After Patrick's comment, though, I started to notice that not everyone drank as hard as I did or was the last one to leave at closing time, but letting loose once in a while sure helped me to let go of, "If you want it done right, do it yourself." Increasingly, though, it was more than just once in a while.

When Patrick and I moved to New York in 1997 and I was

working "satellite" for the Ritz-Carlton Hotel Company's Chicago office out of our bedroom, I'd end each work day at six o'clock. My first stop was our fridge—for that first chilled glass of white wine: *ahhh*. Then a short walk to a nearby liquor store to ensure we had decent red wine for dinner, changing stores frequently so that no one could tell I was drinking a bottle a day. It wasn't always a *whole* bottle; Patrick sometimes drank a glass with dinner.

Once my libations were secured, I'd stop by the grocery store to grab something for dinner. One evening in the check-out line, I eavesdropped on the conversation of the man ahead of me. He was in his thirties, clean-cut, dressed in a Brooks Brothers suit—essentially a male version of saleswoman me.

He said to his buddy next to him, "Now that I don't drink any more, I have the ability to make my actions match my intentions again."

A lightning bolt of recognition coursed through me. He had just described what I was missing each time I drunk-dialed a friend, not remembering our call the next morning. I still successfully managed my obligations by day, but—each evening—I was stomping all over one of the values I hold dearest: genuine connection. And it was getting a little worse every month.

I snuck into the self-help section of Borders near Central Park the next day, buying *Rational Recovery* and every other available book on how to get sober—without actually getting sober. I read them all, highlighting passages and turning down pages. I swore to myself that I'd never again drunk-dial my friends. No more flirting with men on sales trips, either. No more dancing on top of the bar until closing time. But I didn't stop drinking. I told myself it was my elixir—calming me down at the end of another long day as an introvert in an extrovert's world.

Now, though, in Egypt in 2001, I don't have the excuse of Perfect Sales Manager any longer but I crave the relief of the first drink more than ever. That soft layer of fuzziness is like a down comforter smothering the noise and my doubts.

Every afternoon that I'm alone in Ma'adi, with Patrick away, I sip a syrupy white Cinzano or a bitter red Campari before dinner. Or any time after, say, four o'clock, when the sun is low in the sky and another *Long Day's Journey into Night* is looming ahead of me. *Because,* I reason to myself, *I'm a sophisticated woman who lived in Italy and these are sophisticated Italian aperitifs.* I sit quietly on our tiny balcony, the gentle buzz offering me a sense of calm and returning me to my natural appreciation for beauty: *Look at the fiery red blossoms of the flame trees!*

By glass two, I gaze, glazed, at the sunset, my doubts numbed to only the quietest *What am I doing with my life? I didn't sign up for this. Because I didn't know what "this" was.*

One evening, I have almost managed to drown out my endless mental to-do list, but my busy brain struggles its way through the fog to remember just one more thing to do tonight: must find a birthday gift for one of Patrick's colleague's daughters. The booze can't drown out the prick of resentment: *So why am I doing his shopping for him again while he's off in London or Berlin?* Then I remind myself that *I'm* the one who just today volunteered to do the shopping for that little girl. With a sour satisfaction, I add Perfect Present Picker to my mental résumé as I log onto the website of a friend back home who started importing hand-crafted jewelry from Italy.

By the time I log on, I've had the requisite sophisticated Italian cocktail, plus a few glasses of Egyptian wine. OK, so maybe it's more than a few drinks by then, gulped glass by glass by a woman alone in her dusty apartment with her dusty cats. Maybe it's better that I'm alone: I don't need to half-listen to Patrick's telling me about another long, hard day at work while the other half of my mind tabulates how many bottles are left in the kitchen cabinet.

I pour myself one more glass of something. It doesn't matter what it is—anything to silence the voice nagging me: Don't be disloyal to your husband! Remain politically correct and embrace other cultures, even when maybe they hate you! Appreciate the glory of flame trees! Don't embarrass little boys in the street or speak with slouching guards or be impolite to anyone, no matter what! Keep sending home gushingly enthusiastic Trip Reports! Retain your poise when anyone tells you how lucky you are not to have children—which you wanted with all your heart—and wow, *fantastic* that you're writing a book—which you're not doing but keep claiming you've dreamt of doing your whole life!

How could I possibly write a book when I'm so busy living everyone else's life for them?

I hear a roar inside my head: *FUCK IT!*

I pour the dregs from the bottle into my glass, then scroll down through dozens of earrings and stop at a pair of pearls surrounded by petals of hammered gold. *Too expensive for a little girl, but I'd love them.* I put those in my online shopping basket. I see amethyst teardrops. *Hmm . . . too sophisticated for her. Luckily, they're just my style and one of my favorite colors.* Into my basket. *Wow, those big silver hoops? Too heavy for a child; perfect for me to wear with a blazer, though.*

Nothing here for a kid, it seems. I'll look for her another time. I hit the buy button—hard—purchasing three not inexpensive pairs of earrings for myself. I slur out loud to the cats, "Patrick tells me that he couldn't have done it without me. So why not splurge on something special for me, damn it!"

I wake up the next morning with a familiar sour hangover taste in my mouth. *How did I manage to drink myself to sleep one more time?*

Today, though, there's something else—new—in my gut; it's a different version of queasy. I'm standing at the sink, toothbrush in hand, and I can't bear to look at my own face in the mirror. I'm aware that I used food to distract me in the past: Reese's ripped from the package, and ice cream downed by the bowlful. Alcohol is evidently my current security blanket. *Am I really now going to start binge-shopping?* I'd hated the giggles of the seasoned GM's wives who'd brandished Gold Cards, saying, "I'm spending my husband's success." *Is it my turn so soon to use Patrick's credit card against him? Just because he's busy living his professional dream and I'm a little sad and lonely?* I feel disgusted with myself, ashamed—and bewildered. *What am I becoming?*

Suddenly, I feel a tiny flame flaring in my beleaguered soul. It is the clarity to know that something is very wrong and that shiny-dangly, creamy-luscious, fuzzy-numbing isn't making it right. Nothing outside of me will fix what's wrong inside of me: not my parents and friends of a lifetime back home, or a new friend here; not my loving husband; not grasping endlessly at others' lives so I don't have to live my own. I don't know how to fix what's so very wrong, but I do know that I've got to do something different than I've been doing.

Raised by an atheist father and an agnostic mother, I don't believe that I have a right to talk to anything even resembling the divine. But words rush out before I can stop them in a full-out whimpered wail in a dark, cool Art Deco apartment, startling two dozing cats and rattling the empty booze bottles hidden at the bottom of the garbage can.

"Please help me, God," I gasp.

"I'm with you, Child," I hear then. "You don't have to drink again if you don't want to."

Before I can think, more words spill out, this time in a whisper, "Thank You, God."

I have absolutely no idea what's happening. I don't recognize myself. If I thought I was a stranger in a strange land before, that was nothing compared to now. I crawl into bed and pull the covers over my head, hearing six words before I fall asleep, "Rest now, Child. I am here."

I only wake up hours later when Patrick is back from his trip and standing over me, gently caressing my cheek. "*Chérie*, I'm home."

I sit up, groggy, and say, "Welcome home, *amore mio*."

"Thanks," he says, and sits next to me on the bed to add, "I have something to share with you, *chérie*. Corporate finally decided on our move date: we're heading to Sharm el Sheikh next week."

I smile weakly. He asks me, "Are you all right, Margaret?"

After I nod, gulp, and take a deep breath, I say, shyly, "I have something to share with you, too, Patrick."

He takes my hand in his and listens carefully as I tell him about my experience with a voice coming out of nowhere, calling me "Child," which feels so natural somehow—even though I have two actual parents already. I know Patrick won't judge me for talking with God—he's the one who asked for a church wedding in Switzerland. But I feel exposed. This is hardly "Just Doing It." This is the ultimate in dirty laundry. I'm petrified but I manage to squeak, "I don't understand, but I know that I'm done with drinking, Patrick."

"OK, *chérie*," he says, trying not to look wary. I can tell he wants to believe me, but doesn't—exactly. I've made that proclamation many times over the years, stopping drinking but always starting again when I just couldn't manage to stay stopped. I know Patrick would love it if I drank "normally" or at least less, but he's also stood by me—even on the nights when a happily married wife should've been home hours earlier.

Even though he's had plenty of excuses to leave me if he wanted to, I'm still afraid I'll scare him away if I'm not Perfect. I pivot to humor to hide my vulnerability. "So, *amore mio*, seems I've just discovered a relationship with God and now we're heading to where Moses threw down those Ten Commandments? Next stop the Biblical Wilderness!"

Patrick smiles, but I can see he's puzzled by my outburst.

I say, quietly now, "This time, *amore*, I'm really done." I start crying, and he pulls me into a hug. I mumble into his chest, "I'm crying because I'm so excited about the move we've been working toward for so long."

Really, though, I'm sobbing in shock. Not just the whole talking to God thing after forty years without faith. More even than that: *I asked for help and I got it. Just like that?*

SHARM EL SHEIKH

During the next days, Patrick wraps up his pre-opening office in downtown Cairo for the move to Sharm. I pack up our stuff at home in a daze. Just a week ago I was a paragon of brave independence; now each morning after my shower, I sit on the side of the bathtub, press my palms together and murmur, "Thank You, God, for helping me not to drink yesterday." Then I add, "Please help me, God, not to drink today."

I feel weak and foolish, a fraud and a pretender.

I feel like an old skin is cracking off of me, leaving me exposed and raw.

Mostly, though, I feel relieved.

I am lost—and found—all at once, and it's very confusing. I need to talk with someone who might understand. I phone Linda in Chicago, a former drinking buddy and a dear friend. When I'd last seen her, she'd seemed unusually serene. As we'd talked, it was clear that her life had changed for the better, but how? As I'd sipped my wine and she her iced tea, I'd asked her what happened. "I don't drink anymore," she'd said and I remember thinking, *That's bizarre. Why would anyone stop—really stop—drinking?* But my soul must've heard her; a seed must've been planted.

Now, I confess to Linda that I've been drinking more each year, including "a little something" to fall asleep. That I've vowed many mornings never to drink too much again—then drank too much again, maybe not that day, but soon. That I'm starting to get the sweats at night and to wake up shaky.

Then I tell her what happened just a few days ago and add, "It seems too easy to have asked for help and to have gotten it. And, how do you explain this, Linda? All of a sudden, I don't need to drink anymore."

"I call that grace, Margaret. Keep on praying."

"I am praying, Linda, but this is all so new to me. I didn't grow up in a religious household. My mom claimed that we were 'little c Christians: not actually Christian, but with Judeo-Christian values.' My dad endlessly ranted that he was an atheist because of all the violence done in the name of religion. 'Don't look for me in Heaven,' he'd say, 'but in the other place—by Roasting Pit Number Nine with the Green Bay Packers pennant flying and Wisconsin bratwurst grilling over the eternal flames.' I accepted this non-faith as an article of faith for forty years. Am I supposed to drop a lifetime of non-believing because I've started hearing voices?"

Linda responds, "You don't have to start going to Mass—or to a mosque, Margaret. But if asking for help is working for you, you might want to keep on doing that. *You* used the word God, but if that turns out to be an obstacle, just know that the name doesn't matter. Whatever you call the higher power of your understanding is OK." She pauses, and I hear a suppressed chuckle. "As long as the higher power you're envisioning, Margaret, is not *you*."

In a huff, I bark at her, "I don't think I'm *God*, Linda, but I am a magnificent Minister of Domestic Affairs! I keep in touch with everyone, I pay the bills, and I host the parties. Without me, the wheels would have fallen off the bus, Linda. I manage *everything!*"

She says, "I hear you, Margaret, but let's just focus on the drinking for now. How well do you feel you were managing that?"

Ouch, I think, and admit, "Not so well at the end. Actually not for a long time."

"OK," Linda says, "So just for your consideration: a power greater than ourselves might be able to handle that part of our lives better than we can. We can let go of the things outside of our control if we choose to."

My brain screams, *Treason! A crime against The Handbook! When in doubt, hold on tighter!*

"But Linda!" I practically yell, "Who will I be if I don't have it all together? Who will I be if I'm not perfect?"

"Human," she says. "You'll be human, dear friend."

After Linda and I hang up, I press my palms together, bowing my head and venturing in a timid voice, "Hi, God. I'm sorry that I, um, started this conversation with You only in my forties. I just didn't realize that You'd be willing to talk with me. You know: the atheist-agnostic family history and all that." I realize that I'm blathering; I stop.

"Child," I hear back. "I won't leave you if you don't leave me."

After a lifetime of feeling separate and fearing separation, I know I am completely connected to something greater than me. And if I'm a part of "all of it," I can't be abandoned. Not even if every single person I've been desperately trying to please decides to leave me.

I get a glimpse of freedom: a life where not every decision I make is driven by the unconscious need to be needed or approved of by others. I feel the possibility of letting go of an old way of living that worked for me for decades. Or at least I thought it worked for me.

So, once the furniture we bought on behalf of Four Seasons—for this apartment and now for Sharm—has been wrapped and shipped, we take our leave of the suave neighbor. When he leans toward me for a kiss, I manage to shake his hand instead (and thankfully the housekeeper is nowhere in sight).

As the company Peugeot will move with us and we'll be driving ourselves in Sharm, the driver has been re-assigned. I manage to resist writing him a thank you note.

Vee stops by to say farewell, saying "You two are going to be very popular at a seaside resort. I promise we'll see you soon." I manage to believe her.

At last, Nadia and BooBoo are corralled into their green carry-cases which we place inside the car. In the trunk are our suitcases, plus my carefully packed blue Parisian demitasse cups, our Bedouin bedspreads in sunset hues, my fragile new cream and sage-green Italian dishes, and my black evening dress. Of course I'm carrying my turquoise journal, hoping to fill it soon.

After Patrick drives us six hours south to Sharm, we walk into the brand-new general manager's home that's been constructed at the edge of the resort site. First thing my husband does is proudly walk me into a room with a view of the Red Sea. He says, "Welcome to your study, *chérie*. Where you can write to your heart's content!"

I'm ready to write, but first things must come first! Now that we're in Sharm at last, all focus is on the work our "family of two" came to Egypt to do: opening the best resort in the Middle East. I love seeing Patrick as an inspiring leader, kind and encouraging to everyone, as always. "Yes, we can!" is his battle cry, and his army of employees shout it alongside him.

We start each day with breakfast on our terrace, then walk together to the resort's main building, newly built of honey-colored stone. I love these peaceful moments together, greeting his colleagues as they arrive from the employee housing on site.

Once we're in Patrick's office, bright sun bouncing off the Red Sea through tall arched windows, I sit on the opposite side of his desk to help out with whatever he needs that day. Weeks fly by as I edit and proofread descriptions of excursions for the concierge team and menu items for the restaurants: the English, French and Italian are flawless, thanks to me. I pen notes on Patrick's hot off the press stationery, welcoming newly arrived colleagues and inviting their spouses over for coffee. I feel productive and valued, and I'm using my talents as a writer. Sort of.

We start to host parties in the GM's home, with stockpiled beverages: soft drinks for our Muslim colleagues who don't imbibe; wine or beer for the Europeans and North Americans who do. My fingers are now always wrapped around a glass of sparkling mineral water, which Patrick attentively refills for me, perching a slice of lime on the rim. I whisper a thanks to him and he says, "You're welcome, *chérie*. You're doing so well. I'm proud of you." I appreciate his support, but I don't feel proud: I feel grateful. I could not have done this on my own.

One of our party guests inevitably asks why I'm not drinking. "I'm on antibiotics," I say at first. But—after a while—I start to simply say that my life is better without alcohol. And it is: I love waking up with a clear head, my stomach not hurting, my eyes not bloodshot, and with no more earring extravaganzas on our credit card.

As the official resort opening approaches in 2002, a bigwig from corporate visits to ensure that every "t" is crossed and every "i" dotted from a human resources viewpoint. She leads team building exercises, and I'm so excited to be in that freshly painted new ballroom with Patrick and all these incredible colleagues. *Go, team!*

When we break midday, Patrick pulls me aside and blurts out, "*Chérie*, I'm so sorry: I've just been informed that you can't be a part of these sessions, since you don't technically work for the company. I hope you understand."

"Of course!" I rush to say. "I'd never do anything to jeopardize you, or the team, or the resort, or the company, or anyone. Ever!"

"Thank you, *chérie*," Patrick says, touching my hand gently. "I've been advised that you can still help me—help us—if you want to. Just not right now, with this. You know how much I appreciate your help, right?"

"I do know that, Patrick." I gulp back tears and say in the cheeriest voice I can manage, "I'll see you later, OK? I left my backpack in the ballroom. I don't want to disturb anyone: can you bring it home with you tonight?"

Damn it, I felt *useful*, out here in the middle of the damned desert: I was part of the *team*—and now I'm kicked off? Oh, and "I can still help him—just not now, with this?" *What the hell? What am I supposed to do now: my own life?*

When I walk home, I feel dangerously off-kilter. I haven't forgotten how alcohol could deaden my doubts in an instant. In a panic, I call Linda for guidance. She suggests that if I feel tempted to pick up a drink, I "play the tape all the way to the end" instead. When I do that, I remember how the pain would be gone—but only for minutes before being replaced by shame and bewilderment. Alcohol never made my life better for long. It never solved the problems I was trying to drink away.

So, I pray in the mornings for help before busying myself emailing home ever-longer Trip Reports, keeping things light and upbeat. I describe how it's so hot some days that I fear my ears have caught on fire. How I was surprised at a coffee shop along Sharm's Desert Road when wild camels clopped over to nibble the bushes next to where I nibbled biscotti with my cappuccino. How with the resort not yet up and running, I shop at the only grocery store, a half-hour's drive away. I write, "Sheikh Abdullah Super Market: where the occasional carrot is limp, and the sole head of wilted lettuce is a study in forlorn."

Each late afternoon, I pray, "Please help me not to pick up a drink now—at what used to be cocktail hour for me." I make myself another cup of hibiscus tea and read a book. After dinner, I watch Comedy Central on TV and pray again before bed, "Please help me not to drink until midnight." Tomorrow is another day. I'm learning to live one day at a time and grateful to again have the chance to make my actions match my intentions, just like that man I overheard in the New York grocery store line. I no longer squander conversations in a fugue state. I am now present for those I love most. That doesn't mean I don't struggle to admit that many things are outside my control. One of them is our slender gray cat, BooBoo. While fluffy white Nadia is getting fatter and lazier, BooBoo is wasting away.

As a resort destination, Sharm has only an "occasional" veterinarian, who—during one of her visits—diagnoses kidney issues and dehydration and shows me how to administer saline. I'll do anything to save this cat who took months to emerge from hiding when I first got her. I used to joke that I was like Miss Jane Goodall: patiently waiting for BooBoo to trust me. Once she did, though, she'd take naps with me, stretched out on my stomach and looking into my eyes until we both fell asleep. Now I see the shock in BooBoo's eyes as I push the needle through her once lustrous fur, now damp and limp. I feel like I'm violating her trust, but I gut my way past it, willing her to recover.

My days are spent hovering over her, trying to get her to drink a teaspoon of water, or eat a thimbleful of canned tuna from my fingertips. At night, while I encourage Patrick to sleep—it's full-out work for him now—I toss and turn, listening for BooBoo's pitiful mewling. I'm wrung out, exhausted, crying all the time. I phone my mom, and she gently reminds me that I need to have a life for myself, too. I know this is her way of telling me to let BooBoo go. But the vet's away, so I have no choice but to keep our little cat alive, begging, "Please get well."

She doesn't and, when the vet finally returns, I have to admit it's time. When I take BooBoo in, the vet suggests I wait outside for a few minutes: that this is not easy to watch. When it's over, I pet my old friend, smoothing my tears into her fur, whispering her name over and over, apologizing that I couldn't make her better. In an act of silent fellowship, the white-robed Egyptian gardener who tends the spindly plants around the veterinary clinic buries BooBoo there, placing two sticks tied together with twine as a makeshift cross over her grave. On the drive back to our home, steering with one hand and wiping my tears with the other, I scream with grief and helplessness.

When I pull into our driveway, our neighbor is just coming out her front door. She's the wife of Patrick's resort manager, very sweet and a cat lover to boot. She sees my tears and asks me what's happened.

"I'm sorry, Margaret," she says. "I would have been honored to come along to support you. Why didn't you ask me?"

"That's thoughtful of you, thank you," I say, "but I didn't want to impose on you. You have your own life, and I respect that."

She gives me a hug but is shaking her head as she walks away. I'm shaking my head, too, at the realization that my response came directly from The Handbook, which has long threatened me with destitution if I dare withdraw more acts of kindness from the emotional bank account than I deposit.

Hold on, I think. *To keep myself from ending up alone—I've been doing life alone?*

I'm grateful for the distraction of the resort's "soft opening" in May 2002. Ten rooms will be available at first, followed by twenty more and so on—until all two hundred rooms and suites are open and filled with happy Four Seasons guests.

Instead of this careful plan, though, Patrick gets a call from one of the major Middle Eastern stakeholders. He advises Patrick that he needs every room and all the suites ready in just two weeks. Patrick responds, "With all due respect, Your Royal Highness, it won't be possible to open the resort that quickly." That phone call ends with an abrupt click.

Just minutes later, another call comes in to Patrick's office: it's the Four Seasons chairman, founder, and CEO. "Hi, Patrick! How are you? How's Margaret? Glad to hear all's going well there. Just to be clear: the resort *will* open in two weeks. Every suite and every room. We'll do whatever it takes, right?" This last question is clearly rhetorical. It's a *fait accompli.*

Patrick responds, "But I don't know how that will even be possible."

"I don't know either, Patrick, but we'll figure this out. No is not an option."

So, over the next days, Four Seasons colleagues are flown in to help out, and they work as hard as anyone else on site. We love this about Four Seasons; all hands are always on deck to make every hotel and resort a success.

When the Middle Eastern guests arrive, Patrick's job shifts from months of pre-opening to suddenly running a brand-new luxury resort in a full house situation. As the pressure is on to make this visit a success and Patrick's career is riding on it, I ask him where I can help. I reason that this is no longer the forbidden team-building; the team has already been built. Patrick thanks me but says they have everything under control, which is of course exactly what I would have said. But I know that there's work to be done and—when I ask again—Patrick blurts out, "Try the laundry department!" as the Middle Eastern men have brought their six-foot-long white robes and all of them must be ironed before the evening's formal event. *I'm back in the saddle!*

The laundry supervisor is surprised to see his GM's wife asking to help, but he hands me an iron. I start pressing one of the white robes the way my mom taught me: slowly and meticulously. The laundry supervisor urges me to iron faster, bleating, "*Madaam*, hurry up, *bleez*! So many robes!" I speed up, but evidently my pace is still too slow. After eyeing me for another half-minute, he grabs the iron right out of my hand, "Thank you for trying, *Madaam*!"

Right then, the housekeeping supervisor rushes in, calling out, "Who knows how to drive?" He needs help to deliver these freshly pressed robes to guests across the vast, spread-out resort. I raise my hand, he nods, we run outside and jump into one of the resort's brand-new golf carts.

I speed along the stone-paved paths until we reach a very tight corner, where the path is bounded by stone walls on either side. I almost get the cart stuck trying to maneuver it around the turn without putting a scratch on it.

"Please stop here, *Madaam*! I will get someone else to help!"

I get out of the cart and hand him the keys. He's already on his walkie-talkie trying to find a replacement driver as I shuffle away. *I didn't know you could fire the GM's wife, but I've just been fired twice in one day.* Many people would think, "Well, I *offered* to help. Now I can stretch out on our lounge chairs to read. Or I could write." But I'm flashing back to childhood, when my mom's punishment for doing something wrong was not being able to participate in doing the chores with my brothers. *I'm disappointed when I can't do more work?* That feels like a very sad revelation indeed.

I spend the next days behind the computer typing up a Trip Report on this latest fiasco. I wash out the kitty litter box more often than necessary. I straighten belongings that don't need straightening.

When Their Royal Highnesses and their entourages leave after a few days, Patrick and I stand alongside the resort staff to wave good-bye to the limos and motor coaches pulling out along the palm tree–lined Four Seasons Boulevard. Congratulations come from Patrick's bosses. "We always knew you could do it!" This very early, very grand opening has gone splendidly against all odds. Patrick thanks me for all my help, and I bask in his praise and—once again—the reflected glory of his success.

Over the coming year, clients stream in along with journalists and tour operators, travel agents and frequent Four Seasons guests.

We entertain VIPs in the resort's restaurants, and I enjoy most of them most of the time. At a dinner with a plastic surgeon who keeps staring at my face, though, I ask him if he's ever able to just look at a person and not imagine what he'd change with a little nip or tuck. "No," he says, "I'm always imagining improvements." Instead of making a witty rejoinder, I bite my tongue.

Just as Vee predicted, our gorgeous seaside resort—just a quick flight from Cairo and from European capitals—is popular with our Four Seasons colleagues. We're genuinely happy when our professional family visits; we've come up through the ranks with these smart, driven guys (and their smart, underutilized wives). When Vee and her family visit, Patrick and her husband commiserate about how opening their hotels nearly killed them, but they glow with satisfaction. Vee and I catch up over cappuccino like we used to in Ma'adi. She gets me; I get her; I treasure the time together.

Other moments that Patrick and I treasure are with scuba-diving guests, drawn to Sharm by year-round sunshine, water that hovers at seventy-two degrees Fahrenheit, and dive sites populated by a thousand species of fish and hundreds of types of coral. We learned to dive in anticipation of moving here, at this rift between Africa and Asia, with vertical underwater reef walls descending almost endlessly. We feel proud to have picked up a sport in our forties (and I feel relieved every time I manage to pull my wetsuit up over my never-seen-liposuction thighs).

On the resort's gleaming white boat, the skipper cruises to remote dive sites and to Ras Mohammed National Park. The crew gets our dive gear ready. The only thing for me to do is to help entertain the resort guests onboard. I love that we're all barefoot; client Louboutins are left in their rooms. I love that the salty sea air undoes even the fanciest hairstyle. I love that no one can reach

Patrick on his Blackberry once we're underwater (something he loves, too).

When the skipper drops anchor at our dive site, we hear a splash. The dive master, skin tanned and puckered after thousands of hours in seawater, jumps in the water to check conditions: how fast is the current moving, and in which direction. He resurfaces to lead us through a safety briefing: drawing a simple image of the dive site on a white board, then advising us how the dive is expected to proceed.

After that, it's time for the buddy check: "Begin With Review And Friend." B for Buoyancy (for the vest we inflate and deflate); W for Weight Belt (to allow us to sink into the water with a tankful of air on our backs); R for Review (Are the releases on our vests secured?); A for Air (Is sufficient air in our tanks?); and finally, F for Friend (Is my dive buddy good to go?). Only after all that is completed do we pull on our masks, jump into the water fins-first, check in with our buddies again, exchange an OK sign, then release the air from our vests in order to slowly descend, two by two.

On one dive, already eighty feet underwater, our dive master changes course when he recognizes that the underwater current is stronger than he'd originally thought and too strenuous to swim against. He gestures for us to follow him in swimming away from the reef face, into the blue. All I need to do is follow him from one coral outcropping to another. I'm a strong swimmer (with the junior swim team medals to prove it). Against a strong current, though, my skinny feet inevitably cramp up. So I'm swimming as hard as I can, occasionally stopping to pull my fins toward me to relieve the cramping and getting pushed backwards by the current. My breathing is growing louder in my ears as I swim harder to catch up with the group. The dive master is out of sight, and Patrick is ahead of me. "Just keep swimming!" I demand of myself—a hum inside my mouth, filled with the mouthpiece which delivers air from my tank.

I'm deep into the blue now and swivel my head around, search-ing for the reef face we've swum away from—or the one we're swim-ming towards—but I'm disoriented, seeing only luminous sapphire water in every direction. I can no longer see Patrick at all. I'm alone, swimming as hard as I can to try to catch up in what I hope is the right direction, pushing against an underwater current strong as a sumo wrestler, my feet still cramping. I can't swim towards the sur-face; that's the number one safety rule of scuba unless you want to risk nitrogen poisoning. I try to calm myself, reminding myself, "I love water! I love blue!" My rational brain knows that drawing deep breaths is the only thing to do to avoid a full-out panic attack, but all I can manage is huffing and puffing. My terrified bird of a heart is snare drumming and tumbling, my blood pumping at a manic pace. *Have I died, and found myself in some azure afterlife?*

Suddenly Patrick materializes out of the blue. He's swum back to me and takes my shoulders in his hands, his eyes looking apolo-getic and concerned through his mask. He makes a tentative OK sign, which I return, even though I don't feel OK at all—and I know he knows it. I'm frightened, but even more than that, I'm furious. *What was he thinking, swimming so far ahead of me? If I could make him hear 'asshole' underwater, I would!*

He takes me by the hand, pulling me with him against the cur-rent and toward our destination. Only once I see the reef—pink and blue coral, with bright orange fish outlined against it—do I draw a full breath. The dive master is hovering there. He checks my air supply, then looks straight into my eyes until I give him the OK sign as well. Despite my frantic panting, I have enough air left in my tank to continue. The dive master swims ahead of us, but slowly now and sticking close. Patrick doesn't let go of my hand as we swim around the reef face. I want to shake him off, but I'm too shaky myself; I'm just trying to settle back into knowing I'm alive. At thirty minutes underwater, the dive master gestures towards the surface and we start to swim slowly upwards at an angle, stopping at fifteen feet below the surface for the normal three-minute safety stop.

As the crew onboard helps pull me up the metal steps of the boat, my legs can barely support me. I wobble over to the wooden bench on the side of the boat and sit down hard, pulling my mask off my face. Patrick silently brings over a towel to wrap around my shoulders. I stare at him for a minute, really hurt that he left me behind. *Sure,* I think, *I'm connected to the Divine and can't be abandoned on a spiritual level, blah blah blah, but you know that buddies are supposed to stick together, Patrick.*

I know he wasn't trying to hurt me, but I don't feel like the Perfectly Forgiving Wife right now. It's easier to don the mask of Perfect Scuba Hostess. I turn abruptly to the guests, our fellow divers, on board now, too. As the crew passes out cups of coffee and slices of apples and cookies, I ask: "How was your dive? Everything lovely?"

And, really, I think—once I cool down—*everything really is pretty darned lovely.* The resort is filled with guests, so Corporate and ownership are happy. *Maalesh,* I think: never mind. Patrick didn't mean to hurt me. Back to work.

Sharm holds a Road to Peace Summit, hosted by Egyptian President Mubarak and welcoming President George W. Bush, the Kings of Jordan and Saudi Arabia, prime ministers and various entourages. Brawny Secret Service officers in dark suits with earpieces spiraling over their collars lumber across the grounds of the resort ceaselessly.

Once we're seated on the resort's Great Lawn, listening to each dignitary speak in turn under the broiling Egyptian sun, I regret wearing pantyhose under my linen skirt. When I stand to applaud at the end of the speeches, I look down, horrified, to see that I have a dark triangle on the front of my skirt where I've sweated through both nylons and linen. That means there's sure to be some sort of geometric moistness on my backside, too. As I'm never without a scarf, I drape that around me in what must look like the desperate act of an over-the-hill exotic dancer. When Patrick is swept up with Secret Service ensuring the safe departure of the world leaders, I slink home, writing to everyone for the thousandth time how proud I am of Patrick, and I am. The resort's open now and fully operational. Patrick has a cheerful, competent administrative assistant. Even I recognize that he doesn't need me here right now.

After months away from the U.S., I take my first home leave.

These are a perk of expatriate assignments: a round-trip business class ticket for the employee and family to "the home country" every year. Once I've flown from Sharm to Cairo and have boarded the plane onward to Chicago, I employ the system I've developed over years of travel: I bring my carry-on down from the overhead storage bin to use as an ottoman. I swath myself in a shawl, pull on an eye mask, wedge in earplugs, snort Swiss herbal moisturizer into my nostrils as discreetly as I can—and off we go.

Once I arrive at O'Hare, I take a taxi directly to my parents at the Presbyterian Home in Evanston, the same place where I worked as a waitress after high school and on college breaks. My parents meet me at the front door, welcoming me to our round family table, placing blue mugs of black coffee in front of us for a long catch-up. Each night, I inflate an air mattress in their living room; each morning I deflate it and store it away in their front hall closet.

I relish the time together with them and with friends, including my GRRLs, whom I've known for decades: Amy, Kimetha, Linda, Sally and Sally. Over the years, we've compiled top ten bucket lists, built birdhouses, created vision boards, struggled through Pilates. We eat Indian carryout and talk (and talk and talk).

But, even while I'm recharging my deep connection with people I love in Chicago, I'm missing Patrick. Then I'll miss these folks when I'm back in Egypt. I remind myself harshly that no one can be in two places at the same time. These home leaves are a privilege. How lucky am I?

Once back in Sharm, I know I can't replicate the relationships I have back home, but I need to broaden my circle and meet some new people. Patrick embraces the idea of inviting hotel spouses to Four Seasons to revitalize the Sharm Women's Club. It'll be wonderful exposure for the new resort, as hoteliers spend money on Sunday brunches—to explore the competition and get "off property" for a few hours. Patrick is surrounded by dozens of employees so he never lacks for company, but he understands that I'd like a friend here, too: someone to talk with (and ideally not about hotels), even if it's just until one of us Trailing Spouses inevitably moves on.

I reach out to every hotel and resort along our sunny coast, asking the GMs' wives for a photo and some details about themselves. I type up and photocopy a booklet with bios for thirty-eight women: Egyptians from Abdel Aziz to Zeineldein, plus several Germans and Swiss, some Italians, a Brit, Canadian, Danish, Dutch, Filipina, Lebanese, Russian, and South African.

Four Seasons staff members greet the women in our soaring lobby, handing each one a hibiscus-flavored mocktail. They are then toured around the resort (in the golf carts I'm *not* allowed to drive). Once we're all gathered on the Great Lawn, I introduce Patrick, who launches into a warm impromptu welcome speech. As the ladies savor canapés, I add my hope for friendship and my philosophy that we all have the chance to "grow where we're planted." There is polite applause. "Maybe," I continue, "we could all collaborate on creating a Yellow Pages for Sharm—there's nothing like that here." There are smiles all around, but no more applause and definitely no one approaches me to volunteer to help. The ladies sit in clusters, chatting, gossiping while I'm busy fussing over everyone—never sitting down for even a moment.

Between brushing our teeth and crawling into bed that night, I tell Patrick, "I feel satisfied to have done what I could to reach out."

Patrick says, "Good on you, *chérie*. I hope you get a new friend out of today."

But I never hear back from a one.

Thank goodness family and friends start arriving—I can concentrate on being the hostess with the mostest again! With my hard-won Egyptian driver's license, I pick up our visitors at Sharm el Sheikh Airport, just minutes away. Once they're settled in our guest room, with the sunset-hued Bedouin bedspreads on the twin beds, I prepare their first cup of coffee, in our blue demitasse cups.

Patrick's aunt, uncle, and parents visit. A guest in the resort tells Patrick that there's a man from Switzerland who makes conversation with everyone. Patrick chuckles and replies, "Sorry, that's my father!" Patrick's mom is more shy, but giddy to be together and proud of her son. Whenever and wherever Monique and Freddy have visited us around the world, they are far from the rules and roles and duties of home back in Switzerland. Patrick and I are grateful to be the beneficiaries of that carefree vacation spirit, just like I'd been with my parents, who let go of their social constraints when we discovered Italy together.

Marc comes for New Year's Eve. Linda and her partner Annie visit, and we ride horses on the beach with Linda subduing the wildest mare in the herd.

Patrick's sister Jetti and her husband, Otto, arrive with their kids Mirjam, Christina, and Nicolas, who are twelve, eleven and eight. On our first snorkel outing together, the kids swim up to me, eyes wide behind their masks, gleefully pointing out each colorful fish. We eat grilled sea bass for dinner each night at the beach restaurant, our toes in the sand. At home after dinner, we dance to Amr Diab, our favorite Egyptian singer, who croons, "*Habibi*"—my sweetheart.

Near the end of their visit, I take them on the *pièce de résistance* of excursions: "Summiting Mount Sinai." Our driver picks us up at midnight in a van and for two hours across the desert all we hear is

the sound of our tires crunching on gravel road. Huge boulders and
endless expanses of sand glow white in the light of a full moon. The
family dozes, but I cannot take my eyes off the splendor. And also:
I need to stay awake. I *will* get us there safely! (Even though I'm *not*
actually the one driving.) Patrick's back at the resort, busy as ever, so
I'm in charge of our Swiss family's Sinai experience; I've researched
and booked the trip and I will take care of everything. After being
fired from team-building, ironing, and golf cart–driving, at least this
is something I still do well.

The driver deposits us at the base of Mount Sinai at two in the
morning as planned. We'll be riding up most of the way on camelback for the sunrise from the summit. When we emerge from the van
after this peaceful drive, it's chaos in the dark. Camels are braying,
and their drivers are clamoring to have us choose them. "Lady, here
is strong camel!" When the kids are pulled off in different directions,
I panic. What if they're being kidnapped and sold to some Desert
Bad Guy? I yell out their names, "Miri! Chri! Nico!" trying to locate
them in the dark. My ever-calm sister-in-law asks me to relax. And
I do—for a moment—when the kids are led back to us on camelback
and I can see their huge delighted smiles gleaming in the moonlight.

Jetti and I are helped onto camels ourselves, then led to Otto.
He's been assigned the most stubborn beast in Egypt. When we head
up the gravel pathway, his camel lags far behind. The camel driver
gestures with a long stick, hissing at Otto, "Kick him, mister! Hit
him! Kill him if you must!" As though any sane person would whip
a camel up a narrow pathway with a steep drop-off to the side. And
why would you kill an animal you're riding *on top of*?

My heart pounds from the peril of it, and also from the mesmer-
izing sight of dozens of dromedaries winding their way single file up
Mount Sinai, silhouetted against the bright white moon.

Where the path ends near the summit, we dismount and scramble to the top—a large, flat expanse, now covered with other tourists,

including a Korean choir loudly singing hymns into the ink-black sky. Not the serene Biblical experience I'd expected, but . . . never mind. We huddle together on the ground in the frigid desert night. The kids lay their heads in our laps and sleep. I'm very hungry by now, and I'm not someone who should *ever* be allowed to get hungry. I should've brought a snack. I should at least try to nap, too. Instead, I wait—awake—in the hours before dawn, guarding my flock.

Sunrise is glorious, reviving the red color of the rocks of endless mountain vistas. The crowds of tourists take their snapshots then immediately start streaming down the mountain on the gravel path the camels had plodded up on.

But for our descent as a family? I've chosen what I've read is the most picturesque route, called the Steps of Penitence (which really should have raised a red flag to now-exhausted and starving me). We could've strolled down the camel path with 99 percent of the other tourists, but, no! My visitors must have the most authentic and unique experience! My annoyingly fit sister-in-law and the kids scamper ahead; Otto and I bring up the rear. Slow and steady work well at first, but after crashing down six hundred very steep steps— blocks of stone more than a foot tall—my legs are getting rubbery.

"Otto, OK with you if we just stop and enjoy the view for a bit?"

"Sure, Maggie," he says, and we sit on a step to admire the cloud-less blue morning sky —until I see Jetti and the kids waving at us from already far below. What on earth are they doing way ahead of me, their fearless leader?

"Let's go, Otto!" I stand to take just one more step, but the thigh muscles in my legs are shaking uncontrollably and I have to sit down again. *C'mon, Margaret!* I hiss to myself. *Be strong! You're a former soccer player!* (Almost thirty years ago, but still . . .)

Otto sits next to me and points out what he sees in the rock formations in a soothing voice. "Doesn't that look like the Egyptian falcon god, Horus?"

"Thanks for cheering me up," I say, as I try again to stand. No go. "Oh, my God! I can't take one more step." Tears of shame spring to my eyes. *Am I going to have to slide down the rest of the way on my ass?* "Otto, maybe you should go for help."

Instead, he plants himself one step below me and says, "Let me help you."

I resist him, a furious voice inside me boiling, *Better he should just let me die here in this holy place! Go, be with your family. Tell Patrick I love him. Remember me—if you will . . .*

Otto just says, quietly, "Margaret, *s'il te plaît*: please. For once, lean on someone else. Lean on *me*."

He pulls my arms around his neck and—with my whole weight on his back—he literally drags me down the remaining hundreds of steps. One at a time.

Thump.

Thump.

Thump.

At the base of the mountain, Otto helps me limp my way to the tourist van. With the help of the driver, I am lifted in and placed on the back seat. Jetti and the kids gather around me, concerned, then my sister-in-law sees the wounded pride on my face and says, "Give your aunt some space, *les enfants*. She may want to be alone for a minute." But the kids are too young to understand the concept of saving face or about being ashamed to cry in front of others. Instead, they grab my hands with their little hands. They wrap their skinny arms around me, asking, "*Ça va?* Are you OK?"

"*Oui. Merci,*" I say. "Thank you. Please go see the monastery with your parents." They look stricken, bless them, so I add, trying to smile, "*Je suis bien.* I'm fine." I point them towards the Monastery of Saint Catherine, which has risen from this desert canyon for almost fifteen hundred years. I can see they're bewildered at my shooing them away. I'm trying not to sound pitiful as I plead, "Please just go.

I've already seen it. You'll love it." They walk away, the whole family, the kids looking back over their shoulders at me. I wave until they're out of sight.

Then I crumple, sniffling in the back seat of the van. Our driver—without a word—goes to buy me a bottle of cold water at a tourist kiosk by the entrance to the monastery. He hands me a sandwich of pita bread and hummus. "Here, *Madaam*. Is made by my wife." I open my mouth to protest, but he shakes his head and smiles at me, saying, "Eat, *Madaam*. Rest." This is the hospitality of this country: an Egyptian will literally give you the shirt off his back (or the sandwich out of his lunch box).

The driver walks off again, pulling a pack of unfiltered cigarettes out of his jacket pocket. He finds a sliver of shade along the wall of the monastery. I watch him smoke, and when he notices me watching him, he pantomimes eating, which makes me smile. I take a bite and a long pull of water and by the time I've finished the sandwich, I feel the relief of nourishment in my body. I look to the driver, but he's walked away. Maybe he's talking with a friend at the ticket kiosk. The others are all inside the monastery.

I'm completely alone in this dusty tourist van. Groaning, grimacing, I get down on my knees alongside the back seat.

"Here I am, God, humbled before You, thanks to those Steps of Penitence."

I hear a distant rumble: thunder over Mount Sinai—or laughter? "Whatever does the trick, Child. I'm here to help."

"I know that, God, but I want to get better at accepting help not just from You, but also from my fellow humans."

I hear a now-familiar voice, "Finally, Child."

By the time the family returns to the van, describing glimmering icons inside the monastery and the scraggly descendant of the biblical Burning Bush in the monastery courtyard, I've hoisted myself painfully back onto the seat and I'm feeling better. Our driver returns, looks at me once, smiles almost imperceptibly, nods, and starts the engine.

On the drive back to the resort, as the desert stretches out endlessly before us, I even manage a laugh as we recreate our Mount Sinai Experience together. My prowess as a Perfect Guide and Sentry is at an all-time low. And yet, I realize that my dear Swiss family doesn't care. They are happy to be together, discovering and sharing this adventure. Otto is already impersonating his camel driver's frantic, "Kill him, Mister! Kill him!" We are all howling with laughter when we arrive back at the Four Seasons.

I feel vulnerable with my armor off, my sword cast down. But also lighter—that stuff is heavy.

For the rest of their stay with us, the kids help me to hobble around the resort as I recover the strength in my legs. Gently, they pet me and tease me: their middle-aged, humiliated, aching aunt.

Wait, what? They love me just the way I am?

Blood, sweat, and tears: that's what it took to open the resort. The results are spectacular, but everyone is exhausted—Patrick not least of all—now with the grand opening behind us and the pressure for financial return on investment before us. Patrick respects this investors' prerogative, but it's more and more stressful for him every day. There are endless nights comforting him when he feels despondent and pointing out the objective evidence of his success: awards and accolades have poured in for Four Seasons Resort Sharm el Sheikh.

With some of the filters that alcohol layered over my voice off at last, I actually say out loud, "I will follow you to the ends of the earth, *amore mio*, but I won't follow you into utter despair. I can't be the only one to shoulder this pain with you." He reaches out for support to Marc, Jetti, and a therapist—and receives it. It's a reminder to me—again—that people want to help: all we have to do is ask. Patrick is also getting more comfortable with that notion.

A while later, I also say, "I believe, *amore mio*, that you've accomplished what you came here to do. Let's give another Four Seasons GM the chance to take the resort to the next level."

Patrick balks at the notion—it feels like deserting his baby. But he finally agrees that it's time to move on after three years in Egypt, and he asks Four Seasons for a transfer. An offer to move to northern Thailand is extended, negotiated, accepted, and contracted. The home office announcement reads, "Patrick Ghielmetti will be assuming the position of general manager of the Regent Chiang Mai Resort, effective October 9, 2003. He's excited to return to Thailand, a country and its people he learned to love—having previously spent more than two years there before joining Four Seasons." I'd hoped we'd be posted to somewhere closer to Chicago, but I'm also excited; we're heading to a destination everyone describes as a paradise.

Our household goods are packed in boxes then strapped onto a flatbed truck—in a tower ten feet tall with the movers sitting on top. As they drive away, Patrick whispers to me, "*Insha'Allah* on that stuff making it to Chiang Mai in one piece!" and we cross our fingers and laugh.

At the farewell staff party, Patrick and the incoming GM ride in on camelback, there's a lucky draw for prizes, and we all dance until late into the night. Patrick completes the handover to his successor the next day.

When we're driven to the airport, I'm able to hold back my tears until we're in the departure lounge. But when our chef concierge appears there to send us off, I lose it. Not just for him, although he was such an important part of our happiness at the resort—securing last minute EgyptAir tickets and all manner of miracles—but for all the ferociously devoted people on the staff, for the peace and quiet of the red rock Sinai desert, for the aquarium that is the Red Sea.

I email to my parents, "Leaving Sharm = *ugh*. Friends had told us that Egypt would get under our skin, and it surely did. We will carry it with us in our hearts forever. I'll never forget the generosity of the Egyptians—they've shared Ramadan feasts in the streets and invited us into their homes for long, laughter-filled dinners that left us pleading, 'No more food, please!' They've inspired us with their resourcefulness. We can't throw anything out for fear that someone on the staff will find it and repair it and return it to us, tied up with a ribbon. They've touched us with their warmth: the skipper who let our nephew navigate the boat, the chefs who adopted Patrick's mom's recipe for breakfast *Bircher Muesli*, the gift shop manager who conspired with my husband to surprise me on my birthday with a necklace I'd admired but declared was only fit for a princess. Egyptians move heaven and earth to make others happy. It's hard to leave them."

And it's hard to leave the country where I found God—the country where my life changed when I learned that even a brave woman like me can get stronger by getting down on her knees to ask for help. I leave humbler but healthier—and more grateful than I've ever been in my life. I leave embracing IBM: *Insha'Allah*—if God wills it; *Bokra*—tomorrow, or one day at a time in any case; *Maalesh*—no worries (and it's probably not inside my circle of control anyway).

Now I mutter *Alhamduli'Allah*—thank You, God—all the time. I leave not the same as when I arrived.

We board EgyptAir to Cairo one more time: a familiar sixty-minute flight. We say farewell to the staff of the Four Seasons there, with last glances at the dust-covered palms, the jumble of modern/ancient Cairo, my expat hideout at the Marriott Gezirah, the muddy Nile along whose banks we'd started our Egypt journey.

For our onward flight from Cairo to Zurich, we've got our usual two carry-on bags, but now only one cat, Nadia, in her green carrying case. The airline staff insist that Nadia be put through the X-ray scanner instead of me holding her to my chest as we've always done before.

I try a few key words in Arabic, "Cat. Love. In my arms. Please." They don't budge. So into the scanner she goes.

We're worried that we've irreparably damaged our precious pet, but once we've arrived in Bangkok, this ancient cat—formerly slow as a sloth—bounds out of her carrier completely rejuvenated. Patrick says with a laugh, "That zapping gave her a new zest for life! Maybe we should go through the scanner ourselves!"

Patrick's still the partner I want by my side on this next—and every—adventure.

CHIANG MAI

It's not the first time I've been to Thailand. That was in 1992, with my newly minted fiancé. Patrick had fallen head over heels for the Land of Smiles in the late 1980s—from his first step out of the airport into what he adoringly calls the warmth of the tropics.

My first step outside in Bangkok? I'd told Patrick that my hair felt like a mink coat on my neck. He'd heard that my hair felt like a meatloaf on my neck, which was an even more apt description of what I was experiencing. In the taxi to downtown, the windows open, I was overwhelmed by the garlic from street food vendors, which stung my eyes, and blinded by the fluorescent lights everywhere, but thrilled to discover a country beloved by my beloved.

Our destination in 1992 was the Oriental Hotel, our stay there an engagement gift from a very close friend of Patrick's, Armando—a tall, slim, blue-eyed Swiss hotelier like my fiancé. Once Patrick and I had checked in to one of the world's most renowned hostelries and the soft-spoken Thai staff led us to our room, I wondered what the cloyingly sweet smell was—until I noticed garlands of jasmine on our pillows plus bouquets of roses and lilies. Armando had put us on the VIP lists for our anniversary (we wouldn't be married for months yet), our saints' days (he's Catholic), and our birthdays (not even close).

An explosion of senses greeted me the next morning as Patrick took me to the glittering golden Grand Palace, on a rollicking ride in a motorized three-wheeled taxi called a *tuk tuk,* and on a jam-packed public water bus on the Chao Phraya River (leaping up once I realized I'd been sitting in a seat reserved for "Buddhist Monk Only"). On a long-tail boat ride into Bangkok's back canals, we saw houses on stilts leaning precariously just above the brown water where kids splashed and played. Monks meandered across peaceful monastery lawns. To recover from the heat, Patrick took me to visit the Regent Hotel, and we sipped lemongrass tea in its air-conditioned lobby while admiring its painted silk ceiling, a fantasy of pinks, blues, and golds.

Patrick taught me how to *wai*—palms together and raised—as a sign of respect toward "status superiors" and also a greeting, expression of thanks, or apology for mistakes. The highest *wai* is reserved for royalty; nearly as high for a monk; high for elders. He underlined how essential it is to be respectful of the King and Queen. It's not just courtesy: insulting the Royal Family in any way is a criminal offense called *lèse-majesté.* He showed me how to approach a monk for a blessing in a temple: scooching forward on my hands and knees, always staying lower than the monk, never touching him, and never pointing my feet at him (or at anyone else, for that matter).

We took a train to a beach town, Patrick insisting that we travel third-class for "local color." This was my first experience riding next to chickens clucking in the aisles. A bunch of guys played guitar and sang as they passed around a bottle of potent Mekhong Whiskey. One of them perched on the open train window on the verge of tumbling out at every curve of the track.

On Phi Phi Island, Patrick bought fresh fruit on the beach from lithe young women, flirting with them in Thai. They smiled at me, gently touching my skin, saying "*khaw*"—what Patrick told me was the word for white, even though the intense sun was already prickling my skin with pink sunburn and red heat rash. We retreated under a palm tree to protect my skin, over-sensitive from years of Deep, Dark Tropical Tanning as a teenager. When a boatload of tourists was disgorged onto the beach, we cringed as their tour guide screamed, "Follow me!" He added, "Eat now!" in German, French, Italian, and Spanish: "*Essen! Manger! Mangiare! Comer!*" I felt grateful to be following Patrick's lead instead, eating our pineapple in peace in the shade.

Back in Bangkok, per Patrick's promise to me on the roof of Swissôtel Chicago, a jeweler created an engagement ring with Thai sapphires as deeply blue as a night sky, plus two plain gold rings for each of us: for our Chicago and Swiss weddings.

So, having experienced that Thailand a decade ago, the country's not a total shock when we arrive in Bangkok in October 2003. Luxury's not a total shock, either. Patrick has been working for Four Seasons for eight years by now, and we haven't been shy about using the perk of vacationing in the hotels and resorts. When we check into the Regent Hotel, now managed by Four Seasons, I look up and sigh with pleasure at the painted pink, blue, and gold silk ceiling I remember so well from our first visit here together.

Once we're checked into a guest room and showered, Patrick's new colleagues introduce us to the owner of the hotel and his wife, both born in the States, but having lived in Thailand most of their lives. Bill is a famously successful businessperson, and Kathy is beloved for her charm and fluency in Thai and Thai culture. Over coffee, we find that we share a passion for travel and scuba, and we're deep in conversation when they—and everyone around us—suddenly rises to their feet: a member of the Royal Family has entered the hotel lobby with her entourage. Everyone *wais* and Kathy curtsies gracefully. I try to mimic her, achieving a pose which in yoga would be described as Awkward Stork. After the procession has passed, Kathy whispers to me with a smile, "I'll be happy to help you with that if you'd like."

"Uh, yes, please," I respond. I've been praying to accept help from humans, and she's making it easy for me; by not calling attention to my ignorance, she's allowing me to "save face." And her furthering my learning about Thai culture will allow me to grow into an even more Perfect Culturally Sensitive Supporting Spouse.

Early to beat the heat the following morning, Patrick and I stride ten minutes up Rajadamri Road from the hotel to Lumpini Park. The simple pleasure of walking together is a constant in our lives. Here, in this green oasis in the city, there's a paved walking path around the perimeter of the park and palm trees rim an olive-green lake with meter-long monitor lizards basking on its banks in the sun. As we're walking home, a thunderstorm dumps gallons of warm rainwater on us. After three years in Egypt's nonstop sunshine, it'll take some getting used to the once-daily deluge of the tropics. But I have time for that. While I allowed myself only seven days to settle in to Egypt, I'm allotting myself *a whole month* to make Thailand my new home—starting tomorrow. We fly to Chiang Mai first thing.

On the one-hour flight north from Bangkok, I chuckle at the Thai Airways instruction prior to takeoff: "Please do not lie in the aisles." I'm tired enough from the emotion of the move and all the flights that a little nap under the seats sounds tempting.

I'm relieved to step outside from Chiang Mai's airport into Northern Thailand's cool autumn air. It's cooler still after we've been driven a half hour outside the city to the resort, set at the base of tree-covered hills. At the entrance to the resort, a small gazebo protects a stone statue of Ganesh, the Hindu elephant-head god revered as the "remover of obstacles." He's surrounded by tiny statuettes of mice; a mouse was his celestial transportation. I feel a stab of missing my dad calling me Mouse and my mom's bright enthusiasm. They're so far away—literally on the other side of the globe.

But there's no time to think about that. As we step from the van, Patrick's colleagues are lined up to welcome us, *wai*-ing us. We *wai* back, then I follow Patrick's lead in facing Ganesh with another *wai*, this time our palms pressed together around sticks of incense his colleagues have handed us. We close our eyes to offer silent prayers. I'm pretty sure Patrick's is for professional success, which would be more succinct than my mental babbling, "Dear God-in-Ganesh, please remove the obstacles I face in letting go of Egypt, embracing hot, humid Thailand, and, um, I guess every obstacle I can think of and any others which may spring to mind for You."

"I'm on it, Child."

Patrick and I place the smoldering incense sticks upright in a large brass urn filled with sand in front of Ganesh. We're escorted to the guest room where we'll be staying and where our bags are already neatly in a row inside the door. We let Nadia out of her carry-case, she inspects yet another new kitty litter box and new food and water bowls, then jumps onto our bed for her first Thai nap. No need to worry about this well-traveled, security-scanned cat. We leave her to join Patrick's new team at the resort's cooking school for a welcome reception. We all *wai*-with-incense again—this time facing the Spirit House, in front of which two feasts have been laid out by the chefs: one for us mortals, and one for those who are no longer physically here. Whole chickens and fish glisten next to sticky rice; there are bottles of spirits to please the spirits.

That evening, I write my parents a postcard. The photo depicts the view from the open-air lobby: wooden guardian statues—half man, half-lion—oversee the guest room bungalows set on stilts in a half-circle around the resort's rice paddy. My parents will especially love the two resident water buffaloes who graze in the shade: Mr. Sand is a pinkish albino and Mrs. Mud is a deep blackish-brown. "First card is always to you two," I write. "Greetings from our new home: lush green everywhere, lots of noisy birds, striped squirrels and boisterous frogs. Wish you were here!"

The next card is always to Patrick's parents. "We'll be living 'on property' in Residence Eight. It's a three-bedroom apartment inside a northern Thai-style building: a wooden structure with a shaded veranda overlooking flowers and trees. Come see us soon!"

I'm ready to move into Residence Eight, but the former GM's wife is still packing up their things, getting ready to move back to the US. I don't exactly understand why Patrick and I have to allow her extra time to move out: *I would never impose on someone that way.* But it's only for a while and we *are* in a cozy hotel room with a wooden walkway out to a covered dining pavilion. We have a glimpse of the blue swimming pool set in the rice paddies, which eases the ache of missing the Red Sea.

For breakfast each morning in this new setting, we walk two minutes to the resort's main building for grapefruit-like *pomelo* juice, All American All-Bran, and strong local coffee. We sit on the terrace and drink in the view of the hills emerging from the morning mist as denim-clad gardeners arrive for work. When Patrick heads to his office, I ask him to take me to the director of human resources. I tell her that, since I can't be settling us in to Residence Eight yet, "I'd really appreciate if you'd arrange a Thai tutor for me."

She says, "As you wish, *Khun* Margaret." As a sign of respect, Thais preface each proper name with *Khun* (rhymes with soon). This is helpful, as family names can be many syllables long. I add that I'd love to start as soon as possible. She looks perplexed and asks, "Why not enjoy the resort for a bit? Lounge by the pool? Relax after your move from Egypt."

I grind my teeth. I'm a do-er, not a relaxer! "No thank you," I say primly. "I'm anxious to do whatever I can to settle in to Thai culture ASAP."

"This is not really an ASAP culture," she says, "but I'll get you a tutor right away, *Khun* Margaret." She adds, "That means I can expect you to be fluent by next week, right?" She smiles at me and I wonder, *which Thai smile is that?*

Patrick has counseled me on the endless variations, including a smile of determined serenity to accompany the words *jai yen yen:* heart cool cool. This is an essential Thai Buddhist value: maintaining control over my spiritual life includes maintaining control over my emotions. Patrick also specifies an anxious smile when something's gone awry, often accompanied by the words *mai bpen rai,* cousin to the Egyptian *maalesh*—"Never mind, no worries" with the additional Thai layer of "I made a mistake, but please don't be mad. Can we just let it go?" It's essential to respond with *mai bpen rai* in return: "It's not the end of the world. I'm not angry. It's OK." The only polite reaction is to save face for the other, no matter how I'm feeling. This culture already feels familiar to me.

Now, though, I believe that the smile just bestowed upon me is the "I've already seen a hundred expat wives come and go. Let's see how this one works out."

My Thai tutor arrives the next afternoon, ringing the doorbell to our room. She's twenty-five years old with long black hair. We sit on our sofa, pushing aside the cushions covered in cotton with geometric embroidery. I ask her about herself. "My fiancé is English. He proposed like guys do in the movies: on one knee." I smile, remembering my mom telling me that my dad hadn't proposed; they'd just known they were going to get married. I'd found that odd until I fell in love with Patrick. We already knew we'd be making our life together when he proposed with purple orchids on the Swissôtel rooftop.

From her backpack, my tutor pulls grade-school workbooks with faint dotted lines on which to practice my letters. *Shit,* I think, *my turquoise journal. Have I even unpacked it yet? Never mind: to the task at hand: Thai!*

It's immediately apparent, even to a seasoned language-learner like me, that this language is going to be difficult. For starters, there are five different tones: rising, falling, mid-tone, up-then-down, and down-then-up. Get the tone wrong and the word is indecipherable to the Thai listener. While I have a "musical ear," I am making a mistake with every word I parrot—plus the alphabet feels impossible. I loved learning the swoops and flourishes of Arabic script in college, but I was young then. Now, in my mid-forties, Thai's squiggles are forgotten just after I've learned them. Within the first day I master exactly one letter—"*ng*"—by making up a story to remind me of the sound. The letter looks to me like a man holding a fishing pole: he is fish-*ng*. I'm shocked that my progress is so slow, but at least I have the bit of productivity in my mouth.

Over the next few days, I create flash cards of basic Thai words and shyly practice with the staff, all of whom are encouraging (even though they giggle a lot). As it turns out, the most advanced I ever get in conversation with my tutor is asking, "Pencil how much?" She responds thirty-nine baht: about one dollar. "Expensive!" I exclaim. "Discount possible?" She frowns, saying not possible. I end the conversation with "Teacher not nice."

We're laughing as I wave her goodbye, but then it all suddenly seems futile: not just learning a new language, but packing up, moving, creating a home, casting my net wide to meet people, joining a women's group or inventing one, hoping for one kind friend, setting down roots, gaily writing home Trip Reports to prove to myself that I'm fine and everything's fine and I love this lucky life. Which I do, honestly! I fall in love with each place we live in one way or another. But, one day, Four Seasons will call Patrick and ask, "Would you like to move to x y z?" and we'll say yes and I'll be starting over. What benefit will Thai be then? I realize that I won't ever be able to master it unless I spend every available hour learning a language I'll never use in another country. I ask the HR director to thank my tutor and wish her well, but I stop my lessons almost as soon as I've started, handing over my Perfect Language Learner Permit on the spot.

The outgoing GM's wife invites me over to Residence Eight when she's ready to move out, having directed the movers' packing up of their household goods. She wants to show me what remains in the residence as part of the Four Seasons inventory. I enter through the heavy wooden front door and past the two carved wooden elephants standing guard just inside. The wood plank-floored living space is cool and dusky even at midday, thanks to wide canopies shutting out the sun. She shows me the Knights of the Round Table-sized dining table (also wood) with eight massive chairs, then the bedroom, guest room, and patio, ending the tour in the kitchen. Pointing to dozens of dishes and glasses, cups and saucers, a deep fryer, blackened skillets, and a gigantic wok, she announces, "I'm leaving all this in your trust."

What? I think. *None of this is hers!* All this stuff belongs to the owner, just like all the furniture Patrick and I have left behind for his GM successor in Sharm.

"My husband and I hosted a GM's cocktail party here every night for the resort guests," she announces. "We loved it, and the guests expect it."

At the words, "the guests expect it," I hear a taut twanging bark from The Handbook, "Yes! An opportunity to always put others first!" but I'm still smarting from the HR person telling me in Sharm that I wasn't part of the team and getting fired twice and sitting through endless dinners with plastic surgeons imagining me with a better face and to hell with it! Why should I be a good soldier on this one?

I feel a wave rising up inside of me. It's been slowly gathering strength from a decade ago when my shrink in Chicago asked me, "What's the worst thing that could happen if you say no, Margaret?" *The worst thing has always been if I'm not the Perfect This or That I won't be lovable. She might die because I'm such a shocking disappointment to her; I will surely die, having fallen short of the ideal. So, really, it could be a murder-suicide!*

But, I think, *you know what? I am frankly on my last nerve about that bullshit right about now.* With a quick glance upwards, I silently request, "Please, God, remind me that I don't have to please all the people all the time. Help me, please, to speak my mind."

"All I ever wanted for you, Child."

So I say to this woman, standing in front of me, "I'm glad that you enjoyed the parties, but it's not our thing." More honest would be to say that it's not *my* thing as an introvert; my extrovert husband would be delighted to entertain every night, asking the chef to create a luscious dinner—and the barman to create a special mocktail for me. I don't say any of that to her.

She looks stunned. "But you have to do it," she says. Then, more slowly, she repeats, as though maybe I hadn't understood her the first time, "The guests expect it from the general manager and his wife."

She might as well be poking me with a sharp stick, in a very tender, very persistent bruise. I'm just about to say, "I'm sorry," when I hear the voice of another shrink—this one in Manhattan—observing that I apologized all the time (to which, of course, I apologized). But instead of folding now, I stiffen—and my resolve does, too.

"No," I say again. "Patrick and I will entertain clients in the resort restaurants and consider a GM's cocktail party here once a week. There's no way we're having resort guests here every night." She nods, but I can see that her head is moving against her will. My voice is firm as I add, "To each her own, right?"

Whew, just like that, *I speak my mind and no one dies after all?* I feel a weight lifting from me. This has been a long time coming. The next morning, I add to my prayers, "Please help me, God, to do Your will for me today, whatever that may be."

I hear a chuckle followed by a sly, "Would you consider cocktail parties every *other* night instead, Child?" and I chuckle back.

When I wish my predecessor all the best in her move and hug her goodbye, I'm shaking with the effort of not backpedaling and not promising I'll do things her way after all. It's a struggle to set The Handbook aside to be more authentically myself, but I do it.

◞◟

Once Residence Eight is available at last, I march over after breakfast to supervise the move-in. I'm shocked to see that our mattresses have been unloaded from the moving van but left outside—an awful idea with jungly trees all around and who knows how many freeloading snakes hoping for a cushy bed.

"*Jai yen yen*," I say to myself. Heart cool cool. I take the move supervisor aside to discreetly point out the situation. He apologizes with a *wai* saying, "*Mai bpen rai*," which I echo back. He directs his team to bring the mattresses inside right away. These are followed by our worldly goods in dozens of cartons, which the movers open with box cutters. Missing are a few boxes I'd sent into storage before we left New York three years ago. I hate losing *Mr. Mixie Dough*, a cherished book from my mother's childhood in the 1930s, plus a tea set she'd bought when she worked at Marshall Field's—in a turquoise floral design. I tell myself it's just stuff, but I feel the ties that bind me to my roots loosen.

Some Very Important Documents are also missing, which has me going crazy as the Minister of Domestic Affairs. I know the papers will turn up eventually in whatever "safe place" I'd chosen for them before we left Sharm, and won't I enjoy a wry laugh then.

After breakfast the next morning, the bellman helps me move Nadia and our suitcases to our new home. After I've arrived, the housekeeper assigned to Residence Eight arrives, too, letting herself in. She and I introduce ourselves and, of course, *wai*, and she immediately gets to work. She sweeps up after the movers and takes our things out of boxes, placing things in piles in different rooms for me to arrange. She finds fresh linens and puts them on the bed and hangs our clothes in the closets. I'm very grateful to her; our little family will be sleeping in our new home tonight. Going forward, I'd love for her to visit only once a week, but it's a tradition—and an expectation—for Patrick and me to retain the housekeeper full-time and to contribute to her pay.

I appreciate her care of Nadia (now called *Meow*: Thai for cat). I'm grateful for clean dishes, a made bed, fresh laundry, and a sparkling bathroom, but these daily housekeeping chores are done in a few hours and I think, *Here's an idea: she can work in the morning and leave in time for lunch at the staff cafeteria. That would allow me the luxury of her services and also give me time to myself.* But Patrick tells me that she needs to stay "punched in" all day in order to get paid. I have another idea and tell her, "I'm happy to pay you for the full day. You can work in the mornings and study for college in the afternoons."

She speaks English well so she understands my words, but the concept seems incomprehensible to her. "*Mai dai, Khun* Margaret," she says: not possible. If she's paid to clean, she'll clean. So each morning she does her tasks, then each afternoon she whisks the floor clean with a bristly old broom, one centimeter at a time. I spend my days at my desk writing emails, taking a break after lunch to read on our shady terrace with a coffee. I remind myself, "How lucky am I?" Not many people I know have a housekeeper caring for their home.

One afternoon, with the residence already clean, she takes it upon herself to polish my grandmother's demitasse spoons. Before she leaves at the end of her shift, she tells me, "One spoon all afternoon, *Khun* Margaret—so dirty!" What she thought was dirt, however, was gold; she's polished the gold accents right off the silver. Even though I admire her proactivity and her determination, I wish she'd considered asking me if what she was doing was helpful.

I phone Patrick to explain what happened. I'm not sure what I expect him to do; he has bigger issues than a single demitasse spoon, with renovating parts of the resort, rebalancing the budget, and restructuring the whole management team. But, still, I need his advice. He says, "I'm sorry that happened, Margaret. I know these family heirlooms are precious to you. But I'm the general manager for the resort and you're the general manager for Residence Eight. I'm here to support you, but I ask you to *manage* the situation."

"OK," I say, not happily. I'd rather that Patrick handle this; it's still stressful in the extreme for me to be in conflict with anyone. I gird my loins and pick up the phone, telling the housekeeping supervisor what happened, and requesting a brief meeting. She rushes over to the residence and *wai*s deeply when I answer the door. I invite her in, *wai*-ing back.

She blurts out, "Please, *Khun* Margaret: *mai bpen rai*."

I get it; is this really a big deal in the big scheme of things? Of course it's not—and I definitely don't want the housekeeper or the supervisor to "lose face." But I'm determined to express myself—instead of just smiling and nodding. Been there; done that.

In a calm voice and with my best "determined serenity" smile, I say, "I'm not angry." I continue, "Let me tell you what my mother would do if I broke something when I was young. She'd ask me, 'Did you do it on purpose?' I'd say, 'Of course not.' She'd say, 'OK, then just try not to do it again.'"

The supervisor nods but I can tell she's trying to sort out if I'm actually angry after all. She begs me not to tell *Khun* Patrick and I respond that I already have—that we tell each other everything—but not to worry; he's not angry, either. She thinks for a second. "*Khun* Margaret, I will buy you a replacement," she says. "I'll go to the store and find you a spoon."

I know her intentions are pure and she wants to make this right, but that would only add insult to injury—unless Chiang Mai's department store carries antique demitasse spoons, handed down from generation to generation, which I rather doubt.

"Please don't do that," I say. "Your concern means a lot to me, but—truly—I just want and need better communication. Please ask the housekeeper—who is lovely, by the way—to simply ask me if she has questions or if she needs help." I feel the irony of me saying this.

It's so easy for me to suggest this for *someone else*. I take a deep breath and force myself to add, *"Mai bpen rai,"* to reassure the supervisor, and I see her shoulders relax.

When Patrick gets home I catch him up, doing my best to laugh with him about the day's events.

"Well done, *chérie*. That's *mai bpen rai* for you."

I'm feeling proud of this cultural progress until Patrick outdoes me soon after at the Loy Krathong festival. We're among hundreds of people gathered in the evening at a sprawling Buddhist meditation center outside Chiang Mai. Each attendee receives a paper lantern to launch for luck. Once the wick in the center of the lantern is lighted, the lantern slowly drifts up and away into ever-shifting golden constellations against the black night sky. As we gaze up, Patrick's sleeve brushes against the torch used to light our lantern—and suddenly catches on fire. We put out the flames, but before we do, Patrick exclaims, "No worries, *chérie!* Have you ever seen anything more beautiful in your life?"

Really? I think. *The spirit of* jai yen yen *and* mai bpen rai *at the same time?* I tell Patrick I love his enthusiasm, but under my breath, I grumble, "Damned over-achiever!"

When the resort undergoes a name change in 2004 from the Regent to Four Seasons Resort Chiang Mai, I write home to my parents, "Ninety-nine monks were bussed in from the local Buddhist temple for this auspicious occasion." The monks range from youthful and giggling to ancient and solemn, but all are dressed in saffron-orange robes, their heads shaved. They parade past the tables the resort has placed in a circle around the Ganesh statue. At each table, the staff, guests, Patrick, and I place bags of rice or fruit or incense sticks into the monks' bronze metal alms bowls. They aren't begging; by allowing us to make offerings to them, they offer us the blessing of making merit. "So now," I add, "the resort is officially blessed under the new name—and they blessed the water buffaloes, too!"

As the weeks and months pass, I make it my business to get to know a little bit about each staff member. They don't seem displeased by my interest, but they do seem puzzled. I'm not making it easy for them with my American familiarity. I struggle with the Thai world view that we fit on different levels of the social spectrum. It goes against the grain of the American "we are all equal" mythology. Yes, Patrick had told me about this when we visited a decade ago, but *living* here now, I feel it every day. Obviously, I respect the Royal Family and Buddhist priests, monks and nuns. Patrick gets respect as GM of one of Thailand's best resorts—and as the boss. I get some peripheral respect as his wife. But when we encounter Thais with simple education, they ask us, "How old are you? How much money do you make?" Being a Westerner with pale skin means two notches up the scale, which makes me very uncomfortable, but I'm grateful that age is respected. It makes it easier to bear the strands of silver appearing in my hair.

At Songkran, the traditional water festival each spring, Patrick and I—as the elders—are seated on carved teakwood chairs, shaded from the sun by parasols overhead. Our hands are cupped, palms upward. In front of us kneel two of his employees, pouring jasmine-scented water from a silver bowl into our cupped hands. I smile down at his director of human resources. She smiles back up at me, and wishes me, "*Sawasdee Bpee Mai!*" Greetings of the New Year! I repeat those words back to her, then it's my turn to dip my fingertips into the silver bowl and lightly pat her cheek with the jasmine water. This is our exchange of blessings and best wishes. It's the face of Thailand that's beloved by tourists: graceful, respectful, gentle. But we also see another side to the Thai spirit—at staff parties, we hop along in sack races and howl along to karaoke. "This is Thai *sanuk*," Patrick tells me. "The spirit of fun and playfulness."

As the director of HR dips her fingers into the silver bowl again and this time spritzes me over my shoulders, her smile is tinged with mischief. Then I feel cold water on my neck and turn to see her assistant giggling as she pours a trickle of ice water down the back of my blouse. "*Sanuk!*" they both laugh at my ongoing baptism into the ways of the complex, sly Land of Smiles.

I'm balancing earnest and playful, long-term resident yet still a foreigner, VIP but not VVIP. The more I learn, the more I hover between worlds. When a senior manager quits, the employees line up to bid his European wife and him farewell with respectful *wais*. Should I, too, present the calm façade of a Thai—or display Western anguish instead, "tearing my hair out" to show my sadness at their departure? Neither is wholly honest.

I haven't had a drink in a couple of years so I'm squelching my feelings less. I'm a little tired of calibrating and changing to make everyone else happy. Patrick sometimes seems surprised by my expressing myself more, but he doesn't walk away from me—the thing I've unconsciously feared my whole life.

I email to my parents, "I still feel we made the right move here at the right time, but right now I'm adrift. I know I'll find my feet again, but I feel lonely and confused, which by now I know is normal with these moves. I'm no longer shy about asking for help, so . . . please keep your emails coming! They mean so much to me!"

Ever-more lengthy Trip Reports to them follow, describing tropical flora with leaves as big as platters, the delicate scent of night-blooming jasmine. I detail our weekend drives around the neighboring hillside, passing through tiny villages (and around innumerable identical scruffy dogs who scratch themselves in the middle of the road). These are happy excursions for Patrick and me, exploring together and delighting at sights like a thatched-roof hut selling "soup of snake." Patrick loves being behind the wheel of the resort's Mitsubishi and—unlike me—is confident driving on the "other" side of the road. This leaves me free to stare out the car window and take pictures, turning these into Shutterfly slide shows back home and agonizing over which image to choose for our annual holiday card.

On Sunday mornings, he drives us to downtown Chiang Mai, the city itself surrounded by ancient walls and what was once a moat. Two hundred temples are picturesque in their decay; so worn away by rain and time as to seem almost soft, their bricks and wood inviting a caress. While backpackers sit in grungy internet cafés or the moth-eaten used bookstore, Patrick sips a cappuccino at Starbucks and I meet with friends of friends to continue the conversation I started in Egypt: how to clean up my side of the proverbial street and keep it clean; how to continue making my actions match my intentions; how to continue leading a life I'm proud of again.

After Patrick picks me up again, we brave the crowded, noisy shopping mall to reach the Cineplex. Even though we hate the jarring music pouring out of the electronics stores and the fried food smells from the food court en route, it's worth it for a movie on the silver screen. Sitting in the dark while holding hands is one of our favorite things in the world. I learn fast, though, not to get too comfortable in my seat as—before the movie begins—the King's Anthem is played and everyone in the theater is obliged to stand out of respect. For dinner downtown, it's always Giorgio's where we are the culinary beneficiaries of a classic love story: Italian boy falls in love with Thai girl, moves here, and makes the best tortellini this side of Italia.

These treats are a welcome break from trying so hard to be culturally sensitive, which God knows I believe in and I've been struggling to uphold as best I can. I know I'll always be a guest in another's country. I do my best to be respectful. But I'm starting to understand that it's OK to want comfort food—and I love my comfort phone calls home. When my parents pick up, I say, "*Pronto!*"—it's Italian for hello on the phone. This is the sign for them to know it's me calling, so they can hang up and call me back—phone charges are much cheaper from the US to Thailand than vice versa. Dad once asks Mother and me what we talk about on our two-hour phone calls. My mom and I look at each other, burst into laughter, and say "Everything!" at the same time. Ever since she took that fall in Pisa years ago, we've been growing up together as adults. We share more. We share more honestly.

On one of these marathon phone calls with my mom, she says, "I love your Trip Reports, Missie, but I think you'd be marvelous at writing shorter pieces—like a *New Yorker* essay. A page or two." That's my mom's way of telling me that I've gotten too long-winded. Maybe it was the recent Tolstoy-length description of a local pilgrimage site we visited in which I detailed the number of steps from the parking lot to the temple (three hundred and seven), distance from downtown (sixteen point one kilometers), the scene at the top (families picnicking and monks blessing the faithful), the colors of the decorations (millions of tiny mirrored squares in glittering gold, green, blue and red), and—lastly, in a burst of classical music pretentiousness—the sound of the gong being gonged by the pilgrims (a deep *basso profondo*).

If I'm boring even my *mother*—who is interested in *every* detail of my life—I think, *What am I supposed to write now? Should I get back to my novel, started four years ago in Paris?* That feels so far away from me right now I can't even imagine that I wanted to write a book in the first place.

I'm saved from having to figure out what I really want to do by a call from the Four Seasons home office in autumn 2004: The GM in Bangkok is leaving and Patrick is needed there. My efforts can once again be directed to micromanaging another move. I tell everyone I'll be once again "creating a life for myself wherever we are," a platitude I love to spout but which is starting to sound hollow even to me.

A domino effect is triggered within Four Seasons any time one of the sixty-two GMs in twenty-nine countries moves. I scoff when friends in diplomatic service gripe, "We only get six months to pack up!" They know the start and end dates of their assignments in advance, while we get a call simply stating a Four Seasons location somewhere in the world and requesting a yea or nay within a few days, with the actual move to follow within several weeks.

Mother and Dad send me a silly birthday card:

> *We're sending greetings to say hi. Regretfully, we*
> *don't speak Thai.*
>
> *We trust you've found a birthday frock to strut your*
> *stuff in old Bangkok.*
>
> *We wonder if you both are grooving, with the*
> *thought that you are moving.*
>
> *Holy Cow and Sakes Alive: You have reached the*
> *forty-five. HAPPY HAPPY!*

Yes, I realize, *I am grooving.* I'm relieved about this move. Not that it's not stunning in Chiang Mai; it's a paradise for honeymooners—and for Patrick. But I can admit it now; it's not *my* paradise. We've already had a few years in remote resort locations. I need some city!

I separate out what will go into long-term storage in Bangkok, as the GM's apartment there is not nearly as large as Residence Eight in Chiang Mai. We'll only be taking cat and clothes, books and laptops, jewelry and Very Important Documents (discovered in a "safe place" after all). While I feel like I've only just unpacked the last box of our stuff, the movers come and pack it up again. Lastly, I place my turquoise-blue journal in my carry-on.

On the day of the actual move, the staff bids me farewell; Patrick has flown on ahead to Bangkok. Now, Nadia and I are in the resort's Mitsubishi to be driven south. The first few hours of the trip are a

Postcard of Southeast Asia: rice paddies glow green; chickens peck at the side of the road. We make a stop along the way at a roadside restaurant for a slice of jackfruit pie.

When we reach the outskirts of Bangkok, our car is pulled over by highway patrol. The hotel driver is visibly nervous as the officer approaches the car. I roll down the window in the back passenger seat. The officer smiles and greets me, "*Sawasdee Khap, Madaam.*"

Then he says something to the driver, who translates, "*Khun Margaret*, he needs to know what's in the car."

I respond, "Please tell the officer that he's welcome to look in the trunk or to search my bags." The driver relates this back to the policeman, who then peers inside through the car window.

"What's in the green bag?" he asks the driver, who responds *Meow*. The cop tells the driver, who translates again, "I'm sure *Madaam's* husband is a very important man. If *Madaam* would give me his business card, you can be on your way." When the driver relates this to me, I'm thinking, *Oh, hell, no. I am definitely not going to give Patrick's card to this guy—who will show up at Four Seasons in the blink of an eye.*

In a flash of righteous anger and in a fit of out-of-body inspiration, I take one of my own calling cards and a pen out of my purse. On the back of my card, I draw a paw print. I hand the card to him through the car window, saying "For you! From *Meow!*" The cop looks at the card. He looks at me. I can tell from his astonished expression that he now believes he has a crazy foreign lady on his hands—and not the easy mark he may have thought. He steps back from the car and waves the driver on without another word and I feel proud of myself for *not* being Perfectly Culturally Sensitive—for once.

BANGKOK

When Patrick arrived at the Bangkok hotel, all staff was on deck to welcome him. I'm disappointed that my husband and the doorman are the only ones at the front door upon my arrival, but I'm also starting to see that being in the shadow of Patrick's Alpha status has kept me safe. Easiest for me will be to now slide into Perfect Wife who Curtsies to Royalty at Ribbon Cuttings and Such. As long as I play out my roles, no one will ask me what I'm doing with *my* life.

We're living in the GM's apartment on the eighth floor, with views over the Bangkok skyline and the golf course across the street. There's a gleaming dark wood bookcase for my books and framed photos, and the furniture is upholstered in a reddish-gold Thai silk. There's no longer any need to worry about kitty claws: Nadia's listless at twenty-two years old. Her life is winding down, and I want to be prepared for the inevitable. When a tipsy American next to me at a women's club luncheon overhears me talking about Nadia, she blurts out, "No Buddhist is going to be willing to put your cat to sleep. When the time comes, you'll have to kill her yourself."

"Pardon me?" I ask, my voice squeaky. "Am I supposed to hit her over the head with the hammer from my tool kit? Strangle her? Drown her in a rice paddy?"

"Of course not," she scoffs. "Just stockpile enough Valium to do the job."

"But I don't have even one pill like that in the house," I say, "let alone a Valley of the Dolls quantity."

She shrugs, repeats how that's just how it is here, and signals the waiter for another glass of wine.

Having already watched one cat decline, I know when it's time to let Nadia go a few weeks later. Luckily, by then, a new friend has tipped me off to a vet who will discreetly put pets to sleep. I gently maneuver Nadia into her green canvas carrying case one last time and head downstairs. The hotel's black Mercedes is waiting at the front entrance. The driver greets me with a *wai* and takes Nadia from me, *meow*-ing gently at her through the mesh of the carrier, then helping us both into the back seat of the car.

He asks, "I take you and *Meow* where, *Khun* Margaret?" I give him the address of the animal hospital.

This time, I don't leave the room as the vet gently slides the needle in, putting Nadia down as I pet her, tears running down my face. The vet then asks if we'd like Nadia to be taken to a special Buddhist temple where they cremate animals. I nod in agreement and walk out of the vet's, where the driver is waiting. When I hand him the carrying case—empty now—he asks, "*Khun* Margaret, where is *Meow*?"

In order to save face for both of us, I say, trying not to sound panicky, "*Meow* is staying here at animal hospital. She is not well." Both true, but obviously not the whole story. He just nods and drives me home.

I trudge up to our apartment, wiping away my tears before I let myself in. Inside is our part-time housekeeper, who—upon seeing my face—asks, "*Khun* Margaret! You OK?" I nod as serenely as I can. Then she asks me the same question as the driver had, "Where is *Meow*?" As her English is very limited, it's no use trying to explain. Instead, I place my palms together under my right cheek to indicate a pillow, tilt my head onto that pretend pillow, then point skyward. I'm intending to express that Nadia is resting in the Great Beyond. The housekeeper looks puzzled but *wais* me politely and walks away to finish her work for the day.

When I tell my friend who'd recommended the vet, she says, "Margaret, when you pointed heavenward, the housekeeper probably thought you meant that Nadia was taking a nap on a high shelf. She may be looking for her now. To dust her!" That makes me laugh, a little, which I need, after letting go of a companion—cherished for decades—who traveled around the world with Patrick and me.

The next afternoon, when the housekeeper stops by for her daily tidying up, she asks, "*Khun* Margaret! Where is *Meow*?"

Oh, God, I think. *Is this going to be like Groundhog Day with the same question over and over?* Obviously my pantomime of lies isn't working, so I blurt out, "She's dead. *Meow* is dead."

The housekeeper says (a little impatiently, I feel), "I know that, *Khun* Margaret. But *where* is she?" Evidently I'm the one not understanding. Then the penny drops.

"Oh," I say, "Temple. *Meow* at Buddhist Temple." This time I pantomime smoke rising up to the heavens. The housekeeper closes her eyes for a moment and nods. She just wanted to know that Patrick and I had done the right thing.

The verb "to understand" in Thai is *kaojai.* The roots of the word are enter + heart. I want to enter into the heart of Thai culture, but I also want to be in touch with my own heart's desires. I want to remain sensitive to another culture while being true to myself. I'm coming to realize that it's OK to take a break from being *perfectly* culturally sensitive once in a while. When I eat lunch alone in the shade by the hotel's pool, chopsticks in one hand and a book in the other, the Thai server approaches me to fuss, "Ooh, *Khun* Margaret, so lonely! I keep you company!" I know that together is better for Thais. When Patrick and I go to the movies, someone inevitably chooses to sit in the seats next to us—in an otherwise empty theater. *But,* I think, *"Khun" Margaret is happy being alone sometimes. Let me be me!*

And at five feet nine, being me doesn't always fit in Thailand—literally. When I visit a tailor's to get a dress made for a gala event, the tiny Thai seamstress measures me then pronounces, "Oh, sorry! Not enough fabric!" Does she mean not enough of the bottle-green silk I've chosen? Or not enough fabric in the whole country?

When I want to buy panties at the main department store, the petite sales clerk shakes her head and says, "Sorry! No have Extra Extra Extra Large!" *Was that necessary? How about saving face for me, too?*

When I step into the elevator on the ground floor of our hotel at the same time as a white-haired Asian guest, I welcome him to Four Seasons, bowing slightly. We smile at each other and I ask where he's visiting from. "Japan," he replies, then he looks me up and down. After a pause, he exclaims, "You very big!"

"Like Godzilla?" I ask, pointing to myself.

"Yes! Yes!" the old man says. "*Gajira! Gajira!*"

This at least makes me laugh, as does the weekend when Patrick borrows the hotel car to get us out of town for some fresh air and a change of scenery. After driving for an hour, we stop at a restaurant riverside: just a few plastic chairs under a crooked nylon beach umbrella. On the plastic table is a pink plastic container housing a roll of toilet paper instead of napkins. A shy young waiter serves fresh young coconuts as our beverage, then papaya salad and fried fish. We're astounded by how delicious the fish tastes. Patrick asks him in Thai, "Fish comes from where?" The young man points to the brown river, flowing sleepily by just next to us, then walks away to get us our check. When we look to where he's pointed, a bloated dead pig bobs by. Patrick laughs, saying, "I thought I tasted something extra special!"

While I keep exploring and saying yes to every Thai lecture and tour and exploration, I also create Bangkok comforts for myself, joining the American and International Women's Book Clubs, where I'm grateful for the conversations around literature.

I launch an online Four Seasons Spouses and Partners Group in the hopes of helping us all feel more confident as we move around the world. I know it's a cliché, but I propose that we can thrive—and not just survive—in our various settings. Eighteen women say yes to "getting to know one another better" so that's our inaugural topic. Inspired by my friend Chris, a diplomatic spouse, I am more clear than ever that what we offer—as Trailing Spouses and Ministers of Domestic Affairs— is a very valuable skill set: budgeting, managing, supervising, moving, travel planning, PR, marketing, organizing, coordinating. Not to mention the additional responsibilities of those spouses with kids. I'm quite clear that my friends back home do much of this, too, many of them holding down full-time jobs as well. It's just that I'm realizing how much work *I* do—without getting a separate paycheck for it and without recognition (except for Patrick's consistently thanking me and telling me that he couldn't do it without me).

Having given up on Thai, I sign up for French classes at the Alliance Française. This is a commitment to our future happiness— spending time in the French-speaking southwest of Switzerland with Jetti and Otto and their family. Three mornings a week at nine, I walk out the front door of the hotel, greet our doormen, and walk fifty paces past the food stalls crowding the sidewalk, breathing in the stinging scent of garlic I've come to love. With my broad-brimmed hat, long cotton slacks and a white cotton blouse, I no longer pay much mind to the heat and humidity. I walk up a flight of steps to Bangkok's clean, air-conditioned elevated train and travel just three stops for another short walk to the Alliance and my Advanced French class. There's a shady café on the ground floor, where I sit with an espresso and croissant after class, basking in the sound of French around me. I am grateful for these familiar pleasures. Seems that no one's been asking me to be the Perfect Expat—except me.

And, of course, if a croissant in Bangkok is good, one in Switzerland is better.

I hadn't fallen in love with Patrick's homeland when I first visited as a backpacker in 1981. It had rained nonstop, so I didn't see anything of the country's much-vaunted natural beauty, and the youth hostel loudspeakers frightened me with each barked, "*Achtung!*"

My opinion of the country changed when I visited with Patrick for the first time. I'd already met his parents, but in 1992 he introduced me to the rest of his family, and I saw where Patrick had inherited his kindness.

When he took me to the mountains to show me his beloved Alps, I yelped, "Wow! How tall are those things?"

"Over thirteen thousand feet above sea level," Patrick replied.

As a flatlander, I had no context for that number. As a Chicagoan, I cited the altitude I knew best: "They're tall, but they can't *possibly* be taller than the Sears Tower!"

"Actually," Patrick said, "They can be and they are: about eight times taller."

I could see that Patrick was baffled that I didn't comprehend this simple equation, and was reconsidering if I really was the right choice as a life partner (just as I'd done when he'd showed up in ear protectors too nerdy even for me).

But we got past my ignorance and his ear-gear and married in January 1993, just fourteen months after meeting. We had a civil ceremony in the Swissôtel Chicago where we met, then Patrick and I flew to Switzerland for our church wedding in his hometown. We planned our Chicago wedding, but his mom Monique arranged everything in Bern, down to the smallest detail. She was surprised but respectful of my request that my dad walk me up the aisle. That's not a tradition in Switzerland, nor is wearing white for a bride of a certain age who's been living with her fiancé, but so be it. I'd said yes to marrying in a church to honor Patrick's tradition, so I felt comfortable requesting that my traditions be honored, too.

Patrick and I had asked our wee Swiss nieces Mirjam and Christina to be a part of our bridal party. Jetti—pregnant with Nicolas—explained to the girls that we'd like them to carry my long bridal train. When the church bells started to toll, they gripped the lace-edged satin and marched somberly behind me as I walked up the aisle on my father's arm. Once I'd arrived at the altar, though, they would not let go; Jetti had to pry the train out of their clenched fists. I loved their fierce dedication. (I also loved that one niece refused to wear a garland of flowers in her hair. *I get it, lil' girlfriend,* I thought.)

After the wedding, Patrick and I walked from the church to the reception with the whole bridal party following us through the streets and under the arcades of medieval Bern. This cocktail reception was an opportunity for Patrick's parents to invite not only Bernese friends but business acquaintances. I overhead one say, surprised, "*Elle parle français!*" She speaks French. Another added, "*Italiano anche!*" Italian, too. I felt proud to offer an experience of a different American than many Swiss had met.

From the reception, we proceeded to the restaurant where we had our wedding dinner—in a room lined with jade-green silk. Closest family and friends offered not only toasts, but skits, stories, and collages. I was asked to translate the speech of a relative into English, as not many of the guests spoke his native Italian.

He blurted out, "Thank God Patrick is not marrying a Swiss. The Swiss are so narrow-minded." At that point he pantomimed a box. *Oh, boy,* I thought, but hid my surprise and transformed that into, "Thank God Patrick's marriage has us gathered in Switzerland . . . which is um, shaped like this." I pantomimed a sort of an elongated box myself. (Actually, the country is shaped more like a delicious, buttery croissant, but I was trying to avoid embarrassment for my new family and the Swiss guests present.)

After dinner, I waltzed with my new groom and with Patrick's grandfather: a gracious gentleman, dapper in a gray morning coat. My only regret is that we didn't splurge on a hotel for our Swiss wedding night; we stayed in my new in-laws' guest room instead. I'd agreed with Patrick that a hotel room would have been a waste. The departure for our honeymoon the next morning was in only a few hours. But I hated that Patrick and I put rational ahead of romantic (even as I was grateful to be marrying a fellow *frugalista*).

Every time Patrick and I return to Bern in the years after our marriage, I love the meals with his parents and the time with his mom walking through the woods near their home or in mountains nearby. When faced with any beautiful vista (and there is no shortage of those in Switzerland), Monique quotes from a German song: "*Trinkt, o Augen!*" Drink, o eyes! Released from the duties of home and chores for even just a few hours, she—and I—drink in the beauty of the everyday world.

Every time Patrick and I visit Jetti and Otto, I love the time with their kids and with them, strolling the city of Lausanne with its rose-windowed cathedral and markets where the doughy scent of bread fills the air. Along Lake Geneva, a million grapes on terraced vineyards ripen for wine and old steam ships traverse the slate-blue waters, their horns letting out mournful cries as they draw into tiny port after port.

The whole family loves the century-old, family-run Waldhaus Hotel in Sils-Maria, where Patrick worked after finishing his hotel school degree and where we walk for hours in the woods and valleys, dotted with chalets. In Wengen, a car-free Alpine town, Patrick skis while I bask on a mountaintop terrace with a slice of plum tart topped with a peak of fresh whipped cream.

Everywhere in Switzerland, I am enchanted with the Swiss *art de vivre.* It's where long, leisurely meals are the norm and where the first question I get asked at a party may be, "What are you reading?" instead of "Where do you work?" My opinions on art and music and travel are as important as my professional identity (or lack of one). I feel like I am more than what I do (or what my husband does). I feel at home there. Rule-bound Switzerland grows into my Anti-Handbook. It's a place of deep happiness for me.

Suddenly, sadness strikes in the summer of 2005: Patrick's mother passes away—at only seventy. Monique kept reassuring us that the doctors had her illness under control and—from far away in Bangkok—we willed ourselves to believe her. Then one morning Patrick's father phoned him saying, "If you want to say goodbye to your mother, now might be the right time to get on a plane." Patrick was able to make the next flight to Switzerland, but didn't make it in time before his mom passed away.

After a funeral service in church in Bern—with Monique's choir singing her beloved Bach—Patrick honors her memory by climbing Japan's Mount Fuji. She was so at home in the mountains; this pilgrimage just feels right to him. Patrick is grateful that his mom died without the indignity of growing old—and that she is out of suffering. He seems serene.

Not me. I'm angry at myself that I wasn't there for her and stunned to realize that I may not be there for my parents when they draw their last breath. It could happen when I'm near to them or far away; it's not within my circle of control. I pray to know that everyone is in good hands, just not always in my hands.

I have to keep living my life. I head back to Bangkok.

Once back in Thailand, Patrick receives a promotion to regional vice president, which means he's traveling for work more than ever. I don't often accompany him to places we've been to already; I leave no stone unturned when I visit for the first time. "I'm hittin' that place hard," I say—in case I never get back.

There are, however, a few travel temptations I can't pass up:

Farthest northern Thailand, where we breakfast with baby elephants at the new Four Seasons Tented Camp overlooking the hazy blue hills of Burma across the river.

Kyoto, where red-lipped geishas entertain us with music and song—for the most expensive dinner of our lives. We overnight in a traditional Japanese *ryokan* inn with only thin *tatami* mats on the floor as our beds. Patrick falls immediately into gentle snoring while I toss and turn, unable to get comfortable. I grab all the clothes out of my suitcase to make a nest I can lie on, reminding myself that *I'm* the one who insisted on this authentic experience.

Cambodia, where our friends Chris and Manuel meet us to tour Siem Reap's endless temples. As we've booked too late to secure a guide, we take turns reading from the guidebook. Manuel asks us at one point, "At the risk of diminishing your confidence in me as your leader, does anyone know which temple this one is?" I'm delighted to realize that—for once—I have absolutely no idea.

Luang Prabang, where I agree to a five dollar massage, even though the mats are slick with peppermint massage oil leftover from previous customers. There's only a half-curtain shielding me from the men sitting in the next room drinking what I assume is Laotian moonshine, so—when the masseuse gestures for me to pull off my blouse—I say "No, thanks." Not even for the Perfect Traveler.

We even get back to Sharm el Sheikh after giving Patrick's successor two years to make his own mark. The female colleagues we worked with embrace me joyfully; the men offer me respectful handshakes, then clasp Patrick in affectionate bear hugs. It's a deep satisfaction to see the resort thriving. It offers a livelihood for so many Egyptians who can now afford to get married and raise families.

Many have earned promotions, and some are even poised to move around the world with Four Seasons careers.

When we return to Bangkok after these trips and I call my parents, my mom always asks, "Now that you're back, Missie, where to next?" My travel dream is coming true, year after year, trip after trip. I give thanks for that.

I also give thanks for excellent medical care in Bangkok; people come here from around the world as medical tourists. During my 2005 annual check-up, the doctor mentions that I have a slightly irregular heartbeat. This is nothing new to me; I've heard it from every doctor wielding a stethoscope since I was young. But this guy adds in a casual tone, "You might need open-heart surgery—but it's not a big deal." *Maybe not for you, buddy*, I think. I'm terrified and already picturing a long red scar running down my chest.

I recount the conversation to Patrick. What he *says* is that he'll be there for the surgery if I need him to be. What I *hear* is that he has important work to do, but could take time away from that for an emergency. What I *think* is: *What the hell, Patrick?*

Stung, I call my mom. I don't want to worry her, but I need to share about the possible surgery with her. Without hesitation, she offers to fly to Thailand to be by my side. My stoic mother, an old woman who can now only walk with difficulty—*she's* the one who hears my fear and is ready to be there for me?

Luckily, before a scalpel can be wielded, my doctor suggests another test with a cardiologist and that exam rules out the need for surgery after all. Meeting with me after the test, the Thai cardiologist says, "Your heart is very strange—but very beautiful." This is very Thai. I am very charmed and—more than that—extremely relieved with the good news.

But as for Patrick and me? We definitely need to realign. I tell him, for what feels like the hundredth time, "I love Four Seasons, and it's our professional family, but a corporation will never have your back the way I do, and have, for fifteen years. I need you to have *my* back, too."

I'm reminded of when Patrick and I were packing up our apartment to move from Chicago to New York ten years ago. It was the middle of the night; the movers were arriving the next day. As we stood, exhausted, in our study, me gaping at my bookcase and knowing that I couldn't possibly fit all my books into a much smaller apartment in Manhattan, Patrick said to me, "Why don't you just take your favorite book?" Book. Singular.

I turned on him, furious. "You *must* be kidding! That's like me asking you to just take your favorite CD, mister classical music fanatic!"

Patrick said, "Well, a CD is much smaller than a book!"

I thought, *Do you not get me, Patrick?*

It still hurts when I recall doing the walk of shame at the Swissôtel. Instead of letting Patrick escort me proudly to the front entrance after a date and asking the doorman to get me a taxi, I said, "You sleep. I'll be fine." It didn't occur to me to let him take care of me. No, that's not true: it did occur to me. I wanted his care, but I played out my old script of taking care of him instead.

I had done that with every man I ever dated. The relationships would start out fun, but soon enough, I'd slide into my familiar energetic enabling. I remained determined to be the best girlfriend ever, and if anyone's glass got even near half-empty, I chirped, "Don't you worry; I'll fill that right up!" like some frenzied gas station attendant pouring my golden sunshine-y love right into their hearts.

Which of course doesn't work. I thought it was up to me to keep the relationship perfect (or at least to keep it on life support until I could figure out how to make it better). A little part of my heart would always whimper, "This is no way to be treated." I hadn't yet known that it was—also—no way to *allow* myself to be treated.

With what feels like divine intervention, Patrick attends some leadership training with Four Seasons and is intrigued. His boss, Neil, notices his interest and suggests that he attend a personal growth seminar with AsiaWorks in Singapore. When we're reunited afterwards, Patrick says to me, "Close your eyes and open your hands." He places on my palms a pin in the shape of a beetle in a dazzling bottle green. "It's my promise to buy you a piece of real jewelry."

"I love the beetle, *amore mio*," I say, "but I don't need more jewelry. I want more of *you*."

Patrick vows, "I'm committed to being more present."

Before I respond, I pause. I want to be the supportive wife who believes her husband. But I say it anyway, "I'm happy to hear that, Patrick, but the proof is in the pudding. Show me; don't tell me."

I can sense that I've hurt his feelings, but—as the weeks pass—he does show up differently, placing more focus on our relationship and on me. *Hmm,* I think, *whatever this AsiaWorks stuff is, it works.* When Patrick asks if I'd consider checking it out myself, I fly to Singapore for the Basic Training.

AsiaWorks ain't easy and it ain't pretty, but I know the definition of insanity—doing the same thing over and over while expecting different results—so I listen hard to see where I need to change, even when the revelations sting. The training reveals to me how I'm perceived by strangers. I thought I was giving off an air of refinement, but other participants—when invited to share—tell me they see me as arrogant and aloof. "Puckered up," one says, and I think, *Whoa, this is not how I want to present myself to the world.*

I learn just how much my perfectionism drags me down. When I haven't completed my homework on time and the facilitator asks why, I tell him I ran out of time when I was copying my notes more neatly. He shakes his head, asking, "Are you still in grammar school?" *No. I'm forty-five and this is not how I want to spend the rest of my time on earth.* I come to understand that it's me who has trained the people in my life how to treat me.

Patrick and I attend a session for couples at AsiaWorks, the facilitator theorizing that men want to be forgiven while women want to be cherished. I hate gender generalizations, but my heart sighs with how true that feels for me. I tell Patrick, "That's absolutely what I want from you—not just to be appreciated. Not just to be called *chérie*—which I love—but actually cherished, like the most precious gift in your life." I finally tell him, "I don't want to come last on your list anymore." (I still don't yet dare say that what I really want is to come first on his list.)

Then I forgive him for his own unconscious needs—which have driven him as mercilessly as mine have driven me. It's been more than a decade since Patrick and I vowed at our wedding, "I promise to grow alongside you." This is another step on that path.

Yet another is when I tell Patrick, "No more on the constant entertaining. I recognize it's been *me* insisting that we invite over every single possible business prospect."

Patrick says he understands. He saw how wounded I was at a recent dinner party when the sleek-suited Frenchman at my side talked *at* me for hours, only realizing over dessert that he should probably ask me *something*. "What do you do, anyway?" he asked, stirring sugar into his coffee and not even looking me in the eyes. His wife—a fellow Trailing Spouse—answered on my behalf.

"Margaret? *Elle suit.*" Margaret? She follows. Margaret? She's a follower.

It's true, of course, but it's a knife in my heart. I have followed Patrick's career around the world, and I will follow him anywhere. Just once in my life, though, I want to hear someone say, "Margaret? *Elle écrit.*" Margaret? She writes. But that would take me typing more than just my slightly shorter, still nerdily researched Trip Reports. So who's going to change this, Margaret-the-follower?

Oh, confounding, infuriating no-place-to-hide. It's up to me to change me.

I vow to be intentional, like the poet Rumi suggested:

> The breezes at dawn have secrets to tell you.
> Don't go back to sleep!
> You must ask for what you really want.
> Don't go back to sleep!

Maybe, I think, *this is what I really want*, when Patrick gets an email in 2007 from a home office colleague: "Would Margaret be willing to share her ideas for a Transitions Manager?" Patrick had mentioned to her my suggestion for a corporate position to handle employees' moves between and within countries. She's interested in learning more, and I'm ecstatic! All our moves and my years of being a Trailing Spouse can be useful after all.

In my cover letter I write, "It's hard for a GM to do the job successfully if he or she is getting nagged at home." I mention a gem from the international relocation world: "Happy Spouse, Happy House." I outline the return on investment if Four Seasons implements this position, and I propose myself for the job (reminding Four Seasons that I've moved Patrick and me from New York to Paris to Cairo to Sharm to Chiang Mai to Bangkok).

Patrick is supportive, telling me he feels I'd be perfectly suited for this work. I feel that I've presented a well-thought-out proposal. The home office colleague responds that she'll keep me posted. I never hear back.

I feel deflated, just as I'd felt when Patrick had a short-term assignment in Istanbul years ago. I'd proposed myself to the GM there for an ad hoc sales assignment. He barely bothered to let me make my pitch before he said, "I hope you'll enjoy spending your days in the Spa, Margaret." Just as my Sharm Women's Club fell flat—no one but me wanted to put together a Yellow Pages. Just as my recent Four Seasons Spouses and Partners Network fizzled out. I'd asked participants to share their advice for fellow expats, but it never gained traction. Maybe because I'd answered my own questions instead of allowing the others to respond?

I feel pathetic: a little girl walking home alone from school, surprised when no one wanted to be friends with a Teacher's Pet like me. No one wants to play with me, even when I think I'm bringing the ball to recess.

I do again what I've always done under duress: throw myself back into old familiar roles. Perfect Hostess it is—to our visiting friends and family. As ever, I have the Perfect Itinerary ready. Upon arrival, we'll walk to the nearby Erawan Shrine ("Let me show you how to *wai*"), then home to the hotel for a power nap ("I'll wake you from your jet lag coma for a refreshing swim in the pool"). The next days include touring the Grand Palace ("No sleeveless tops"), the floating markets ("Offer half of the selling price"), and the Reclining Buddha Temple ("Don't touch the head of the Buddha"). I orchestrate taxis and tips, meeting places and meals ("Patrick will meet us for dinner").

Seeing the wonder in our guests' eyes makes me happy. But—as with Paris, Cairo, Sharm, and Chiang Mai—I have essentially memorized each hour of the itinerary. With a jolt, I realize that I just can't bear doing this for another several years. I just can't accompany every guest on the exact same outings every time, even though I love each and every one of them and I'm grateful that they came to visit. Instead, I prepare a binder with my touring suggestions (still obsessively, compulsively detailed, needless to say). I settle visitors in on rollaways in our living room or in a nearby guest room. I accompany them on Day One, but often that's it.

"But will they have a Perfect Stay without me?" I fret. My instinct is still to tag along everywhere, dashing to open their maps for them and paying their tickets. If I worry that one friend, or guest—or even a stranger I see on the street!—might be lost for even one minute, I want to be the one to save them.

In fact, our guests seem happy to be with me *and* happy on their own, or with their partner or kids. This triggers in me an old fear: If I'm no longer valuable, who am I? And will I be loved?

I feel an aching sadness in my heart: *I have been asking myself these same questions forever.*

I ask, "Please help me, God—when the time is right—to release my outdated defense mechanisms: You know what they are. I can be controlling—please help me to hold lightly to things and to other people's lives."

"Even Patrick's life?" I hear.

I want to say yes to that—and I know I shouldn't be bargaining with the Divine—but I say, "Uh, sorry. May I get back to You on that one, God?"

On the 2008 anniversary of the opening of Four Seasons Hotel Bangkok, I've just flown back to Thailand—twenty-four hours in transit—from one of my home leave trips to Chicago. I'd been seated next to a woman who told me she has an unusual job: curing people of a fear of flying. She claimed that she can cure anyone, unless their sub-conscious desire to hold onto their fear is greater than their conscious desire to let go. "Aha," I'd said, then was speechless for the rest of the flight, this impacted me so deeply.

Patrick hadn't actually requested that I come back, but a part of me still feels it's my duty as his Perfect Partner, even though it's increasingly frustrating to feel like I'm always rushing between Patrick in Bangkok and loved ones in Chicago. "Be here! Be there! Be here! Be there!" How many times have I flown back or forth because I was certain I was needed across the world? The comment of the woman on the plane makes me wonder—maybe the world might not stop spinning if I let go. A reminder that I may be the one holding on to my fear of abandonment if I'm not the Perfect Wife.

It's pre-dawn (which my body thinks is pre-dinner, with Asia twelve hours "ahead" of Chicago). I haven't gotten much sleep and there's no time for breakfast or even coffee. I dress in an outfit specific to these kinds of occasions: a heavy embroidered wraparound skirt and a blouse of stiff cream-colored silk, its elaborate golden embroidery jabbing me around the neckline.

First, Patrick and his team and I pay homage to the Royal Family. We all sit on the carpeted floor on the hotel's mezzanine level, facing a statue of a former king. Our heads are bent towards the statue, our palms pressed together in a *wai* high on our foreheads in a sign of maximum respect. I am tipped on my left hip, my bare feet tucked behind me to the right to keep them from pointing at royalty. I'm terrified of a leg cramp: I cannot have my feet shooting out towards His Highness or my wraparound skirt flying open. I murmur gratitude toward the king, but also a prayer, "Please, God, no Sharon Stone today!"

Once respect is offered—without incident—Patrick leads us downstairs to the shrine just outside the hotel: four white pillars protecting a gleaming golden deity. The chief of Bangkok's Brahmin priests is there as the spiritual guide for this auspicious occasion. He's dressed all in white: a cruise ship captain-type jacket, puffy pants that fasten just below the knee, knee socks, and tie-up shoes. His very black hair is pulled back in a ponytail.

In front of the shrine, the hotel staff has set up a table covered with offerings: apples and Chinese pears to bring financial luck; boiled eggs for never-ending success; golden-tinted desserts for prosperity. The priest starts chanting in Sanskrit and each of us is handed five lighted incense sticks, which we hold between the palms of our hands, saying a silent prayer before placing them upright in front of the statue. There are fifty sticks of incense smoking away just a foot in front of us.

The Brahmin drones on. I know he's inviting the gods and the previous kings of Thailand to bless the hotel, but all I can make out is the occasional mention of our hotel (*Foe Sea-SUN*) and my husband's name (*Pa-TICK Ghee-meh-TEE*). With the sun now up, the temperature climbs by the second. I'm starting to perspire (The Handbook does not condone the word *sweat*), headache-y from lack of caffeine and sleep, hungry and—while I hate to admit it—resentful. I've learned that "holding on to a resentment is like drinking poison and hoping the other person dies." But here I am now, standing behind my husband, *wai*-ing respectfully, growing woozier and more nauseated as the incense incessantly curls around my face.

Suddenly, my vision narrows; I feel like I'm straining to see through a peephole. I feel queasy and wobbly and think, *Definitely do not want to do a face plant onto the offering table—that could only mean bad luck for the hotel and Patrick. I should probably just fall backwards into the bushes surrounding us, hoping that I won't be noticed.*

While I'm contemplating this and trying not to unceremoniously hurl, I feel a steady hand under each elbow, and a deep voice whispering in my ear, "We're taking you inside, Margaret." I try to protest, but two of Patrick's tall European colleagues lead me away into the hotel lobby. They lower me into a soft armchair where I droop, mouth slack.

A young Thai server rushes over to help me. "Oh, *Khun* Margaret! Are you all right? So pale. Your eyes! Can you see me?"

"Hmmhhh?" is all I can say.

She brings me a glass of water, a croissant and—bless her—an espresso. Staring blindly, I take in all three greedily and—in this cool, calm space, with the pressure off my heat-swollen feet—I start to regain my focus. When I've also regained my strength, I rejoin the group outside, watching Patrick do something no one does better:

being fully present in another's culture, respecting it, and building a team. The colleagues who'd saved me flank me again, nestling close to my sides.

It felt good to let myself be taken care of. (That they were strong, handsome men didn't hurt.)

I vow to myself that—next year—I'll get my rest, wear light cotton clothes and flat sandals, eat my breakfast, and drink my coffee pre-Brahmin. Or maybe I'll skip the anniversary entirely. Maybe I won't fly back from my parents and friends just to stand behind *Pa-TICK Ghee-meh-TEE* when he doesn't need me there.

That evening, I say to Patrick, "Starting from today, I will be by your side when I add value. I will not be by your side when I don't add value." I'm nervous as I say it, knowing that The Handbook will be in an uproar. Worse than that, I'm *still* worried on some level that Patrick will be frustrated or disappointed or angry and will leave his not-so-Perfect Wife at last.

Instead Patrick says, "Thank you for the times you choose to be with me, *chérie*, but I respect that. You know I want you to have your own life, too."

Oh, God. I've been imposing all of this on myself. I thought I was playing out these old roles for him—because he needed me to. And that his needing me—everyone's needing me—would keep me safe.

But everything I thought was keeping me safe has just been keeping me hidden.

I start to make different choices: not attending every single Thai Royal meet-and-greet (when Patrick has a phalanx of colleagues to assist); not inviting ever-more clients over (we've done our part to promote our hotel and there's an entire sales and marketing team).

Instead, I spend more time with the friends I've made: Anne and Pam, Bangkok book club buddies, and my "Brown Cows": Kathy, the hotel owner's wife, plus Sherry, Therese, Shannon, Ros, and another Kathy. All of them are smart and funny, in their forties and beyond, and here for the long-haul with husbands working in Thailand. They don't need a thing from the Four Seasons GM—and they don't need me to say that he's perfect. I come to enjoy an occasional bitch session about our perpetually working husbands. It's not, I'm surprised to discover, the hallmark of a disloyal wife to let off steam in confidence to other humans who understand. The Handbook may not be happy, but I am.

My Herd meets once a month for lunch or one of our Famous Brown Cow Adventures. On a muggy day in 2008, we board a ferry departing from a swaying old wooden dock in downtown Bangkok. After half an hour of our laughing and chattering, the ferry has chugged across the broad brown Chao Phraya River to a rural island for a bicycle tour in the country. Several visitors from Holland have signed up for the tour as well, all middle-aged women like us, except one thirty-something man. The Dutch ladies introduce him to us as a policeman, and we women of a certain age try not to stare at his arms, covered with elaborate tattoos—and muscles.

Once we disembark onto the island, we're met by our tour guide: a trim young guy in bike shorts. He assigns each of us a bicycle and offers to help adjust the height of our bike seats. All my friends let him help, but—even though my bike seat is so high I can barely touch the ground on tiptoe—I thank him but wave him away. My Brown Cow girlfriends, who've known me for a few years at this point, give me the Look: the look when others know something about you that you don't really know about yourself or maybe don't like to admit. While I'm obsessively precise about travel *planning*, I like to say that I "wander in wonder" once I'm actually exploring. I don't pay much attention to the technical aspects of my surroundings. Like maybe I should let someone adjust my bike seat to fit my height?

Instead, I shoot my friends a dirty look and turn to listen to our guide, who starts his orientation spiel. "First, we'll be cycling on some bumpy back roads then we'll head into the coconut grove, riding on a raised concrete pathway, with canals on either side. Single file, please, at that point, as it's very narrow. Not to worry, though," he adds with a laugh, "no one's ever ridden off the pathway."

We all chuckle at that then pedal away from the ferry dock, past makeshift roadside stands with wrinkled old ladies selling coconuts. Barefoot kids in T-shirts and shorts run out from dirt yards to wave at us; ragged dogs run uncomfortably close to our heels, barking then backing off.

I bring up the rear of our group: cruising along, smiling at everyone and everything, taking mental pictures, waving with one hand. *I'm wandering in wonder!* When we head into the deep, cool, green of the coconut grove, we roll onto the pathway, single file. The pathway at only three feet wide *is* very narrow. It's also very raised: six feet up from the canals. There's no railing like we'd see in the States and no "Beware" sign, but no worries either; we've all been riding bikes since we were little kids.

A thousand coconut trees loom around us with smooth, slender grey trunks, their green fronds swaying high in a blue sky. I hear birds chattering, and I catch a whiff of frangipani nearby, their blossoms like waxy white stars, their scent like buttery sugar cookies baking. I close my eyes to luxuriate in that tropical perfume just for a second, then a few seconds more.

When I open my eyes again, I see that the pathway just ahead of me turns at a sharp right angle. I wrench my handlebars into the turn and instinctively take my feet off the pedals, wanting to steady myself.

Next thing I know, I'm on my back, legs upraised, my bicycle suspended above me, caught only by the hem of my jeans. Evidently I lost my balance, tipped on one tiptoe, flipped over in the air, and now have won the prize for first person ever to have ridden right off that pathway. I roll my eyes right and left, and see that I'm lying on thick green vines. When I look up, my Brown Cow girlfriends are gathered on the walkway above me, peering six feet down at me, doubled over with laughter. "We're laughing with you!" they say, but they are definitely laughing *at* me and only after taking *several* "souvenir photos" do they ask, "Would you like a hand?"

"Yes, please," I squeak. As soon as the words are out of my mouth, peering down at me, too, is—oh, thank you, Lord—the Dutch policeman! He'd heard the commotion and had run back to offer assistance. Now, wordlessly, he lifts my bike off of me, setting it on the pathway. Then he reaches back down with his gorgeous tattooed arms, which I grab like I've never grabbed anything in my life. He effortlessly hauls me up out of those vines, bows silently to me, and walks back to his own bike.

My friends are now alternating between giggling and guffawing. Sherry asks, "Margaret, seriously, though, do you have any idea how lucky you were—where you landed?" Not really, until I look down to see that I'd fallen onto a perfect nest of tangled vines—instead of into unappetizingly murky canal water. My friends show me their photos. Their favorite is the one in which my face is contorted with fear, my hands desperately reaching up for salvation from the swamp.

I'm shaken up, but I manage a laugh with them as Ros checks under my blouse for leeches on my skin—or snakes coiled around my bra straps. I'm relieved to hear her say, "No creepy crawlies!" with a giggle.

Sherry is holding a packet of her never-without-them sanitizing wipes. I ask her for one and she crows, "You're always making fun of me for being a princess, but now you want what I have? Say pretty please."

I'm dying to get whatever swamp slime may be on me off of me. "I swear to you that I'll never tease you again, Sherry! Could I just have one wipe?" She waits until I add, "Pretty please!" I hear the Divine chuckling at my not just asking for help from humans—but *begging* for it.

Sherry smiles, triumphant, pulls a wipe from the packet to hand to me then asks me, earnestly, "Margaret, would you at least consider looking where you're going from now on?" I know my friends worry about me—this is not my first incident on our many adventures together—but my feeling is that this is who I am. I don't want to miss out. I want to live my life fully, even if that means that sometimes I fall.

And as I've been helped, once again, by a strong, handsome man, I hear another chuckle from the Divine and "You're welcome, Child."

After almost five years in Bangkok, Patrick gets a call from corporate HR in April 2008: our Thai time is coming to an end. Our next destination is Prague. Europe, here we come! We'll be so close to Switzerland and at least closer to Chicago. I buy Kafka's book *Amerika* and a basic Czech-to-English phrasebook. I start dreaming of drinking strong black *kava* along the banks of Prague's River Vlatava.

Then Four Seasons decides that my husband is needed elsewhere after all. I'm frustrated until Patrick mentions the new destination they're proposing. Now I'm thrilled! I call my parents and rush to say, "*Mammà!* You'll never guess what's next for Patrick and me. Get this: We're moving to Chicago!"

She pauses, then asks softly, tenderly, disbelievingly, "You mean Chicago-Chicago?"

"Yep, as in just up the road from Dad and you! Patrick and I will be taking you two out for lunch soon. We never thought we'd see the day, but isn't this fantastic?"

My mom and I are then speechless with emotion, a rarity for us. I want this move back to my hometown. My parents are in their eighties, and they're definitely slowing down. Our nieces there, Katie and Meghan, are growing up, with college and boyfriends to hear about. My brothers Pete and Charlie and their wives Rita and Mary Ellen are there for Packers watching and Wisconsin bratwurst from the grill. My brother Hal and his wife Sarah are just one time zone away in Virginia. So many friends are in the US, too. I start to request bids from three moving companies as I've done so many times before.

Before our departure, though, I'm happy that Patrick and I get to celebrate one last Songkran—Thailand's springtime water festival. We dress in old T-shirts, jeans, and flip flops, then taxi to the heart of Bangkok's backpacker neighborhood, the epicenter of the festivities. We join hundreds of Thais and tourists walking toward a free street concert there. As we walk, strangers approach with greetings for the new year. "*Sawasdee Bpee Mai,*" they say as they softly rub white jasmine-scented paste onto our cheeks, a traditional gesture to ward off evil in the new year.

Simultaneous to this gentle tradition, we are being bombarded by water—from every side, as is everyone else. Kids shoot super-soakers at us. Even toddlers skitter towards us, carrying tiny plastic buckets and dumping water on our feet. Armed only with pink and blue plastic water pistols bought at 7-11, we are completely outgunned. I'm soaked and smeared with jasmine paste and having a blast. Then I notice the gleam in the eye of a Buddhist monk. He holds a garden hose tight against his rust-red robe, points it directly at us and *drenches* us. I'm shocked and delighted and laughing so hard I have to bend over to breathe.

We follow the sounds of a band playing Thai pop music on nearby Khao San Road. This one-block-long lane has been closed off at one end by a chain-link fence with a makeshift entry gate. Stationed there is a wiry Thai policeman wearing reflector sunglasses and a skin-tight chocolate-brown uniform. Patrick whispers, "Cap'n Badass!" to me and we chuckle, but it does seem like a smart idea to control the number of partygoers entering that confined space.

We file in through the gate and past the cop into a sea of people dancing to music blaring out of loudspeakers on the raised stage. The black-haired, dark-eyed lead singer is bouncing around the stage, singing his heart out: some Thai version of a song by Rihanna or Madonna—or a mash-up of both. The vibe is very *sanuk*. Fun.

It's also very crowded. Initially, young Thais *wai* to us, smiling, excusing themselves for stepping on our toes. Suddenly, people start getting shoved against us. Looking around, I realize that we're completely walled in by buildings on either side of the street, and there's another chain link fence at the other end, and evidently Cap'n Badass is letting in more and more people without any regard for the fact that there is literally no more space for even one more person.

As we get wedged in tighter and tighter between bodies, people stop *wai*'ing us and start pushing; all of us struggling just to keep our footing. I hear shrieks and bleats as though we're livestock in a pen and say to Patrick, "I feel a stampede coming on." You can smell the animal fear in the air. "We could die here," I say, clutching at him just to stay upright. I feel angry at myself for not having been on my guard and Perfectly Prepared for this somehow. There is nowhere to go and nothing we can do about it.

Looking up to the stage, it's clear that the lead singer has just realized what's going on in the crowd, as he gestures for the band to stop playing and says into the microphone in a quiet but firm voice, "*Jai yen yen.*" Keep your heart cool cool, even when you feel like screaming.

The tension between bodies melts away. *Immediately.* We start to move as a mass toward the exit, but wordlessly and calmly. I'm shuffling behind Patrick, my arms wrapped around his waist, glued to him, until we're safely out of Khao San Road.

We trudge for blocks in silence, finally finding an open sided *tuk tuk* to convey us back to the hotel. Along the way, revelers splash us with water and we are restored, at last, to a sense of the day's *sanuk*.

Back inside our home, showered and dry, safe and warm, I tell Patrick how incredibly grateful I am that disaster that day was averted with three little words—*jai yen yen*—and that I think the world could use a lot more of that restraint. "But," I add, "I already have quiet and serene at my disposal. I want a broader range of emotions in my life."

I add to my daily prayers, "I know I can be cool to the touch, God. Please help me to also be warm." Even as we're getting ready to leave Thailand, I'm learning a lot from the culture—including what I don't need to learn.

Before our departure date to Chicago, I take one more trip together with my Brown Cows, this time to a winery. On the drive out into the Thai countryside, we laugh and joke as ever. At the winery, my friends partake in a tasting of local vintages while I sit silently on the terrace, staring out at the vines, tearful at the thought of leaving them. When they amble towards me, polishing off their glasses of wine, they stop when they see me crying. Sherry says, "You're leaving, aren't you?" I nod miserably. My Herd engulfs me in a squishy love-filled group hug, telling me that they knew this day would come, and promising that we'll stay in touch.

I hope so. I want to believe that we aren't just "friends for a reason or a season" or the harsher "friends du jour." At the same time, I'm realizing that I've been working so hard at this my whole life. Others will stay in relationship with me, or they won't. If they don't, I won't shrivel up and die. I'll miss them, but I'll survive.

I hear God say, "That's right, Child. Trust that."

When my Brown Cows drop me back at our hotel, I burrow into the stack of moving company quotes on my desk. Within weeks, our things are packed and stacked onto a container ship—this time sailing across the Pacific. At our farewell party in the hotel's Grand Ballroom, Patrick and I are presented with a set of Thai ceramic dishes in glittering gold, fuchsia, and green to remind us of the temples, orchids, and rice paddies. Our final gift is a handcrafted wooden spirit house; we'll carry the spirit of Thailand back to Chicago.

As Patrick and I sit on the stage, his colleagues kneel before us one at a time. Each one ties a white string around Patrick's wrist, then one around mine, as they whisper wishes for our health and safe journey and I cry onto their gentle hands.

BACK TO CHICAGO

On our first day back at the Ritz-Carlton Chicago, Patrick says, "We've come full circle." This is the hotel where he started his career with Four Seasons in 1995, chompin' at the bit to become a general manager. Today, he'll reunite with colleagues we've known for thirteen years and meet new ones, too.

"It's full circle for me, too, *amore mio*," I say, as I head to my first stop: Evanston to see my parents.

After forty minutes north in our Mini Cooper—up Lake Shore Drive, Sheridan Road, and Lincoln Avenue—I'm sitting at the round Davis family dining table. It's heaven to drink black coffee out of the old blue mugs and catch up in person, knowing that now I'll be able to come out here whenever I want without getting on a plane.

On the way back downtown, I make a quick pass through a discount store: I always manage to find something small to buy there when a few bucks are burning a hole in my pocket. I tell myself that our shipment won't arrive for weeks (although we are traveling with suitcases filled with clothes). When the woman ringing me up doesn't even glance my way, I think, *"Mai bpen rai"*: *It's not a big deal.* When the floor manager screams at a young man stocking shelves, I find myself appalled, wanting to yell back, *"Jai yen yen"*—*calm down!* When a couple shoves me on the escalator as they push past, I think, *This is not fun "sanuk" at all!* I run out clutching a flimsy plastic bag with a ten-dollar scarf and—once I get home—phone my mom.

"Well," she laughs, "maybe that wasn't the smartest way to start your re-entry."

She's right.

Let me get smarter, I think. I remind myself how other former expats had warned me that the biggest culture shock is upon return to the home country and how some people will say, "You've finally been moved to America? Your husband must've done something right!" I'm happy to be back, but that's not how I see the world. I determine to consider this move back to the US as adjusting to yet another "new" culture.

My first move is buying guidebooks on Chicago—to see my city anew. Next, I join International Women Associates to be around people whose worldview does not end at the city limits. I sign up with an international relocation company to offer cultural orientation programs for expats moving to Chicago.

For my fiftieth birthday, Patrick invites my family to brunch at North Pond Restaurant and they celebrate me with poems, photos, and collages. Patrick also invites my GRRLs to dinner at Green Zebra. They present me with a scarf with a peacock feather design, as they know I believe one simply cannot have too many scarves. Patrick gives me an easel and art supplies, wishing me creativity. At half-a-century, I feel beyond grateful to be known for who I am by those I love.

I'm thrilled that they can come stay with us, too: the GM's apartment has a guest room. Kimetha gifts us with a guest book, and family and friends fill its pages over the coming months with appreciation of our views of Lake Michigan and the Windy City (plus the nonstop meowing from Giorgio, the chatterbox rescue cat we adopted before leaving Bangkok). So that guests may explore on their own, I have bus passes and maps ready—plus a brand-new binder, "Enjoy Your Chicago Visit!"

My heart feels happy and full and our Chicago posting is going well except for two things: I hate to admit that I miss the cachet of being an exotic expat, and I'm ashamed to have become the GM's wife who's gotten used to her groceries being whisked out of her hands by the doorman and brought to her apartment by the bellman. I used to state, "I never want to get spoiled." Too late for that.

Oh, and Patrick realizes that he no longer wants the job we moved back to Chicago for. He no longer wants the job he dreamt of since he was seven years old. The role of general manager has changed over the decades. It used to be the debonair double-breasted host in the lobby, greeting guests; now Patrick spends his days on budgets, marketing, owner relations, and seeing the hotel through the financial crisis of 2008. He's not with people: he's stuck behind a computer or on the phone. When he tells me how he's feeling, I say, "I'm sorry that you're unhappy," but I think, *Didn't we just move back to my home town, where I can be with so many people I love?*

I find myself muttering the Serenity Prayer over and over. "Grant me the serenity to accept the things I cannot change, the courage to change the things I can, and the wisdom to know the difference." I try to accept what's true for Patrick *and* have the courage to act on what's within our circle of control. One morning over coffee, I say, "*Amore mio*, we need some outside perspective. It's time to get help from objective professionals to figure out your options."

Patrick agrees. Chicago friend Linda and her wife Annie recommend Rita as a life coach, and Patrick starts to work with her. Rita's partner, Michelle, is also a coach and I'm surprised and delighted that—at this age—we make deep new friendships with these amazing women, sharing long breakfasts around our glass dining table with the sun glinting off the lake. After sweet rolls and fruit salad, Patrick drags out a white board for brainstorming possible next careers. In the spirit of no idea is a bad idea, Patrick calls out, "Opera singer!" (He has a sonorous baritone voice.) "Dog walker!" (He's never met a pooch he didn't love.) "Cruise ship director!" (He'd love the endless scuba opportunities, and it's perfect for an extrovert.) Innumerable friends pitch in with ideas, but nothing's clicking for Patrick.

Michelle, champion of imaginative imagery, asks, "OK, Patrick, so how about if you pretend you're a frog? Frogs leap from one lily pad to the next, but they're still in their favorite pond: hotels in your case. They just have to start with that first jump."

Patrick nods.

Another morning, Michelle proposes that Patrick bring all his shoes into the living room. Onto the floor, he dumps shiny black loafers, tan desert boots, scuffed tennis shoes, battered black rubber flip flops. Michelle asks, "So which shoes do you want to wear in your new job?"

Patrick grabs the flip flops without hesitation, smiling broadly. "These!" he says, "Or barefoot would be even better!"

"Now we've got a start," Michelle says. "You need to find a job in hotels where you can be barefoot or almost barefoot—at least part of the time."

The Divine is listening, it seems, as Four Seasons offers Patrick the GM position at a resort on the Pacific Coast of Mexico. "I can already feel the sand between my toes!" Patrick says.

Even though I thought the whole idea was to get Patrick off the GM track, I want to keep an open mind. "Let's check it out," I say, typing in the destination's website on my computer, thinking, *All I need is something like the Community Services Association back in Ma'adi: maybe they'll have a book club. I could refresh my high school Spanish. I could learn to make piñatas! I just need a place where maybe I can meet one like-minded acquaintance.* But— while the resort and the destination look majestic—and I'd enjoy whale-watching in the bay once or twice—there's no town to speak of. No bookstore, library, or museum. Definitely no community center.

For almost a decade, I've said yes to every move offered to Patrick, but by now I know what will work for me—and what won't. "I'm really sorry, *amore mio*," I say. "I can't do this. First of all, it's a job that we agree no longer fits for you. And it's in a location that will suffocate me."

I can see from the disappointed look on Patrick's face that he feels that a lifeline is being yanked away. He says, "But it's on the water, which we both love. And such a short flight; you could come back to Chicago often. I'd like this, *chérie*."

"I know you would, Patrick, but I wouldn't. Besides, we've agreed to try never to jump from the frying pan into the fire." We've talked a lot about this by now: letting go of the notion that any one job is ideal, but staying determined to find something that will be an improvement. We need to keep searching for what will work for Patrick as a professional in transition—and will work for me at this stage of my life.

More emails are sent out to more friends, asking for thoughts and referrals. Peter responds with classical music contacts and Fran with travel industry names. We update Patrick's LinkedIn profile and his résumé. It feels like I've added Perfect Career Counselor to *my* curriculum vitae and—while The Handbook still approves, crowing, "Put others first!" and I *do* want Patrick happy—I also need a break.

My eyes light up one day when I notice an ad for Second City Chicago's "Improv for Adults." The year-long series of classes in improvisation is starting soon. I'm intrigued by the notion of doing something completely different; Patrick's intrigued when he hears Second City's claim, "We want you to have fun like a five-year old." We both sign up and go to class every week for a year.

Level A starts with games to build trust and exercises to instill Second City's signature spirit of "Yes, And." Later in the year, there's a student show and—in one scene on stage—I sing a lullaby to my new prison cell-mate about a devil with a blue dress on. The audience howls with laughter and I'm ecstatic. By year-end, the focus is on longer scenes, and the intimacy with my scene partners is palpable. Our instructors all along have reminded us that the best improv is not about trying to be funny; it's about listening to your scene partners and being real. Improv is a heavenly place to be for me. I learned to listen hard from my mom and to riff in words with my dad. I feel depth in connecting with people and joy in reconnecting to my creativity.

I add to my daily prayers, "Please help me, God, to use the gifts you've given me, without shame or timidity. I'm strategic and organized, and I honor that. But also, God, I'm creative and artistic. Please help me to share that in some way today. It appears that I can be entertaining, too." I get a smile back from the Divine.

When Patrick and I have completed Levels A through E, I start to investigate auditioning for the next higher level at Second City. But in August 2010, Patrick phones me, yelling, "People! I'd get to focus on people again!" He's gotten wind of a position that's opened up with Four Seasons: Vice President of Human Resources for Asia Pacific, based in Singapore. "I want to throw my name in the hat for this job, chérie! What do you think? Could you get on board for this with me?"

I pick up our old globe to find Singapore and sigh when I see that it's about as far away from Chicago as you can get. But Patrick's passion is what I've been hoping for him: moving towards something, not running away. I'm anxious as I log on to Tourism Singapore's website. We visited from Bangkok many times for AsiaWorks but had never really gotten to know the place. Expats had talked about it as simply "Asia Light," but I'm intrigued as I scroll through details of a symphony orchestra, bookstores large and small, award-winning Changi International Airport, diverse cuisines, cultures, and neighborhoods.

I've learned by now that I have the capacity to say no to Patrick, but this time I say yes.

He applies for the job, Four Seasons recognizes that his years in operations will be a unique asset for this position, and they say yes to him, too.

Patrick's excited, but starts to question himself. Is he really going to diverge from the career path he's been dedicated to for decades? When we're having lunch with Adrienne, another insightful-delightful new friend, she asks, "Patrick, don't you think that—after twenty years of doing one thing really well—you've earned the right to try something new?"

"Yes," Patrick responds simply, and I see the release this offers him: to see his past as a success, and to now consider something different.

I call my parents in trepidation. I know how hard our leaving will be for them: they're getting more frail with every year. But my dad says, "Mouse, this sounds like an excellent fit for Patrick and you. Singapore sounds like a real city, which I know you both love."

My mom says, "We always knew we couldn't keep Patrick in Chicago for long. The world needs him out in it." Then she adds what she's always added, "Missie, go!"

So I write to family and friends: "We're off to the Lion City! I'm very proud of Patrick for having followed his heart. This presents a wonderful opportunity for him to blend his passions for hotels and people. He'll be traveling 50 percent of his time, as there are twenty-two hotels and resorts in Asia/Pacific and several more in the pipeline. We already miss everyone, but we look forward to living in vibrant Singapore and exploring even more of Asia. I want to see Mumbai and Malaysia . . . and we'll get to China's Great Wall at last!"

All true. But two years in Chicago have gone by too quickly. Leaving is hard. I can feel my reluctance at the prospect of packing up again but at least, this time, I don't feel like I'm being swept along by unspoken rules and roles and forces outside my control. I'm making choices.

My heart is starting to pitter-pat with excitement and curiosity, too, at the thought of a new destination and a new culture. Patrick and I are setting sail again.

I print out color-coded labels that I tape to every single thing in our apartment. Red is for the hotel's permanent inventory—this furniture does not move. Yellow items will go into a mover's van to our apartment in Chicago—Patrick's insisted on renting a small place, saying "Enough already with you sleeping on an air mattress in your parents' living room on home leaves. They don't need your Energizer Bunny energy—and you don't need their six o'clock bedtime." Green items will be packed and loaded onto a container ship to sail *back* across the Pacific to our new home, arriving in around six weeks.

At the end of packing-up day, the Chicago move supervisor tells me, "Ma'am, we've never seen anyone this organized. You're better at this than we are." After four continents of moves, that might just be true.

SINGAPORE (and INDIA)

When we land at Singapore's Changi Airport in February 2011, everything works smoothly—a far cry from some of our past postings, and a pleasant change, as I no longer feel the need to prove my expat credentials. Patrick and I just sit back and relax in the hotel car on the highway into town. A canopy of trees, their tangled black branches stretching into a blue sky, shades our way alongside miles of beachfront bike and walking trails. Twenty minutes from the airport, we are at our home-away-from-home during our arrival time: the Regent Singapore, a Four Seasons hotel. We know the GM and his wife from Chicago and are once again reminded how we love reuniting with our work family around the world.

The next day, I visit the bunker-like American Club to pick up my Women's Association membership card. On the way out, I notice a silver-haired woman in a caftan slumped poolside, staring into the middle distance with a full bottle of wine to herself—at ten in the morning. I get her, but I'm grateful that I no longer *am* her. I also know that some expats will never leave this bubble if they don't have to. That won't be me.

Patrick and I visit the Ministry of Manpower to apply for his work permit and my dependent's pass. The smiling young lady processing our application rubs hand cream onto our thumbs in order to get a clearer thumb print. "Free massage!" she says. We've heard how efficient Singapore is, but it's already exceeding even those expectations, plus we're starting to see the sassy Singaporean sense of humor. Opening a bank account and setting up a taxicab debit card are just as easy, and the lack of stress feels grand, but also strange. I hear an old tune on a distant record player: I should be working harder to earn my keep and Patrick's appreciation—even though I've learned that he's grateful we've made this move together and wants me to be happy, whatever that looks like for me.

The search for an apartment in this astronomically expensive real estate market feels more familiarly all-consuming. Our agent is armed with our budget and wish list: modern, bright, and walking distance to Patrick's office. This doesn't feel too demanding, but my hopes nose dive when she shows us units so mildewy that my eyes sting or so poundingly loud with nearby construction that I can barely think. Patrick and I agree to increase our budget slightly, and suddenly one building soars to front-runner status: a slender white high-rise tower overlooking a long swimming pool shaded by palm trees. It satisfies our requirement for proximity to Patrick's office at a five-minute walk. There's a guest room, a study, and floor-to-ceiling windows in the living/dining room. A small balcony overlooks neighboring single-family homes with terracotta tiled roofs and green lawns; high-rises sprout in the distance. The apartment is move-in ready, which is essential as our container has already arrived and cleared Customs and now languishes expensively in storage. As we walk around the apartment, Patrick whispers to me, "I love it," and I whisper back the same.

The only thing we insist on is installation of a dishwasher. The owner's agent seems perplexed, asking, "Won't you have a live-in helper?" No, we won't have a housekeeper staying with us 24/7, even though many expats do. Our agent negotiates the dishwasher and the deal, including a price reduction because we're willing to live on the "unlucky" thirteenth floor.

Four Seasons human resources arranges a Newcomers' Orientation Tour for Patrick and me and I'm delighted (albeit irritated that one of my best transition manager ideas is being put into practice without my getting credit for it. But, *mai bpen rai*—never mind). The British expat who is our guide drives us around, pointing out grocery stores, pharmacies, florists, and especially bookstores: giant Borders, sleek Kinokuniya, and indie charmer Books Actually. Along Orchard Road, a tourist and shopping mecca, the sheer quantity of high-end stores is eye-popping and the number of Ferraris and Maseratis on the road is mind-boggling. Patrick and I explode with laughter when we see a man drive by in a pricey convertible, holding onto the steering wheel with one hand, and his toupée with the other.

Within days, Patrick and I have established our favorite morning walk: out of our apartment, past the fortress-like American Embassy, and onward to the vast Botanic Gardens. Upon passing through its entrance gates, we breathe in the butter-cookie scent of frangipani (the same intoxicating smell I still blame for my Bangkok canal incident). Black butterflies flitter around red-trunked lipstick palms. We speed-walk the three mile circumference along wide sidewalks, first passing sweating tourists clutching damp maps as they emerge from the orchid garden. Elderly ladies dance solemnly to traditional Chinese music, their crimson fans whacking open and shut to punctuate their moves. We hear the strains of disco from a boom box and see a trim Singaporean man in his sixties dressed in white leading a dozen seniors in dance moves. As we pass, he waves to us, smiling. We wave back, he runs over, and we introduce ourselves. On our walks every day after, we greet him and he calls out, "Hi, Patrick and Margaret! Enjoy your walk! See you tomorrow!"

"We look forward to that, Jeffrey!" we respond. We've jumped from one lily pad to this new one and it already feels like home.

But I can never resist jumping onto a plane: to join Patrick someplace new-for-me that his work travels take him or back to Sweet

Home Chicago. It's wonderful, this gift of bouncing around the world, but I'm never quite sure where I am. I'm smiling—and I mean it—but my head is spinning.

Waving Patrick goodbye as he sets off on his inaugural business trip to China in the new job, I feel a twinge of old resentment that he'll be gone as I handle our move-in. After eleven years of this, though, I also feel a certain elation that I'll get to do it my way: Every single one of my beloved books will be on display, *ha!*

On the first day of March 2011, the movers arrive promptly at nine, the "captain" first Christo-wrapping in brown paper the exposed surfaces along the move-in route before a small army of barefoot movers start bringing in cardboard box after box, calling out the number on the label on the box. My job is to check off that number from the master list and direct the movers where to place the boxes. We have 193 pieces coming in, and I'm grateful for a unique feature in Singapore apartments built after 9/11: a bomb shelter in the unit, perfect for our suitcases and plastic tubs filled with holiday décor, scuba gear, art supplies, and dormant files. Before departing, the move captain presents me with the perfect housewarming gift: a French press coffee maker and Javanese java.

After I check out of our room at the Regent and schlep our valuables over to the apartment by taxi, I explore nearby Tanglin Mall. The grocery stores there sell mystifying local favorites like crab-flavored chips. I look forward to trying Singapore's exotic cuisines, but I'm also happy to see our comfort foods: Illy espresso, Kashi cookies, Amy's frozen pizzas, bananas (super cheap), and blueberries (so costly as to be rationed like caviar).

I return to our new home carrying the Italian essentials: spaghetti and olive oil plus cherry tomatoes grown in nearby Malaysia. I cook myself the Inaugural Bowl of Pasta—just like I did back in

Cairo, only this time no bleach, and there's real Italian (really expensive) Pecorino Romano cheese. I slurp spaghetti and gaze out at the city lights, Skypeing with my parents afterwards: my evening is their morning. I "tour them around the apartment" by walking around with the laptop. This visual tour is Patrick's brainstorm, and they laud him once again for being a genius: Patrick can do no wrong in my parents' eyes.

The next day, the doorbell rings and it's the Friday morning "helper" we've hired through an agency. I request of her only that she please let me know whenever she has questions. I'm grateful for the help, but—please—no more demitasse spoons polished to within an inch of their lives. Over the next week, I pick up my Singaporean mobile phone, the vendor telling me that I'm lucky my number includes the very auspicious eight, as the sound for eight in Chinese sounds similar to the words for prosperity or wealth. She says, "Beijing's Summer Olympics started on 8/8/08 at 8:08 plus 8 seconds." The cable guy comes to our apartment to hook up the equipment we need to get BBC World News and Turner Classic Movies. A handyman comes over to hang our pictures and mirrors.

At the mall, I buy myself a photocopier/printer/scanner, forcing myself back home to RTFM (read the f***ing manual) and congratulating myself wildly when I get this new contraption to work.

Everything's going too well; there's bound to be a snafu. It takes the form of the only unpleasant encounter since our arrival. I'm in a taxi and—as family is such an important value here—I ask the taxi-driver about his children. He tells me with pride about his sons and daughters and asks me how many children I have. When I tell him we were not blessed with children—which still hurts me to say—he snaps, "Your fault! You should have asked God for children." He ends with a strange and awful curse, "Now you are going to be lonely and sad."

When I tell my mom about this on the phone, she suggests that

I fabricate a lie to use in all similar future encounters: "And don't forget," she says, "to make my make-believe grandchildren Harvard-bound *geniuses!*" Patrick and I agree over Skype: If that one horrible man is the worst thing about settling in to life in Singapore, we're officially fans.

Which means I can turn my attention back to Chicago. My mom doesn't want to dwell on it (God forbid), but she tells me she may have pneumonia. Patrick returns from his trip; we catch up over dinner; I then head to the airport myself. My taxi driver, a very gentle soul this time, asks me, "You mommy's girl going home?"

"Mommy's and Daddy's girl," I say. I'm anxious to get back to them, but there's no rushing this trip. First it's a four-hour flight to Hong Kong, next it's thirteen hours to California, then one last flight ("only four more hours") to O'Hare, where I grab a taxi to our apartment, peel off my black travel clothes, shower, brush my teeth, and fall exhausted onto our Chicago bed as it's too late to visit my parents. The next day, though, first thing, I hop into our car and drive out to see them. It's surreal to be in Singapore one day and Evanston the next—and I give thanks for jet planes.

In their late eighties now, my parents no longer meet me at the door. We still drink coffee and catch up, but it's a new normal. My dad is consumed with worry about my mom, who refuses to talk about how she's feeling. Her version of The Handbook won't allow her to say anything that might even resemble a complaint. I try to respect that and to focus on the fact that at least she's recuperating.

On that trip home and every other, once I've left my parents and have driven back downtown, I take a long walk along Lake Michigan from North Avenue to Fullerton to counteract the airplane food and jet lag and allow me to clear my head and murmur my prayers. I pause to look back at the city: the Drake Hotel, the Palmolive Building, the John Hancock. In March, the lake is an icy blue, but flowers will start to bud up soon and the paths will become a blur of joggers and cyclists. My eyes fill with the shimmer of our blue lake.

I open the mountain of mail that collects while I'm gone, paying our US bills and strategizing my chore list. It's what every other adult does; I just do it on two continents.

Patrick and I find a Chicago apartment to buy in December 2011, thanks to our friend and real estate agent, Annie. I see dozens of places with her, but only make a choice when our friend Rita says, "Patrick and you are all about the view." That allows us to drop everything else on our must-have list and find a permanent home overlooking Lake Michigan and the city. Rita dubs our vista "where God meets man," and Patrick and I count our blessings: a home in a city we love that doesn't need to move.

At the end of every home leave, I fit in one more visit to Mother and Dad before I close up the apartment and head to O'Hare. To keep me from breaking down in tears I chirp, "See you on Saturday!" no matter what day of the week, and no matter that I don't know when I'll be seeing them next. Denial *does* work.

And—while I'm missing my parents before I'm even on the plane—now I can't wait to get back to Singapore to be with Patrick. When he's there, that is. His travels read like an atlas—from Macau to Marrakesh to Mumbai, where my new favorite photo of him is taken: Patrick drinking *masala chai* tea on the street with colleagues. His smile says it all; he's out in the world—with people. During one trip to another M—the Maldives—Patrick tacks on a weekend of after-business scuba with Armando, now the Four Seasons GM there (and our friend who'd filled our Bangkok hotel room with flowers almost twenty years ago). Patrick gushes to me on a Skype call: "So many manta rays gliding all around me." I've seen them with Patrick; mantras are magnificent, as is the warm, crystalline water. "I love the Maldives so much," he says. "I want to move here!"

He's joking—mostly—but I'm not when I respond, "You must be

fucking kidding me, Patrick. We just moved to Singapore. No way I'm moving from a city I already love to an island the size of a football field, no matter how gorgeous it is. A hug for Armando and a kiss for you. Sweet dreams, *amore mio*."

Every day that he's in Singapore, Patrick walks home from the Four Seasons Asia Pacific office after work and takes a swim while I make dinner. We've found the perfect small round table and chairs for our balcony and—this close to the Equator—we can eat outside every evening, candles flickering and bare feet on the tiled floor.

Since we're now in the same city as AsiaWorks, we gorge on even more personal growth work. In a program called "Mastery," I come to understand how I still tend to act as a sentry: watching over others and making sure they're safe, even driving myself to a breaking point to care for them because I won't give up. I see how my best qualities are my worst in excess. My dogged determination is a strength but—when over-used—a weakness and a convenient excuse; in a hand holding a sentry's sword, there's no room for a writer's pen or turquoise journal.

Patrick and I entertain now only when we want to, occasionally hosting informal bratwurst parties, and inviting Patrick's HR team over to celebrate Chinese New Year. One colleague says, "We all know that you've just gotten off the plane from across the globe, Margaret. Patrick, you've just returned from who knows where. But here you both are—dressed in red and welcoming us into your home." I glow from their appreciation *and* I say yes when they ask if they can help with the cooking and the cleaning up.

Our time in Singapore is happy with nonnegotiables like weekend dim sum at Imperial Treasure Noodle and Congee House, where we're welcomed as regulars (and almost always the only foreigners). The servers bring us round stacking boxes holding hot steamed dumplings filled with scallops, prawns, mushrooms, greens. Sometimes they tease me, asking, "You want chicken feet this time?" but one taste of gnarled yellow claws years ago in Hong Kong was enough; I don't need to secure more international traveler bragging rights.

Once a month, we go to the Arab Street neighborhood, its al fresco restaurants filled with local Muslim families. We eat creamy hummus dotted with whole chickpeas in a little lake of olive oil and pita bread fresh from the oven. The restaurant plays our favorite song from Egypt—Amr Diab's *"Habibi"*—which mingles with the minor-key call to prayer from the Sultan Mosque, its giant dome glowing dusky gold at sunset. Next door to Singapore's oldest mosque, there's a holding pen housing a hundred wooly sheep and a dozen curved-horn goats to be sold for the feast at the end of Ramadan. Asking price for a sheep is $443; goats are a bargain at $395.

During the Hungry Ghost Festival, the spirits of discontented souls are allowed out of Hell to mingle with mortals who appease them with food, money, and entertainment. In a visit to an ancient Chinese cemetery, standing in the long grass and taking Trip Report notes, I whisper a question to the woman next to me: Does she feel sharp stinging on her legs? She nods and says, "Ants!" In my Trip Report home, I write, delighted, "I can now officially say I've had ants in my pants!"

At *Thaipusam,* Hindu devotees walk a three-mile route carrying a burden as a demonstration of faith. One white-haired man looks straight out of a mythology pageant, carrying a trident, walking slowly but determinedly, his shoes fitted with nails (pointing *up* into his feet). Not for the first time, I end my Trip Report with: "We're not in Kansas anymore, Toto."

At an American Women's Association drop-in coffee at a nearby Starbucks, I meet a new arrival who whines that she's worried about the food in Singapore. I think, *Girl, you should've been with me at the open-air butcher's in Cairo if you wanted to worry!*

And, joy! I have friends here. Susan and I haunt every patisserie to find the best chocolate cake in Singapore (when she's not finishing her upcoming book). Niva and I tour museums (while she's not finishing her upcoming book). They inspire me as explorers and authors.

I have volunteering I love, too: greeting newcomers at the Friends of the Museum's Monday Morning Lectures. We learn about Chinese Zodiac, Terracotta Warriors, Ancient Proverbs. My favorite proverb is, "You cannot discuss the ocean with a frog inside a well: it is confined to one space." At another lecture on Islamic architectural arts, I swoon over the dazzling blue ceramics from Samarkand. They're intended to represent the "enameled azure dome" of the heavens, but I think, *Wait, what does that color remind me of?*

But I don't have time to write in my old turquoise journal. I want to keep seeing the world with Patrick while Mother and Dad are still at least reasonably well.

After all these years traveling together, Patrick and I have refined what works for us. I'm the navigator, and he's the driver. He asks, "Just tell me when to turn right or left. I will never blame you if you're wrong, but make a decision." I like an old-fashioned fold-out map; I don't have my Orienteering merit badge for nothing.

When we take a vacation to Portugal and Spain, after touring Lisbon, we're heading to southern Spain's Andalusia region. We'll visit Cordoba and Granada but first up is Seville. Our Lisbon rental car comes equipped with a GPS, and Patrick suggests, "Hey, this time, let's try it, and skip the map." Against my better judgment, I agree.

We drive south from Lisbon—past fields of cheerful sunflowers and over sloping brown hills—then east towards Seville. GPS lady is directing us in Spanish (which we both speak, a little), but it's all highway at that point (so, frankly, a bit of a no-brainer). As we approach Seville we see a familiar road sign in Europe, a bull's eye, which indicates "This way to the center of town." Boy, I want to just follow that sign, but GPS lady has other plans for us. "*Sigue adelante!*" she calls out, so we keep going straight ahead on the highway. I trust that she knows a better exit—one that will lead us more directly to our hotel. As we curve around Seville, we can see the faint outline of the city on our left, far away, and getting farther away, but we await her instructions to head towards the center.

Those instructions never come and—all of a sudden—we're on an enormous suspension bridge leading away from Seville altogether and far up into the sky. Only then does GPS lady announce, "*Date la vuelta!*"

I'm thinking, *You can't turn around on a bridge*, and certainly not one plodding along with several lanes of traffic. I'm feeling quite irritated with GPS lady and—to make matters worse—once we're in the middle of this bridge, our car starts to beep. I say, "Patrick, please slow down. I'm sure the car is trying to tell you that you're going too fast." Patrick likes to push the speed limit.

He says, "How could I be going too fast? We're stuck in traffic on a bridge." Then he adds, "Anyway, it's beeping because we're low on gas."

Now I'm mad at the GPS lady *and* at my husband. "Oh, great, Patrick! Didn't I suggest that we get gas, about an hour ago—and you said no?"

Patrick says, "Yes, but the tank went from low-ish to empty-ish awfully fast," and I have to admit that is true.

All the while, GPS lady is repeating, "*Date la vuelta! Date la vuelta!*"

I start yelling at Patrick, "She wants us to turn around! Just get off anywhere!" And—once we're over the bridge—he does just that, right—thank heavens—into a gas station there. Patrick pulls up to a pump. I leap out of the car and run into the Mini Mercado to *buy a map*. The dark-eyed young check-out clerk offers me directions towards the city center, which I actually understand. I return to our car feeling better; my high school Spanish has worked with a handsome Spaniard . . . and Patrick's filled up the tank with gas.

Back in the car, we nod at each other: the equivalent of a marital reset button. I open my crisp new map on my lap and settle into my familiar role: navigator to Patrick's driver. Soon, we're back over the bridge, off the big highway, and deep into the winding old streets of Seville.

Now, I respect Patrick's need for me to tell him when to turn. I do rather well at following his driver's demand, but I'll admit that I get distracted by architecture, art, history, beauty; these are why I travel! So—once we're in a huge traffic circle, swirling with cars, a splashing fountain in the center—I really should be telling Patrick where to turn. Instead, I call out, "Ooh, look, *amore mio*! I think that's the cigar factory from the opera 'Carmen!'"

Patrick yells, "I don't *care* about that right now, Margaret! I'm driving! Just tell me where to go!"

"Sorry!" I snap back and try to reorient myself, but in my distraction I've lost our place on the map.

Suddenly GPS lady wakes up from her siesta and starts hollering, "*Gira a la izquierda!*"

"We *are* turning left, bitch," I scream at her. "It's a roundabout for God's sake!" Furious, I rip the GPS right off the dashboard, roll down my window, and hold the GPS outside in my fist. "How much would it cost to replace this damned thing it if I throw it into the fountain we kept circling around?"

Patrick glances over in disbelief. "Margaret!" he yells. "Focus!"

Gritting my teeth, I stuff the GPS into the glove compartment, where we can still hear her yammering on: "*Gira a la izquierda! Ahora mismo!*" Turn left right now! I really have to figure this out. I unfold the map some more. It now covers my side of the dashboard and windshield.

"Make a decision!" Patrick barks.

"I'm trying to!" I bark back.

As we circle the roundabout once more, Patrick speeds up angrily, the map slips out of my hands, and over the steering wheel. Patrick yells, "That's it!" then swerves left down a tiny street and stops the car dead.

That's when we see that we are on a one-way street—going the wrong way. *And* when we see the black-haired Spanish policeman on the same street, leaning on his polished black motorcycle, his tall polished black boots crossed at the ankle, smoking a cigarette. When he sees us, he gazes at our car for a moment, taking in the Portuguese license plate. He stubs out his cigarette in a leisurely way and starts walking toward our car with a swagger, unfolding his little booklet with slow pleasure, getting ready to write the *turistas* a juicy traffic ticket. Patrick screams at me, "How did this happen?"

I scream back, "Because of your stupid GPS!" By then the police-man has strolled up to our car and is peering in at us through the windshield. I can't believe we're going to get a ticket and I scream at Patrick, "What a nightmare!" while crumpling the map up into a huge messy ball. "I mean, seriously, Patrick, why on earth couldn't you have just let me buy a map in the first place? Now we're going to have to pay God knows how much—do we even have enough Euros? Oh, yippee!"

The cop watches us, slowly shakes his head then gives Patrick the most sympathetic look *in the world*. I know he's thinking, "*Hombre,* I'm married, too. You have enough problems for today. You don't need me adding to your pain." In fact, he looks straight at Patrick and dramatically mouths the words, "*Vaya con Dios.*" Go with God, *amigo.* Then he closes his little notebook and swaggers back to his motorcycle.

Patrick starts up the engine again and drives past the cop very slowly and carefully. Suddenly, we can hear GPS lady from inside the glove compartment, "*Usted está en su destino.*" I am just getting ready to smash her to smithereens when we see that our destination—our hotel—is actually right at the end of the street. Patrick and I burst into laughter and—once we've checked in and dropped our bags—we head out to the nearest plaza for an espresso. Holding hands, we chuckle over today, remember trips past, and dream of where to go next. We make a good team (most of the time). We're still on the journey, fulfilling our travel destiny together, seeing the world.

Until, in 2013, my world shifts.

My mom's past of two packs a day has caught up with her. She quit smoking years ago, but now she's coughing up blood sometimes, and gets pneumonia again. In April, the pulmonologist detects "white infiltrate" in her lungs; an X-ray reveals a malignant tumor. Mother now has an oncologist who recommends radiation, but she can only start in late May. I commit to being in Chicago then, but for now I fly to Beijing for a visit that Patrick and I booked long ago.

Our guide shows us Tiananmen Square and the Forbidden City before driving us outside Beijing to the Great Wall. The scenery of endless jagged mountain peaks and spring-blossoming trees is as spectacular as this wonder of the world. On the way back to our hotel, the guide suggests (and we decline) local delicacies: Scorpions on a Stick, Smelled Bean Curd, the Donkey Rolls about on the Ground, and Mung Bean Milk "known as delicious food hard to swallow."

The next day is work for Patrick, and a National Museum day for me. The driver guides me to the entrance; I'm the sole Caucasian in a sea of tourists. "So many people!" I say.

"China!" he replies with a smile.

Once inside, I'm museum-giddy as ever, my molecules jittering around at so much creativity. In the entrance hall are massive oil paintings of patriotic scenes (like George Washington crossing the

Delaware River, only ten times larger). I wander happily for hours through galleries of ancient bronze vessels, delicate porcelain painted with pink peonies and blushing peaches, and flowing calligraphy on long scrolls. The museum claims to have more than one million items in its collection, and it feels like I've seen most of them.

Just before closing time, I head to the gift shop—actually just a few shelves in the middle of the marble-floored lobby—selling replicas of the precious works inside the museum. I'm searching for just the right gift for my mom—not a souvenir but a talisman, to protect her as she undergoes radiation.

I notice a jar made of carved bronze-colored metal, topped by a lid with a small Chinese "foo dog" in a ferocious guardian stance. Perfect: she loves dogs; the color is perfect for her room; and it's a meticulously crafted work of art. There's a small sticker on the base with Chinese characters and the number three thousand: the price. I do some quick math in my head, exchanging from Chinese *yuan* to dollars. I figure it costs around fifty bucks, which seems surprisingly inexpensive for such a finely-crafted item of substantial heft. I think, *Maybe the prices are state-subsidized, to support artisans creating objects of beauty that tourists take back home—spreading Chinese culture around the world.*

That explanation satisfies me. I carry the jar over to a skirted table near the wall, where a young woman is standing, shining black hair around her shoulders. She doesn't speak a word of English and I don't speak Mandarin, but I pantomime a box. She nods and rummages under the table, extracting a cube covered with cinnamon-colored silk and embroidered with golden dragons. As she nestles the jar into the padded red satin interior of the box, I think, *That box is almost as gorgeous as the gift itself!* She then gently lays the box into a shiny red shopping bag and I think, *This is an unbelievably good deal!*

After she places my credit card receipt inside the shopping bag, she says, "*Xie xie.*" I return her thanks and head out the exit door, where the driver is waiting for me. I'm feeling very pleased with my purchase and with myself.

In Patrick's and my hotel room, I fish the credit card receipt out of the bag to secure it in my wallet. Glancing at the receipt, my mental calculator runs over the figure again. *Three thousand yuan is actually less than fifty dollars,* I think. *It's more like forty-eight dollars.*

Suddenly, my heart leaps into my throat. *Oh, no! Did I just pay forty-eight dollars, or...oh, my God!*

It kicks in that I got the exchange rate colossally wrong. I log on to my laptop and our credit card account and there it is: *four hundred and eighty dollars.* There's no way to return it; the museum is closed, and we're leaving Beijing tomorrow morning.

I take a deep breath and call Patrick on his mobile phone, "*Amore mio,* I'm so sorry! I thought I was buying a gift for Mother—for fifty dollars. But I left off a zero."

Patrick reacts exactly how my mom did when I made a mistake as a kid and came to her to confess. He's heard me tell this story about my mother many times after twenty years of marriage. "Did you do it on purpose?" he asks, and of course I say no. "Well, OK," he says, with a sly smile in his voice, "and try not to do it again."

He adds, gently, "Truly, though, *chérie,* don't worry about it. What's most important is that you're going to make your mother very happy."

"Thank you for that, *amore mio.* For saying that. For knowing that."

"Besides," he says, "at least you didn't leave off *two* zeroes!"

I'm carrying the gift when I return to Chicago in May, handing it to my mom first thing after I walk in my parents' door. I recount the story, prefacing it with, "*Mammà,* I'd never normally tell you what I paid for something I've bought you, but I'm going to need you to really love this gift."

She chuckles at the story as she opens the silky cube of a box, admiring the golden embroidered dragons then lifting out the heavy bronze jar. As she holds it in the palms of her hands, she says, "Thank you, Missie. I really, really, *really* love it." This expensive gift has been transformed into a priceless masterpiece.

After that sweet beginning to my visit, though, I jump straight back into helping my brothers care for our parents: taking Dad to the bank, picking up the dry cleaning, doing the laundry, cleaning out the bird bath, topping up the bird food, and getting to the grocery store (with my mom calling out from her bed, "Don't forget the coupons!"). I keep the attic as organized as a Swiss Army store room (including the horrible task of clearing mice from the traps) and sort through the mountain of catalogues my mom strews around her room, which had always been neat as a pin.

Sometimes, my parents are still up for indulging in one of their great pleasures: lunch out, ideally followed by a scenic drive along the Skokie Lagoons or up Sheridan Road to Lake Forest College, with Mother pointing out where on campus she's lived—and Dad remembering visiting her there as they were falling in love in the forties.

One spring day, my brother Charlie is folding up my mom's walker to place in the trunk of my parents' car; we'll take them to lunch together today. I'm standing behind my mom, holding the passenger door open for her. She puts her left leg into the car but her right leg—too weak to hold her—gives way. As she falls backwards into me, I put my arms around her but can't keep us upright, and we crumple to the ground as slowly as I can manage. Rain starts to fall and Dad, helpless to do anything else, holds an umbrella over us as we sit on the pavement, trying to catch our breath. Petrified that my mom's been hurt, I ask, "*Mammà*, are you all right?"

"Yes," she replies, "but could you please remove your hand from my breast?"

We both laugh, Charlie helps us up, then pulls her walker back out of the trunk. With my dad still trying to protect my mom with the umbrella, we all walk soggily and shakily back into their townhome for a lunch of leftovers from their fridge. That's the last time she ever walks to the car; it's wheelchair only from now on.

Once her radiation starts, my brothers Charlie and Pete and I take turns getting her to Evanston Hospital every weekday. She charms everyone with her interest in them—from the women at the entrance to the receptionist in the waiting room to the nurses in Radiation. She is charmed in turn by her affable young oncologist, who tells her, "Mrs. Davis, thirty radiation treatments is the maximum. You can choose to do fewer."

"I'll do all thirty," my Just Do It mom responds firmly. "I will do whatever I can to feel better."

Between hospital trips, my brothers and I run as fast as we can with new chores added: sorting out the medical bills; ordering oxygen and checking the tanks; soothing her radiation-burned skin with steroid cream. Exhausted and fragile, she doesn't eat the food we place before her. We plead with her to drink water and at least a daily protein shake.

I find myself filled with dread and panic. I want her to get well. *No—I need to make her well again.* I have let go of so much, but I'm certain that I inherited The Davis Family Handbook just so I could be ready for this challenge. *I've got this!*

The radiation shrinks the tumor, but Mother gets another respiratory infection that takes her back to the hospital in an ambulance. At the end of this second in-patient stay, her oncologist tells her, "Mrs. Davis, there's nothing more we can do to make you better." She shakes his hand and thanks him. She insisted that he be honest with her—and no one says no to my formidable mom.

Afterwards, once we've gotten her back to my parents', we're sitting around our round family table, the afternoon sun glinting off my mom's soft silver hair, and she says, "No more trips in an ambulance. I want to stay here."

"Here" means their townhome so she can look out at the oak trees and the birds. With all the calls I'd made to my parents—from wherever we've lived around the world—and us talking for hours, at some point in our conversation, my mom would inevitably say—with so much delight, "There's a beautiful new type of bird on the patio today!" And I'd think, *I don't believe that you can have a new bird every day in suburban Evanston, Illinois; I think that's more of an Amazon jungle kind of thing.*

But I've had decades of seeing her see—and create—beauty everywhere. I am desperate not to lose her, but I do respect her wishes. My parents had always been clear with my brothers and me about what they wanted at the end of their lives: no extreme measures. Mother would say, "Let's talk about this now; then we can talk about more interesting things." So we know what she wants when she says what she says.

I phone Patrick, blubbering. "I miss you, *amore mio*, and I was going to come back to Singapore now . . . but . . . but . . ." My voice ends in a pathetic whimper. "I don't know what to do, Patrick."

He responds softly, "I *do* know, *chérie*—be where you need to be now."

So, almost every day, I drive up to Evanston, praying, "Please stand by me, God. Help me to do this. It's hard to watch someone you love slipping away. I feel like I'm losing control over the situation, God."

I hear, "Still with the control, eh, Child? I'm starting to feel you don't trust me. Try to let go."

I'd love to let go. At least by now I *think* I'd love to let go. But how can I? It's day in, day out, for months on end: all the previous chores plus, now, showering with Mother when she'll let me, buying puppy pads to protect her mattress, changing her sheets, and changing her.

One day, Charlie and I are at my parents together. They're resting in their rooms while we prepare lunch and set it on the table in between endless sips of black coffee. We're both running on fumes. "I'm grateful to be able to do this, Charlie, but I'm so tired."

He nods and says, "I know. It's not just tiring, it's *wearying*." He adds, "Re-read *Henry the Fifth*." He means Shakespeare's lines:

We few, we happy few, we band of brothers;
For he to-day that sheds his blood with me shall be my brother . . .

Charlie's reminding me of the privilege of fighting for what we hold dearest, even though the battle we are fighting is to lose her.

But it gets to be too much, even for our little army. Soon after that day, I ask, "*Mammà*, can we please get some help?"

"Why, Missie? I've got you." By this, I know she means not just me. But I'm the one there, kneeling by my mother's bed, begging her.

"Please, *Mammà*. The wheels are falling off the bus." She shakes her head. I grit my teeth. "Mother, you've *heard* me talk about Buddhist monks: how when I place an offering of money or food into the monk's bowl, he is allowing me the blessing of giving. *You* need to allow us the blessing of giving—giving help—to *you*! Please let us get help for you, Mother."

She looks at me, smiling softly, and says, "Hmmm. Whippin' out Buddhist philosophy on me. What next, Missie? *Zoroastrianism?*" And we both crack up. Then I lay my head on her sunken chest and cry.

Over the decades, we've worked hard to get to know one another. By now, we've learned each other by heart. I know this is her way of telling me that she gets it—and will let us do what we need to do.

So we get help through an agency: a woman who helps keep my mom fed and clean, and who gives Dad and my brothers—and me—a break.

Given the blessing of this in-home help, I ask my mom if she's OK with me taking another trip away with Patrick: to India with our friend Armando. He's an expert on the country, and we've been dreaming of taking this trip together for years.

Of course my mother says yes to my travels; she always has. Her helper takes me aside and says, "She's stable now. She could be around for a long time. I can tell that she wants you to take this trip." That's true; this is the woman who's told me forever, "Go!" So, despite my instinct to be by her side, I go.

Patrick and I land in Kolkata in June 2013 and check in to our British colonial-era room in the Oberoi Hotel, with a carved-wood four-poster bed and adorned with a painted portrait of a bearded and bejeweled Maharaja. We smile at one another: we're in India! *Namaste!*

Over a breakfast of fresh mango the next morning, I share guide-book tidbits. "The National Classification of Occupations includes Snake Charmer, Complaint Attending Man, Wigman, Tea Gardens Pruner, Hand Dehairer, and Hand Fluffer." We examine our hands to ascertain if they need fluffing before I continue, "There are eighteen languages recognized by the Constitution, not to mention over 1,600 minor languages and dialects." For polyglots Patrick and me, this is a linguistic gauntlet thrown down.

The *Times of India* headline trumpets "Monsoon!" but no drenching storms ensue, just steamy heat. Indian friends had advised us against travel in summer saying, "It'll be hot as a furnace." I'd assured them that I'd be cool with that—not, perhaps, the best choice of words, as temperatures are forecast to soar over a hundred humid degrees daily.

The hotel's assistant manager offers to show us around Kolkata, taking us to visit where Mother Teresa worked and lived. "We have been created for greater things: to love and to be loved," Mother Teresa had said, and I gasp, *Mammà! That is so my mom.* I'm away for just one day, and I'm missing her and worried about her, even as I'm fascinated by everything I'm seeing.

As we walk Kolkata's back lanes, children scamper, cows lumber, and a shy calf can just be glimpsed inside a house. Dogs trot by, panting-hot. For only a few rupees at a roadside stand, we buy fresh *khati* rolls: "tortillas" fried on a griddle then filled with cheese and hot peppers. Determined this time to say yes to street food, I've packed a supply of what I've long suggested to every traveler: Pepto-Bismol & Co.

Armando arrives in Kolkata and introduces us to the thirty-year-old man he's hired to be our driver across northern India. He also proudly introduces his car, a tomato-red "Ambassador"—the brand of car used as Indian taxicabs in the olden days. I ask Armando hopefully if his car has air-conditioning, and he replies, "In theory only. But at least we've got these for the road ahead." He brandishes a giant fold-out map of India and Bollywood soundtrack CDs. As we drive away from the hotel, "Ambi" attracts a lot of attention: thumbs-up from other drivers and shouts of "Nice car!"

Once we're out of the grit of the city but still on a major road, we zip past green fields, palm trees, power plants, a brick factory, and a roadside hostelry called Hotel Bubbles. Men in madras plaid stand on the top of trucks cruising down the highway; ladies with black braids down their backs ride side-saddle behind guys on motorbikes.

After a couple of hours, Armando announces a "P and T" break at a *dhaba*, a basic roadside snack joint, frequented by truck drivers and travelers by bus and car. The skinniest man I've ever seen cooks bread for us on a heated metal dome, then slathers it—hot from the oven—with *ghee*, clarified butter. The "T" is *masala chai*, the foamy spiced milky tea in a terra cotta cup one of the best things I've ever tasted. As for the "P," the simple toilet out back is clean but swarming with mosquitoes. I'm righteously relieved to have insisted that Patrick and I take anti-malarial medication. Armando clicks a photo of me emerging from the WC, clutching the Handi Wipes I carry with me on all my travels now. I growl, "You men don't understand how easy you have it in this department!"

He laughs and says, "I warned you that this trip would be no-fuss."

"Armandino," I say, "those are fighting words for me. I'll show you just how much I don't need fuss."

I do need seat belts, though, and I'm very grateful that Armando retro-fitted "Ambi" with those, as we are up close and personal to endless oncoming trucks, each one brightly painted in cobalt blue, golden yellow, and fire engine red. Hand-lettered signs on them read "Horn Please" or "Obey Traffic Rules" (ha!). Some trucks have "I Love India" emblazoned on them. I already love India, although I am really hoping not to die on these highways. Vehicles swerve into our lane, and we into theirs. We pass one another with inches to spare. I'm terrified and exhilarated and muttering, "Please God, I'd love to see another day in India if that's all right with You?"

"OK," God says. "Enjoy the ride."

Eventually, some four hundred kilometers later, we arrive in Bodhgaya, where the Buddha found enlightenment beneath a bodhi tree almost three millennia ago. The guys venture into a simple no-name hotel and ask to see two rooms. Patrick reports back that the bathroom is rudimentary but promises to meet our sole conditions: "clean with hot water." After checking in, we buy huge bottles of lemon-soda (to gulp thirstily after hours in an only theoretically air-conditioned car), then walk across the gravel parking lot to the temple complex. Kids peddle trinkets, and a few scraggly folks have their hands outstretched. I'm grateful for Armando's suggestion that—instead of scrambling for coins or feeling guilty—we send a donation after the trip to a friend of his in Mumbai who helps keep poor kids in school.

We leave our shoes at the temple's shoe depot and follow the crowds heading inside the temple complex. Along with hundreds of pilgrims, we wander the grounds and the gardens. Monks from around the world circle the temple, dressed in robes of orange, ochre, and maroon. Some chant softly; some click strings of beads. There are nuns, too, including one woman who prostrates herself before the main temple building, rises to her feet to move forward a few paces and prostrate again, repeating endlessly. We pause for a long time near the famous bodhi tree, or rather its descendant. After our years in Thailand, it feels momentous to experience something so important to Buddhists.

For dinner, we eat in a makeshift restaurant in the tourist bus parking lot. The plastic chairs are only feet away from the resting motor coaches, but it's worth it for the delicious curried lentils. Patrick and I are in bed by eight, pulling the blanket over us, delighted—and surprised—that our room has AC.

The next morning, when Patrick picks up the blanket that had fallen onto our hotel room floor, he yells, "Cockroaches!" as a herd of black insects scatters *clackety-clack* across the tiles. I'm able to identify them as friendly Jiminy Crickets instead, and we both feel better. It also provides us with our Hotel Rating System for the trip, with Five Crickets the pinnacle. This hotel had the potential to earn Two Crickets (one for Proximity to Historic Site and a second for Unexpected Air-Con), but loses one for Cold Water Only When We'd Been Promised Hot and a second for, uh, Clattering Insects. So this no-name establishment will languish forever in our minds as a Zero Cricket dud.

As we set off again, the road rivals Chicago's avenues in potholes. I appreciate the occasional break to stretch our legs. At noon, Armando buys us juice extracted from sugar cane by an old man with an ancient metal press roadside. We pass people working in the fields or taking their lunch in the shade of trees. After driving for hours with Armando consulting his map and murmuring directions to the driver, we are stunned to read the sign, "Welcome to Bodhgaya!"

We're drenched in sweat but laughing our heads off at having driven in a huge circle back to where we started this morning.

It's gonna be a long ride to our next destination, Varanasi, but I don't care. It's a huge relief that it wasn't *me* navigating this time and—as Patrick and I always say—"If you don't get at least a little lost when you travel, you're not getting your money's worth." We're on an adventure!

When we finally do approach Varanasi on the highway, we pass a truck with a sort of triple-decker bunkbed setup, like the trucks that carry shiny new cars to a dealership. This truck, however, appears to be carrying three levels of white-shrouded bodies en route to cremation in Varanasi along the banks of the Ganges River. For Hindus, *Ganga* is Mother; the devout bathe in her waters to wash away a lifetime of sins. If they can, they come here at the end of their lives, as dying here offers liberation from the cycle of birth and death. If at all possible, they send—or better yet bring—their dead to be cremated alongside this sacred river. I feel my heart in my throat, thinking of what awaits me back in Chicago.

The driver gets "Ambi" and us as close as possible to our riverside hotel, then Armando says, "We'll have to walk for a bit." He opens the trunk and hands Patrick and me our luggage: identical black backpacks with little wheels, which are handy on pavement but virtually useless on ancient cobblestones. As Varanasi dates back more than three thousand years, there are *lots* of cobblestones. As one of India's holiest places, there are also *lots* of sacred cows (and sacred cowpats: we step carefully over those).

We also step carefully over mostly naked men, stretched out on the ground. These are *sadhus*: wandering hermits considered holy men, their bodies smeared with ash, their foreheads dotted with sandal-paste, their possessions a bowl, a staff, and a blanket. I know all this from my guidebook reading; however, I do *not* know if they are sleeping or dead, awaiting cremation the next day. Armando looks at me, reads my mind, and says, "Sleeping." As he leans in to say that, he sees the stunned look on my face and grabs my backpack with a wink, hoisting it onto his back. I'm afraid he'll accuse me of being high-maintenance, but he takes me by the hand instead, whispering, "It's OK. Just come with me."

When we arrive at our hotel, we can't see the Ganges below in the dark, but we can see many more bodies strewn along the concrete path that runs along the river. "Sleeping?" I whisper to Armando, smiling weakly, and he nods yes.

Patrick and I find that our room is matchbox-small, but clean, with psychedelic-colored Hindu artwork on the walls. The clattering air-conditioner is cantilevered over our bed, but it feels better to risk dying crushed by cool versus melted in our sleep.

We're up at four the next morning to perform *puja*, the pre-dawn offerings and prayers of respect. Armando, Patrick, and I walk down to the *ghat* just below our hotel. *Ghats* are the steps and landings leading down to holy water. Varanasi has eighty-four of them, and by the time we've descended to the water's edge, there are already dozens of pilgrims in the river. Some are somberly engaged in ritual bathing, but many are whooping in joyful abandon. One fellow floats around blissfully in an old black rubber inner tube, just like we did as kids in Lake Michigan. There are children in swim suits and grandfathers wearing loincloths over skinny frames. One brave Japanese tourist in a Speedo pulls on goggles, plunges in, and is roundly applauded by his Indian fellow-bathers. I expect the Ganges to *look* a lot dirtier than it does, but still, we've been advised not to dip even one pinkie into it.

Wooden rowboats bob about, painted red, blue, and yellow. Armando chooses a smiling skipper, and I step aside as Patrick and he negotiate a price for a boat journey with that special bantering back and forth of people who love to bargain. Once aboard, we are rowed a hundred feet out from the shore. The sun rises, glowing, turning the whole scene rosy salmon pink. The buildings along the river look like crumbling candies: a temple to Shiva in the soft green of salt water taffy; a centuries-old mansion in Necco Wafers pink.

We buy tiny tinfoil cups with candles and flower petals and set them on the water to float away with our wishes. My wish is really a prayer, "Please, God, make Mother well again," even though I'm aware that she's eighty-five with lung disease and a malignant tumor. I also ask God to please look after my parents while I'm away.

"Thanks for weighing in, Child, but I'm already on it."

Our boatman rows us past the "burning *ghat*" where bodies are burned seven days a week, twenty-four hours a day. There are huge piles of logs and lots of smoke. A white-shrouded corpse is on the funeral pyre. The closest male relative is standing by, his head shaved, dressed all in white. The body has been doused in the Ganges and anointed with clarified butter to help it burn faster. It takes about two hours for the body to burn, after which the family takes some of the ashes, leaving the rest at the river's edge. I can't help but mumble, "Ashes to ashes; dust to dust." I can't help but feel this is our common cultural heritage and, somehow, the most natural thing in the world.

Upon disembarking, we walk through Varanasi's alleyways, gingerly squeezing past a sacred cow blocking our way in one particularly narrow lane. We pass bright murals, small shrines, shops opening up, street sweepers, and more wild-haired holy men. Armando leads us to a rooftop café, and we are transported from close alleyway to open-air breeziness. We breakfast on thick brown toast, papaya jam, omelet with Nepali cheese, lethally strong espresso for me, and tea for the guys. In this town dedicated to death, I feel grateful to be with people I love and very alive.

And—in just the few hours since dawn—I feel different about caring for the dying. The families here have done all that they can for their loved ones. That's what I want to do. It's instantly clear to me that my job is to stop fighting to keep Mother alive or to make her well again. My job when I get back to Chicago will be to help take her all the way home.

I pray, "God, please help me to do my best to help fulfill Mother's wish to die at home."

"I will, Child."

Once we've returned to our hotel, packed up, checked out, found "Ambi," and set off again, the driver navigates through this ancient town to the highway. After this transcendent visit, my journal simply reads, "Diesel fumes = *argh*," but it really should read that my life has been changed.

We drive on to Lucknow, a gritty city of two million, arriving in the early evening traffic-chaos and checking in to the Art Deco Hotel Capoor's on what Lucknovians considered "their Champs Elysées." Patrick negotiates an additional "top sheet" for us (as a barrier against cricket-laden blankets).

We're here to experience Mughal cuisine: the food of the ancient Muslim princes. When we arrive at the market area, filled with fluo-rescent-lighted food stalls and milling crowds, the smell of roasting meat emanates from Armando's favorite spot. It's a literal hole-in-the-wall which sells kebab that has been mashed into a paste, a dish devised long ago for a Mughal ruler with nary a tooth in his head. A throng of male customers stand around a huge metal skillet, all of them waiting for their food. My journal reads, "Meat Paste = *ugh*."

Next is Chicken Biryani, and I will myself not to fixate on the state of the silverware and the plate-washing, plus the plastic buckets on the ground for chicken bones. I prefer seeing where dishes and cutlery have been washed (in clean water, with soap bubbles abound-ing). Another journal entry that night is "Bones in bucket = *yech*."

Luckily, we finish our meal with *kulfi*—Lucknow's creamy ice cream in pistachio or saffron. This is the only time I observe Patrick nervous about the food. He whispers, "I thought we were supposed to avoid dairy in this climate!" but I don't care. I want ice cream. I've come a long way from our early travels to Turkey years ago: I'd read a terrifying travel magazine article about how red snapper is not a clean fish. When we'd see it on the menu, I'd hiss at Patrick, "No way!" and he'd roll his eyes at me. I feel triumphant, just this once, to be more adventurous than my husband.

The road out of town the next morning is, again, chaos. There is honking, garbage rootled by pigs, and two dead dogs along the side of the road. But then we are out of the city and immediately into farmland, with fields divided into square green plots. A minaret is painted in a green checkerboard pattern. Men work at ancient foot-pedaled sewing machines along the road. Cow patties dry in the sun in meter-high pyramids. A teenager on a motorbike carries a watermelon on his lap. We pay tolls at official toll booths but also at homemade stands run by local "entrepreneurs." At one booth, there's a sign "Complaint Book is available in Booth 5," and we all laugh when we see that Booth 5 is empty. At another, the ticket agent gives us plastic-wrapped hard candies in lieu of coins for change. We gobble those, giggling, and head towards one of the New Seven Wonders of the World, the Taj Mahal.

After hours of driving, we arrive at last on the outskirts of Agra, a much bigger city than I'd expected. As we approach the entrance of the Oberoi hotel, we wipe our faces with endless Handi Wipes, each one coming away filthy. We have soot inside our ears and in the crooks of our arms. My hair is stiff and wild as a Varanasi *sadhu*'s: I pat it down the best I can before we arrive at our hotel, but in my Einstein-in-a-baseball cap look, I am definitely not the Perfect Luxury Hotel Guest. When we enter the lobby, passing ramrod-straight guards in crisp white uniforms, the GM greets us and—when we apologize for our appearance—is gentlemanly enough to exclaim how he would never even have noticed the dust covering us.

After a very long scour under the shower, we head over to one of the most graceful structures in the world. The Taj Mahal exceeds my very high expectations with its effortless floating fragility and strength and its iridescent pearly hue. I'm dazzled by the workmanship on the façade; flowers of blue lapis lazuli, black onyx, red carnelian, green malachite are set into the marble. Calligraphy of Koranic scripture runs up and around arches and back down again. It took twenty-two years and twenty thousand artisans and builders to create this sixteenth-century masterpiece—a Mughal emperor imagined it as a memorial to his favorite wife who had died after giving birth to their fourteenth child. Our guide tells us a favorite joke of his: A woman touring the Taj with her husband asked hubby when would he build her such a tribute. To which the husband replied, "My dear, I am completely ready to do so. The delay is entirely on your part." Patrick turns to look at me with a smile, and I shoot him a warning look.

On our departure day, we pack our freshly laundered clothes. Some items have been returned to us with unsurprising notes from laundry: "We regret that we were unable to get items clean."

Now that we've completed the northernmost part of our thousand-kilometer arc, Armando is heading back to work with "Ambi" and the driver. Patrick and I thank him for having shepherded us on this once-in-a-lifetime experience, then we head southwest on the best-yet road: a four-lane highway with easy traffic. We're now in an Oberoi-rented car with a driver and, while the air-con feels delicious, the road full of cows now looks merely "cute" through the cool glass windows. I am brimming with gratitude to have had several days fully immersed in India.

On we drive into Rajasthan, and, after a visit to Jaipur, its buildings a soft pinkish-red color, we retreat to yet one more Oberoi hotel for a long siesta. When we awaken, we phone Evanston to see how my parents are. Dad answers the phone, "Hello, Far India!"

My mother responds to my concerned questions with, "Keep enjoying your trip, Missie. I'm fine."

I want to believe her, but I know very well what "I'm fine" can mean.

Before we depart Jaipur, an Indian friend emails to suggest that we add just "one more stop," quoting, "'Brahma dropped a lotus flower on the earth and the town of Pushkar appeared.'" Heaven help me! We have already traveled hundreds of kilometers, sweated buckets, survived holy hermits and sacred cows. But we're definitely not gonna say no to seeing *that*.

When we check into the Pushkar Palace, I pretend to feel charmed. It must have been very grand—a century ago. We are clearly the only guests in the whole hotel, but get a cheerful welcome from a chubby young man in a lopsided maroon turban. He leads us to our room on the fourth floor, and points to town, "Only five minutes the walking."

We gaze out at dozens of small Hindu temples curled around tiny Lake Pushkar. From each temple, the steps of *ghats* lead down to the lake so that pilgrims can bathe in that sacred water, which they're doing. We hear high-pitched laughter and see a line of ladies in saris of dazzling reds and oranges. I'm reminded for the millionth time in my life: This is why I travel!

Dumping our bags, we're just heading out to the most important temple in Pushkar—dedicated to Brahma—when it starts to pour down rain so thick we can't see a foot in front of our faces. *Maybe this is a good thing*, I think. *We've had no down time on this trip, so this gives me the chance to rest*. We retreat into our room, and I stretch out on our bed to read. Reading is not possible, however; the bed is lumpy, and there's only one dim light bulb overhead. The air-conditioner, which had been rattling loudly, suddenly shudders to a halt. I lay there, sweating, until the rain finally stops after an hour.

Patrick asks, "Shall we go to the temple?" and we head out, but at the hotel's entrance, chubby guy chirps, "Waiting for thirty minutes, please. Let the rain to be retreating." Back up four flights of stairs to droop into a rickety rattan chair to wait. When a half-hour has passed, and Patrick suggests that we try—a third time—on the temple, I lose it.

"Patrick," I wail, "I cannot do this! I just can not!"

He says, "*Chérie*, you've been a great sport this whole trip. We don't need to go out if you don't want to." I think, *This is easier for him. He loves the heat and humidity. He doesn't need to re-charge as much as I do.* But I see how much he wants to go; I really want to go, too. I rally.

At the hotel entrance this time, chubby guy says, "Most excellent, Sir! Most excellent, Madame!" The narrow streets we walk toward downtown are lined with old buildings, the façades crumbling, but also carved and painted in bright colors, giving an idea of how magnificent Pushkar once had been. My familiar "I love to travel" bounce is returning to my step—until we reach the main street that leads to the Brahma temple. It is completely flooded from the heavy rainstorm. Locals wade through knee-deep cocoa-brown water.

"Patrick, I'm *not* walking through that water in my only footwear. And don't you dare even *think* about going barefoot, mister!"

Instead, Patrick does the local equivalent of hailing a taxi. He flags down an eighty-year old guy wearing only a white loincloth and pushing an empty wooden cart. The old guy is stick-thin with wisps of white hair, resembling a human Q-tip. Patrick gestures toward the famous temple, the old guy nods, we climb aboard and whisper to one another in delight, "A pushcart in Pushkar!" After pushing us through fifty feet of sloshing brown water, Q-Tip tips us onto muddy ground right in front of the temple. Patrick gives him a few bucks, and we're all happy.

Out of respect, we take off our desert boots to enter the temple. After ten days of visiting every sacred site possible, the soles of my feet are rough and cracked (and feel filthy, even though I wash them rigorously each night). "You know, *amore mio*," I say, "I'm not crazy about going barefoot again." Patrick nods, sympathetic, but eager to explore. As I walk up the steps, which are slimed with mud—and whatever—I mutter, "This temple had better be stunning." Well, it *isn't* particularly stunning. And the second room we enter is filled with *bees*! They're buzzing around, supping on syrup left by devotees.

I storm out, yelling, "I don't care if those are sacred freakin' bees. You know I'm allergic!" Patrick follows, nodding, and retrieves our desert boots. I stare at them, unable to move. "*Amore*, I just cannot put my filthy feet back into my boots!"

Patrick wordlessly leads me to a fairly clean step and helps me to sit down on it. He takes his own socks to gently wipe off my feet, then helps me into my desert boots. It's one of the kindest things he's ever done in two decades of a very kind marriage. With this simple gesture, I feel *cherished*.

By then, the water has retreated, and we're able to walk back through town, hand in hand. Shopkeepers smile at us. Cows mosey by us. Back at the Pushkar Palace, the chubby guy guides us to the rooftop terrace and—at a plastic table with a tiny votive candle on it—serves us a meal of lentils and spiced vegetables. Stars emerge, evening breezes wash over us, and it washes over me how travel can be so challenging—but sweet and sacred with someone I love.

We really should have stopped looking at helpful emails from Indian friends, as one more writes, "You simply must see the ruins of India's largest fort. The Victory Tower at Chittorgarh is not to be missed." I'm thinking, *Oof*. Instead, I say OK with as much enthusiasm as I have left in my wilted body.

I can see why our friend has insisted we visit, though, once we're gazing up at the nine-story tower, covered with elaborate carvings of gods and goddesses, weapons, and flowers. I'd never heard of Chittorgarh, but Indian tourists clearly have; it's crowded with folks busily snapping photos of the dozens of wild monkeys roaming around the base of the tower, each monkey as big as a beagle. I shudder as giggling tourists place their hands just above those furry cinnamon-brown heads. "See, I am petting him!" I hear more than once.

Dozens more monkeys have climbed up onto various levels of the tower, and are busily grooming one another. There is an enormous amount of flea-flicking going on. I feel a little bit queasy and whisper to Patrick, "I'm pretty sure those monkeys are rabid!" But, still, when Patrick asks me if I want to climb that tower, I say, "Hell, yes!" The surrender of Pushkar is far behind me, lost in a blast of FOMO: Fear of Missing Out.

In Patrick and I go, taking off our desert boots once again to leave them outside the entrance. We've just started up the 157 steps when a dozen young Indian men cram in right behind us, very courteous, very smiling, but exhibiting a very non-Western sense of personal space. We let them squeeze past us and keep climbing, but just when I think I'm *not* claustrophobic, I'm confronted by the fact that perhaps I *am*. I squeak, "I don't love enclosed spaces, right? But I can do this!"

Patrick calls out, "Super, *chérie*: two thumbs up!"

It isn't helping that it's a little smelly in there; the tower is *hundreds* of years old. By the time we arrive at the dim landing to the third story, I am feeling decidedly heroic, but—as I look up at the steps to come—I say, "Patrick, it's completely dark up there." There's *no* light coming in above us. We'll have to use our hands to *feel* our way up along the moist, much-palmed wall—a wall that is black with mildew and the sweat of a million tourists' hands.

"Patrick, I still want to do this. As long as there are none of those monkeys inside this tower." I'm just adding a light-hearted "Ha ha ha" to reinforce that I'm no quitter when—cue pissed-off-monkey-shrieking-noise from just above us in the pitch black. My old familiar Handbook voice commands, "Don't miss out! Just Do It!"

But I hear my own new voice, *You know what? Fuck FOMO. I don't want to go up there.*

I turn on my heels, yelling, "That's it, Patrick! I'm outta here!"

He calls back, "You all right?"

I'm too focused on descending the sweaty, slippery steps to respond. As I'm groping my way down, a monkey leans in through a window-slit—yellow teeth bared, hissing—and takes a swipe at me with a withered leathery paw.

I scream, "Yo, I'm leaving your freakin' tower! Gimme a break!"

At the base of the tower, I grab my boots, stumble out into the bright sun, and collapse onto a bit of wall in the shade of a scrubby tree twenty feet from the tower. I rub my sweaty palms dry on my pants legs. I gulp in hot—but open—air. As I gulp, my photo is taken a lot: I appear to be the first Caucasian some tourists have ever seen, as there is a lot of stunned staring at me, which turns to shy smiling when I smile.

I wait for Patrick, catching my breath and smiling for photos for half an hour. Then I get nervous: Where *is* Patrick? I'm ashamed to say that I'm wondering if he's being raped by monkeys! I don't even know if that's possible, but that's what I'm wondering. So now I'm feeling anxious about my husband—and also ashamed that I wasn't brave enough to reach the top. I could be there now, enjoying the view, or helping fend off rabid monkeys. Whatever happened to Just Do It?

"Child," I hear. "Listen to your heart. You don't need to be blindly brave any more. Brave(ish) is enough sometimes."

I'm just about to ask, *Really, God?* when Patrick emerges from the base of the tower, surrounded by young men, all of them laughing. After he shakes their hands, he grabs his boots and walks over to me, beaming, saying, "Everyone took my picture at the top of the tower. Some ladies up there even put their babies in my arms for photo-ops."

I ask, "Who on earth would take a *baby* up there?" and he laughs.

"Point well taken, *chérie*. But it was fun. I'm sorry you missed it."

Normally, I'd be feeling jealous by now—of the experience Patrick had that I wanted to have, too. Instead, I am really enjoying the moment. First of all, with all these cameras on us, it feels like we are Celebrities in Chittorgarh. Most importantly, though, I realize that it's OK for me not to have kept up with Patrick; not to have reached the summit; not to worry about being less than—or left behind; not to be brave if I don't feel brave.

It's taken me over fifty years—but it's time for me to feel what I feel. Ask myself what I want: Go all the way up, or not. Set sail, or rest safe in port—occasionally at least.

When Patrick and I fly back from this land of over a billion people toward tiny Singapore, I finish up my Trip Report for India. "*Namaste* means hello, but also goodbye. *Yatra* means journey, but also pilgrimage. This trip was all of that: the everyday intertwined with the sacred. It has not been an easy trip, but I wouldn't have missed this proud, dignified, big-hearted country for the world. My dreams are now scented and colored with a spice blend of cardamom, cinnamon, cloves, and cumin."

My guidebook ends with an ancient poem, "If there is a paradise on earth, it is this, it is this, it is this."

India has shown me that *this* means staying present in the here and now. Exactly what I need to know as I head back to care for my mother at the end of her life.

The next month, July 2013, my mom enters into hospice care: not curative, but "for comfort only." No one knows how much time a hospice patient will have, but my mom far outlives even optimistic projections, carrying on—even as she weakens, month by month. She so clearly wants to stay with us, and I stay on in Chicago, driving to my parents daily, pleading along Lake Shore Drive, "Stand by me, please, God."

"I'm here, Child."

Patrick in Asia is incredibly supportive of my spending months away from him in Chicago, and I'm so grateful when he joins us at Christmas. We sing carols around the old family table with Charlie, Mary Ellen, and our two American nieces. Meghan is on the keyboard and Katie is holding Mother's hand, when she's not getting up from the table several times to walk away, her tears overwhelming her. When we sing "The Twelve Days of Christmas," Mother belts out "Five Gold Rings" at the top of her battered lungs, telling Charlie the next day with a smile, "That nearly killed me—but it was worth it."

It *is* worth it to be together. But it's very hard, and I need something that's not pre-grieving my mom and not missing Patrick nine thousand miles away once he's back in Singapore. I call Second City, but there's no improv class that fits my schedule. On a whim, I sign up for "Beginning Storytelling." I've loved stories since Dad read to me every night before bed.

After years of compiling encyclopedic Trip Reports—and helping Patrick with strategic business writing—I can feel the left and right sides of my brain duking it out with this return to the creative writing I've always loved. My Strategic Brain has developed over the years into a world-class synthesizer of information and bullet point champion. It has also grown into an arrogant bully. "I'll take over from here," it blusters to my tender daydreaming Creative Brain, who whispers to me a reminder that we've been together since birth. *True,* I think. I thank Strategic Brain for all it does for me but ask it to please take a break. Maybe go out for a cup of coffee? I know it won't be able to nap.

With Strategic Brain stepping aside reluctantly, I encourage

Creative Brain, talking to it as though I were its Montessori teacher. "What would you like to do today? Put on a puppet show? Putter around with crayons and construction paper? Tell a story in haiku?" At this, Creative Brain is beaming—one of its gifts is making up poems on the spot.

In my first storytelling class at Second City, my synapses firing in espresso-level excitement, I write a story about our recent India experience, with "Monkey Tower" as the title. After I read it aloud during class, the instructor says, "Whoa, you don't *look* like someone who'd be telling that story, Margaret, but now I'm gonna be thinking of you as Indiana Jones!"

My heart leaps with joy at that—and during each class session. Storytelling, it turns out, is not just the life preserver I need so desperately; it's love at first sight! I get to be like Harriet the Spy: observing and writing. I get to share my travel stories—and the fact that my life has turned out like intrepid sailing dog Scuppers, who roamed the seven seas. I love my teacher, just like I always did. I love my fellow writers. I forget my sorrow and exhaustion if only for a few hours every week.

On Sunday mornings, I walk from our apartment back over to Second City for a free storytelling show. As the "Live Lit" scene is still relatively new, I have the chance to leap up on stage to tell a story at a moment's notice. I channel the wisdom of my storytelling teacher Deanna, who reassured me, "Don't worry about forgetting your story: it's your story." As it turns out, I make people laugh (and not only my friends, who turn out in droves, bless them, telling me, "Shine!"). I feel a deep satisfaction when audience members tell me that my story touched them.

I'm having fun. I'm expressing myself. I'm connecting. My stories have meaning for others—and for me. "Thank You, God," I say, "for answering my prayers." I hear a little cough and a rumbling *Ahem*. I add, "I meant to say as You always do."

When producers ask me to perform in their storytelling shows, my response is always yes. I tell in the hushed silence of a used book store, in a coffee shop with Chicago's elevated train rattling so loud overhead that my words are obliterated, and at a center for the blind, where an elderly man falls asleep right in the middle of my story, and I remind myself, *You can't please all the people all the time.* I keep on telling.

I start to participate in Moth StorySLAMs, writing a five-minute story to fit the theme then polishing and practicing it until I can tell it in my sleep. That's when I know I'll be able to bring it to life on stage. When I talk with people in line to buy tickets, sometimes they ask me what I do. For so long I told people I was a Trailing Spouse or the Minister of Domestic Affairs. I said it jokingly, but I wasn't laughing. Now I respond, "I'm a storyteller."

It's time, in spring 2014, to also share this part of me with my mom. Hospice has told us, "There's just a while left for her," and it hits me: I have shared with her 99 percent of me. It's time to share the rest, before it's too late. That 1 percent is also who I am—and want to be—in the world now.

I've already told my mother that I'm taking a class in storytelling and that I like it very much. "I know that, Missie," she says. "I see that you're happy." But I haven't dared tell her that I love having an audience and the audience seems to really like my stories.

So I bring my laptop out to my parents' with a video of me live on stage at Second City. I'm very nervous about what my ladylike mom will think about me telling a big, dramatic story about an ancient, dark tower in India, surrounded by wild and probably rabid monkeys. In the story, I sweat, yell, and cry in a most unladylike way. But my mother has let me see her—all of her. She hasn't hidden herself from me at the end of her life. I won't hide myself from her one second longer, no matter what I'm afraid The Handbook will be whispering in her ear.

I sit next to her on her narrow bed, holding her slender hand. I tell her, "I love you, *Mammà*."

"I love you more, Missie. And more."

That gives me strength. I take a deep breath and press play on my laptop. I cringe when I notice how terrifyingly center stage I am. But, as Mother's watching the video, I'm watching her. She has a soft smile on her face, tears in her eyes. She gasps when it's scary and chuckles at just the right places. When the story's done, I press stop, but not before the audience's applause.

"Missie," she whispers, "I'm just so proud of you for sharing your stories."

When my mother speaks that single smiling sentence, decades of keeping myself quiet and small to stay lovable start to fall away. Finally, I get it—just how much she's always wanted me to have my voice and be myself. She just never had the voice herself to tell me that. Or maybe The Davis Handbook's voice simply overpowered hers.

After all the months of wondering when it will happen, hospice in April 2014 says, simply, "Soon." Patrick gets on a plane from Singapore. As he sits by Mother's bed, she tells him, "I adore you, Patrick." After one of her familiar sly pauses, she adds, "Most of the time."

My brothers and I try to keep Dad calm. He's frantic to be losing the love of his life and helpless to know what to do. "How about Winnie the Pooh, *Papà?*" He sits by the side of her bed and reads from this touchstone of their sixty-six year marriage of comradeship, determination, family, fights, and love.

We are now wetting Mother's lips with a sponge—and giving her morphine every few hours. When Charlie and Mary Ellen change her, my now-tiny mother wraps her hands around my very tall brother's neck so he can lift her up with gentle strength. I ache with love to see this tender intimacy.

This, as it turns out, is where The Davis Family Handbook is genuinely heroic, helping us to stay strong and keep going, even when our hearts are breaking.

This is completely, genuinely brave and I am proud of it.

The hospice nurse tells us, "Your mother doesn't want to miss a moment with any of you." *So true!* Then she adds, "She won't leave if you keep pulling her back to consciousness. You're holding her here." So we vow not to talk to her, stroke her silver hair, or adjust her coverlet that doesn't need adjusting—she hasn't moved for days. I whisper, "Go when the time is right, *Mammà*. Go." I want her to feel free.

On the morning of April 5, Patrick and Meghan and I are just awakening. We've slept in my parents' living room on a flotilla of air mattresses. I make the coffee, and Meghan goes to look in on her grandmother. She returns to the living room in tears, saying, "I think she's gone."

I hug her, then go to my mother's room. Yes, she's gone. As Meghan phones her parents, I go into Dad's room to wake him up. He sits up, groggy, when I sit on the side of his single bed. I put my arm around him, and we sob with grief and exhaustion after losing one of our best friends. I phone Peter, who says he'll be right there. I phone Hal in Virginia to let him know. One of us calls the hospice nurse, who arrives straightaway, telling us to take all the time we need before we call the funeral home.

The hospice nurse guides Peter, Charlie, Mary Ellen, Meghan, Patrick, and me in gently washing Mother's face and hands with a soft cloth. She helps us to dress her in a Talbot's jacket she loved: patchwork in soft blue, green, yellow, and pink. We lay a skirt over her and pull nylons up her slim legs. We slide onto her slender feet the saddle-brown Ferragamo loafers she'd never worn. Just a few months before, when I'd been helping her clean out her closet, she'd told me, "I'm saving those for springtime." It's springtime.

I feel numb as I phone the funeral home. They quietly take her out in a black body bag on a gurney. Patrick and Meghan see the hearse off, holding each other.

In the coming days, we console Dad, return Mother's medical equipment, clean her room, toss the remaining catalogues . . . and pick up her ashes from the funeral home.

Two weeks after she died, we offer "A Celebration of the Life of Onnie Davis" in the Presbyterian Home chapel. D. C. friends Don and Daniel have flown in and are handing out the programs we've made up. The cover shows a photo of Mother around the time she met Dad: an eighteen-year old with dark hair in waves around her smiling round face and vivacious dark brown eyes. On the back cover is a photo I took of my smiling parents in Portofino, behind them the muted colors of the old houses around the port, and behind those the deep green of umbrella pines.

For the program, Charlie has written, "She stayed current with world events, enjoying lively debates on social and political issues. She was a champion for the underdog and believed that we are all individuals who can take great pride and pleasure in the active contributions we make to our world. It will be through her contributions and compassion that she will live on in our hearts." We mention how she became an ardent supporter of the Packers when she married Dad, how she loved travel, and also how she loved hearing about others' adventures.

As our friends and family are reading the program, an organ interlude plays. The minister offers an opening prayer and a meditation. We all sing "Amazing Grace," which Mother loved.

Patrick sings a baritone aria from Bach's *Passion of Saint Matthew*: "*Mache dich, mein Herze, rein.*" Make yourself pure, my heart.

Mary Ellen reads from the Bible, Proverbs 31:10–31: "Who can find a virtuous and capable wife? She is more precious than rubies . .

. She is energetic and strong, a hard worker . . . She extends a helping hand to the poor and opens her arms to the needy . . . She is clothed with strength and dignity, and she laughs without fear of the future . . . When she speaks, her words are wise . . . She carefully watches everything in her household and suffers nothing from laziness."

Hal, Peter, and Charlie offer remembrances; Katie and Meghan offer tearful references to Pooh and Piglet.

When it's my turn to speak, all I can do is grip the lectern and weep. After years of advising bereaved friends, "If all you do is stand there and cry—that will be enough," that's what I do. Until, at last, I find the words to honor my *Mammà*—how she taught me to love and be loved. I am beyond grateful to be surrounded in this moment by those who loved my mother—and who love me.

That summer, Charlie, Mary Ellen, Meghan, and I kayak far out onto Lake Michigan to scatter half of Mother's ashes. I'm so glad that we could return my mother to water, earth, and sky. I place the other half in a Ziploc bag in case my brothers Hal and Pete want some— and also because I'm not ready to let go of her completely. I promise myself I'll do that once I hear from her that it's time.

To honor her and delight her spirit, the family plants a tree near their townhome with a small plaque reading, "In Memory of Onnie Davis." Dad pats the bark of her tree with affection and murmurs something to my mom with a smile.

I miss her every day, but now my biggest concern is my dad. I'm quite sure he'll die of grief any moment now. The hospice agency's grief counselor gently redirects my thinking. "Your father is over ninety. He realizes that he's near the end of his life. He's either in despair or integrity about the life he's led." I know my dad's devastated over losing his girl, but he's led a decent life. Recognizing that brings me a lot of comfort. It's been four years of caring for my mom, and it was the greatest privilege of my life; we have taken her all the way home.

It's time for me to get back to my home: Patrick. I fly back to Singapore.

Patrick and I are both wiped out because we were apart so much and so often for so long. But also because, once again, his job no longer fits. He has had four years of what he loves: people. He has conducted HR visits across Asia Pacific, recruited at hotel schools, and helped decide which GMs move where and when. But, by 2015, the job of vice president, human resources Asia/Pacific has shifted to strategic planning. He's behind a desk again and miserable.

As a frog having leapt from one lily pad to another, he feels confident he can leap again and negotiates with Four Seasons to become a consultant in the realm of leadership training. He has been learning to facilitate this work, which integrates the personal growth work we both love. I feel relieved that Patrick sees a way forward—without our even needing to drag out the white board (or the flips flops). His heart is speaking for him.

As soon as Patrick's replacement is found, Four Seasons announces that he'll assume the role of global leadership trainer, bringing to the program his ". . . wide operational experience as well as his deep understanding of people, their motivations and what they need to develop and grow. He'll relocate to Chicago in 2016 with his wife Margaret, but as ever, will be wherever he is needed."

So, after five years in the Lion City, we'll be moving back to the Windy City, leaving expatriate life behind—maybe for good this time. I'll be in Chicago, which I love, but I'm already shocked at how hard I'm holding on—again—to my identity as an expatriate. I have a lot of pride wrapped up in how well I negotiated all our moves and how well I managed to embrace other countries (most of the time).

I'm also shocked that, while I didn't marry Patrick for his title,

I have to admit that I liked saying that my husband is a VP with Four Seasons. I've long said, "It doesn't matter how high up you've climbed on the ladder if the ladder is on the wrong wall." But now we'll be stepping off the corporate ladder entirely for the first time in our lives. It's positive, and yet, as the saying goes, "Change is good; you go first." This is a big change for us.

Now that I've learned that Patrick can handle all of my true emotions, I let loose with some serious bitching and moaning. "I hate to leave Singapore. It's exciting *and* it's easy. The people are smart and funny, it's a fascinating city, we love the music and museums, we still have so much to see in Asia, and we get to go barefoot in January." Patrick reminds me that we also love Chicago (most months) and we always knew we weren't going to retire here in Singapore. But he admits that he'll miss it, too.

"I hate giving away all our stuff." It's not actually *all* of our stuff, but a significant amount. We don't need it in Chicago with our already furnished apartment. Patrick's also sorry to see some of our treasures go, the table and chairs we've sat at each night for dinner on our balcony in particular. But we give those away to our friends, other items to colleagues, and I take trips daily in a taxi with a trunkful of items to donate to the local charity.

"I hate losing the perk of staying at Four Seasons." Patrick has no comeback to that one. Saying goodbye to those very favorable conditions stings for both of us.

I whine on, "Why do I have to give up everything I love? I've lost my mom, and now all this."

Patrick says, "I know, *chérie*; it's a lot. Even though I know you're also happy about returning to your hometown, right?"

I'm reminded of Linda teaching me years ago that when the glass is half full, it's also half empty.

And vice versa.

"Yes, *amore mio*, I'm happy about returning to Chicago. I'm happy that you have work you love again." And, having lived the better part of two decades like a turtle carrying around its shell, I'm happy at the thought of taking things out of the carefully labeled plastic containers I've moved them in around the world and giving those big battered bins away.

We give notice to our landlord that we're leaving in a few months. I collect bids for an international move one more time, buying red, yellow, and green stickers for my Trademarked Moving System. On our own Nostalgia Tour, Patrick and I visit everything we've come to love in Singapore. We say farewell to hotel comrades and close pals, grateful that our friendships will endure. We say goodbye to friends at AsiaWorks, our dim sum pals, and Jeffrey in the Botanic Gardens. As a parting gift, Patrick's office gives him an antique map of Asia (which Navigator me adores). We thank his team not just for their Singaporean efficiency, but for their good humor and warm care of us.

With preparations set for our departure in early 2016, I take my final home leave to Chicago for Christmas 2015. I've seen on the website for the Moth that they have a StorySLAM on the evening I arrive in Chicago. During my flights traversing the globe, I rehearse the story I've written on the theme of "On a Dime." I'm careful to mumble quietly so as not to disturb the passengers around me on the plane, and I keep my hand gestures discreet to avoid the attention of air marshals.

When I'm finally in our Chicago apartment, I log on to the Moth to buy myself a ticket to the StorySLAM. "Noooo!" I shout— it's sold out. I'm furious with myself for not having bought a ticket earlier, but I was engrossed in all that needed to be done before I left Singapore.

Damn it, I think. *I want to tell this story, and I'm more than ready!* But I'm also jet lagged and stale-smelling after three airplane flights. Maybe it's a sign that I'm supposed to rest tonight?

Tomorrow will be time with Dad, and that'll be tiring all over again.

It's too early in the morning in Singapore to reach Patrick, so I call Linda. I know she'll offer both sides of the situation to consider. I'm practically yelling as I explain my predicament, "Linda! What should I do? Relax at home? Or rush over to the Moth and hope that I can get on the waitlist to get in?"

Linda listens intently until I've talked myself out. "Well," she says, "it sounds to me like either choice is perfect: self-care at home or going for it at the Moth. Listen to your heart, Margaret, and maybe remember to check in with your Higher Power."

I feel a gentle nudge on the small of my back; God is weighing in without my even needing to ask. "No time to lose, Child. The show starts soon. Let me hear you roar." I have my answer.

"Thanks, Linda," I shout into the phone. "I'm gonna brush my teeth, find a taxi, beg to get in, hope that my name gets called, and pray that I get to tell my story!"

"OK, then!" she says with a laugh. We hang up, and I do just that.

When I get to the Haymarket Pub, my heart pounding, almost in anxious tears, the cohost is standing by the front door. "Hi, Tyler," I gasp, "Any chance the waitlist has cleared?" He waves me in with a smile and a nod, and I nearly weep with relief.

I sign the release form, put my name on the list, then visit the ladies room, where I close myself in a stall to mumble my story—just once more. Back in the bar, I weave my way through the noisy crowd to the farthest corner of the room to hide by myself with a mineral water.

When Tyler and his cohost, Don, start pulling names from the hat, I applaud the other tellers, but block out their stories. I'm afraid that my own story will get squeezed from my memory if I let theirs into my brain, even though I can hear my friend Deanna reminding me, "Don't worry about forgetting your story. *It's your story.*"

Don reaches in the hat again and calls out, "The next teller is . . . Margaret Ghielmetti! Come on up!" he yells to the crowd. "Make some noise! Show her some love! This takes guts!" I weave through the cheering crowd toward the stage. "Let her through! Make her feel welcome! Keep it going for Margaret! Here she comes!"

And, finally, I'm standing in front of the microphone. There is a sea of faces looking up at me. I will myself to smile at them and to take a deep breath. I want to savor this moment of my audience breathing with me, breathing encouragement into me, buoying me up. I used to fear that crowds would wrinkle their noses ("What's that old lady think she's doing up there?") but their expressions are open and eager. We are all hungry for real stories.

I begin. I tell a story about Patrick's and my infertility and our struggle to stay married when the pain of that ordeal nearly destroyed us, singly and as a couple. I share how everything changed for me "On a Dime" when our therapist—almost twenty years ago— gifted us with the image of us as a beleaguered turtle couple. The Moth crowd screams with laughter, then sighs when I end my story by saying that's when I knew that Patrick and I—our family of two— was going to make it.

When I'm finished telling, I pause again to take in the roars of applause as I head back to my seat. I'm so grateful to have shared something so painful, but to have also given my audience some amusing moments in the midst of heartbreak.

I can listen, now, to the remaining stories without rehearsing my own. I feel proud to be in the company of storytelling peers who honor this art and polish their craft. I tell myself that I've told my story the best I can. I've told my truth. That it's not whether you win or lose: it's how you play the game. But then, oh, dear God, the scores are tallied—and *I've won*.

When Tyler and Don call me up to the stage for a hug and photos with the score sheet, I'm beaming from ear to ear and call out, "This is one of the happiest moments of my life!"

Afterwards, as the crowd starts to disperse, audience members stop me with congratulations and comments. One says, "My sister went through that, and I never knew how hard it was for her husband and her." Another, tearful, touches my arm, saying, "Thank you for telling my story." One dazzlingly pretty young brunette approaches me, shaking my hand. "I'm Sophia," she says, "I loved your performance. You remind me of my colleague on 'Chicago P.D.' You could play her funny sister."

"Oh, thanks," I say, in a daze from my win and the praise. "Your appreciation means the world to me." When I get home I search for her online. It turns out it was Sophia Bush who approached me. In the old days, I would have dismissed her interest as, what, pity? A fluke? Now I feel thrilled that a Hollywood star liked my performance.

I'm also very excited that I've won a Moth StorySLAM because that means I'll get to compete in a GrandSLAM—on a new and different theme—in front of an audience of a thousand people. The Handbook would still have me believe that all of this is "airing my dirty laundry in public." Instead, I know now that this is connecting with other human beings through my art—and I feel deeply satisfied.

Soon Patrick and I will have moved back to Chicago, where there are storytelling shows cropping up on every corner. I'll be able to get up momentum on rehearsing and telling my stories, something I didn't manage to do with the packing, moving, and shuttling back-and-forth-and-back-again.

I'll even have time to write. I'll return my turquoise journal to its rightful place in my hands. All the pieces are in place for an exciting new chapter in a familiar place.

Except.

Except my father—who had always been so supportive of me—is becoming more demanding by the day. My filters may be slowly lifting from me, but my dad's filters are completely gone. When I tell him about our move to Chicago Dad simply states, "Good. Now you can spend more time with me."

CHICAGO ONCE AGAIN

I am committed to making sure Dad knows he's beloved; it was so easy to lose sight of that when we were caring for Mother. She blazed like the sun all the way to the end; Dad now gives off a faint light like a crescent moon. Hal still sends him cartons of books on history, which Dad used to devour. Now he looks at them and says, weakly, "That's nice," but he's not reading history anymore—he's listlessly watching the History Channel. Pete and Charlie build him a whole model railroad in what had been Mother's room. Dad appreciates this labor of love, but dimly. It's clear he's checking out of life.

I struggle harder each day to make Dad happy, trying anything to make conversation. He can be roused to talk about our Packers, but it's a far cry from the hours we used to share as a family—swearing at our coaches when we lost and sweating out a win. It's a far cry from the summer Shareholder Road Trips with Dad and my brothers and sometimes Meghan or our nephew Hunter, when we'd follow a familiar routine: a bit of driving around Green Bay to revisit Dad's childhood haunts followed by dinner at the Union Hotel with 1940s big band music playing softly in the background. On the day of the actual Shareholders Meeting, Lambeau Field's parking lot would be filled with tailgate parties before we arrived. Once inside the Atrium, Dad would say, "This trip is about being together," and I'd nearly faint from joy, then scramble to find a fellow fan to take our annual keepsake snapshot. My favorite is the one with Dad holding a replica of the Super Bowl trophy: I am beaming, my arms around my family like an octopus, ridiculously happy to be with my team.

That was when Dad was still able to care for himself, shaving each morning with a boar bristle brush and smelling of Dial soap when I kissed his smooth cheek. Now, in 2016, he's allowed a mustache to straggle across his face. I tell him it gives him a rakish air, but in reality I'm shocked by how disheveled and unkempt he looks, which triggers a reaction in me to take even better care of him: a daughter taking care of her daddy.

I add to my prayers, "Please help me, God, to set goals for *today* and achieve them." I simply don't have the bandwidth to consider bigger dreams. To help my tired and frazzled brain remember, I list my commitments starting with the same sound: Father, Feller, Friends, Physical Exercise, Food, Family, Fun. When I realize I haven't yet mentioned Faith, I start over. Without faith, none of this is possible.

My friend Michelle gently says, "Margaret, you're certain that if you set down even one thing you're juggling, you'll never pick it up again. But you will, my dear." I say OK, and I set down Fun.

When Dad starts to need a catheter, it's heartrending to see him so frustrated and sad, his arthritic fingers struggling. It's no longer viable for him to stay in the townhome where Mother and he lived for sixteen years. He needs to move one step higher on the scale of care that the Presbyterian Home offers.

With Dad's permission, my brothers and I set up an appointment with assisted living. When the pearl-necklaced director asks Dad how he feels about this move, he replies, "It's time, but it's not what I wanted. I've always known that the Presby would be the final address, but I was supposed to just croak in the townhome." The director looks aghast, searching my brothers' and my faces for shock, but we're smiling to ourselves and I'm thinking, *I'm so proud of my father for being a nut.*

"Yes, Dad," I say, "that was the deal. We had the pillow made for you, embroidered with the words 'Croak in the Townhome.' But you went off-plan." Dad shakes his head in mock shame, and my brothers chuckle. But these moments of Dad's peculiar charm and humor are getting increasingly rare as his spirit diminishes.

Back at the townhome the next day, we start to identify what will move to his much smaller new apartment and what will get donated. My dad doesn't really care much about things—except his books. I gently Marie Kondo him, holding up one book at a time, asking him if it sparks joy. At first, he just whines, "This is too hard; *these are my books!*" But, slowly, he gets into the swing of it, singling out books to delight my brothers. "Would they like those?" he asks. Yes, they would, and I sort into stacks for Hal, Peter, and Charlie. "And, Mouse, you'd like the books on travel and Italy, wouldn't you?" Yes, I would. What Dad keeps are treasured tomes on Winston Churchill, ancient history, and our Green Bay Packers.

In February, Pete, Charlie, and I get Dad moved into a sunny apartment still on the campus of the Presbyterian Home. I feel intense sadness breaking up the home my mother so carefully curated, but we recreate our parents' home as best we can. The round wooden dining table where we've passed so many family meals remains the heart of the home. On the walls, we hang Dad's favorite artworks: Hal's pen and ink of a massive tree from our yard growing up, and a painting of a man in the woods; a photo Dad took in Rome that had been published in the *Chicago Tribune*; a color illustration of Winnie the Pooh holding Piglet's hand.

We donate odds and ends to the Presby resale shop (and I try not to buy them back, my excuse being that I'm a sentimental "keeper"). We share family treasures among us, my brothers and I each choosing what Charlie calls "touchstones"—and I know Mother would be pleased. But I also lug a Mini Cooper–trunkful of Mother's clothes to Patrick's and my apartment, even as I'm reminding myself that her things are not *her*. Since Marie Kondo worked with Dad on his books, I try it myself, half-heartedly. But how can I donate her tan trench coat? She wore that on every trip we took together. The Alpine hat with the jaunty green feather Dad bought her in northern Italy? It makes me look like the Jolly Green Giant, but I can't give it up. I squirrel things away under Patrick's and my bed, in our armoires, and in the back of closets.

"*Amore mio,*" I tell Patrick, "I know you love a streamlined home, and I promise I'll go through everything—someday. But I can't let anything go yet. I can't let *her* go yet." At our wedding twenty-three years ago, Patrick and I chose, "Love is patient; love is kind," as so many couples had before us. When my husband reassures me that he understands about my keeping Mother's things, I know that he doesn't understand at all. But I love him for his kind patience—and for lying to me on this.

I take turns with Charlie and Pete visiting my 94-year-old Dad every day, asking God to stand by me. "Please help me, God, to do Your will for me, whatever that may be, just for today."

That still includes doing the *Chicago Tribune* Sunday crossword puzzle with Dad as we've done religiously for years. My father used to regularly astonish me with his mental storehouse of esoterica. "Wait, Dad, how the hell do you know that the name for a female lobster is a hen?"

He'd smile and say, "I just know." Our puzzling is a calm and happy sharing between two word nerds.

Some days, we reminisce about trips to Italy with Mother. I ask him his favorite moment from his favorite city, Rome. "Our first day," he says, "when I saw the Colosseum and I thought, *I'm actually in The Eternal City.*" He adds, "Oh, and when we got shot at as we walked home after dinner."

I laugh, remembering a man who ran past us on the tree-lined Via Veneto—carrying a bulging white canvas bag; he looked just like a cartoon burglar. A Roman policeman ran after him, firing off shots in the general direction of the bank robber. Dad called out, "Take cover!" and Mother and I crouched behind a flower box. We laughed together afterwards—realizing that a foot-tall planter probably hadn't offered us much protection from a shoot-out. My parents' willingness to accept the uncertainty of travel set the mood for our many journeys.

Only now do I think to ask Dad about the childhood football games I loved so much. "Papà, did you tell my brothers to let me run the ball in for a touchdown sometimes?" He nods, and I add, "Wow. And there I'd always thought I'd been a Packers-worthy athlete. Thanks, Dad."

"You're welcome, Mouse," he says with a smile.

Another day, Dad shares a disappointment that's been haunting him: the additional care he needs now is more costly than he'd anticipated. "I really wanted to leave you kids something."

I kneel by his bed, looking up into his brown eyes until he shyly returns my gaze. "Papà, you've already given me what any child wants: your kindness, sense of humor, intelligence, and integrity."

Oh, and love. He has given me love. Even if he doesn't have the words to say it, I do. "I love you, Dad."

He pats me on the head, saying, "It's nice that you feel that way, honey."

It's a tender moment, but quickly effaced by his frightened crankiness as I'm departing for the day. "Don't forget to call me!" he yells, even though I've called him daily from every place I've been around the world every single afternoon since Mother died. I feel so angry and so sad at his outburst that I never want to see him ever again—in that moment. But I do love him, and I'll be back by his side tomorrow.

When people tell me, "You're a saint!" I nearly explode, protesting that I don't want to be a saint. And yet *I'm* the one who doesn't take off the Perfect Daughter halo (polished to a gleaming shine) even when it pinches. I'm the one putting on the heavy angel wings each morning (fitting them over my Super Woman cape). I'm even considering layering another petite pair of wings on top of the ones already weighing me down.

It's *me* not giving myself even one day off. The Handbook is gloating and, by fifty-seven years old, even I know that's not a positive sign. I also know when I need help—it's Therapist O'Clock. In my first session with Ellen, she asks, "May I walk you back in time to when you were a little girl?" And in a sort of waking hypnosis, I find myself at five years old, half a century ago. Ellen gently asks, "What does it feel like in your home?"

I mumble, "I'm in our white house with the dark green shutters. My mother is caring but strict. There are lots of rules and expectations, and I need to be careful not to make her mad. Otherwise, she'll shut me out." I pause then add, "I feel my dad's sadness and hurt. I comfort him when he's down. I distract him to cheer him up."

When Ellen gently brings me back to the present moment, I tell her what I didn't know as a five-year-old, but I've learned over the years. My dad had a happy childhood until his parents divorced and his mother died. My dad went from being a bright-eyed, smiling little boy in short pants to a teenager who coped with his feelings by developing a keen wit. He earned a degree in journalism, served in World War II, then—one afternoon back home in Wisconsin—his step-sister introduced him to a pretty sorority sister. My dad always said, "I took one look at your mother and thought, 'I'm gonna get me one of those,'" but it was my mom who asked him out on their first date. They only made it to the dance just before it ended at (*ahem!*) midnight.

They're radiantly happy in their wedding photos, my dad's lanky arm around my mother's elegant round shoulders. Along came

three sons in the next six years and then—surprise!—they found out
Mother was pregnant with me. She confided in the wife of the family
doctor that she didn't think she could handle a fourth child. The
older woman told my mom, "You have no idea what a blessing this
new baby will be." But four kids *was* a lot. At a certain point—when
bills piled up and activities overwhelmed—my mom could or would
no longer make the effort to buoy up my dad when his old sadness
overcame him. She turned her bright enthusiasm away from him,
abdicating that part of her role as a supportive spouse in order to do
the million other things a busy mother does.

I tell therapist Ellen, "My mom quit college when she married my
dad, and I'm sure she was frustrated intellectually. My dad was not
doing work he loved, but rather keeping food on the table. They were
not living their dreams. I feel bad for them."

Ellen's response echoes what I've learned from my friend Laurie's
book, *Baffled by Love*: that it is, in fact, the parent's responsibility to
care for the child, not the child for the parent. *Oh.*

"Margaret," Ellen adds, "you are making excuses to take care of
everyone."

I insist to her how essential it is for me to be compassionate.

"You don't need to worry about that, Margaret—you *are*. But when
you go into compassion overdrive, I don't trust you anymore: it's no
longer about caring for the other. Compassion is your gateway drug
to enabling and people-pleasing to reassure and soothe yourself."

I have enough shrink sessions under my belt to recognize when
my therapist has hit a bullseye.

"What I suggest for you," Ellen continues, "is benevolence. The
roots of the word are *bene* from the Latin meaning 'well,' and *volere*
meaning 'to want or wish.' You can want the best for your father—
and wish him well—without tipping over into compassion overdrive."

I also know that *com* means "with" and *passion* is from the Latin
for "suffering." I see how I still—after all these years—dive headfirst

into the lives of those I love: straining and scrambling to keep them happy; rushing to do whatever it takes to make them un-hurt and make things all better for them. I've been playing out this role for decades. The music is familiar and the dance awaits; all I need to hear is the scratchy old song. When I jump in, I know who I am again and what to do. Even if I've left myself depleted, I've ensured you won't leave me. "Ellen," I say, resigned, "I've tried to change this. It seems to be how I am."

"Maybe up until now," Ellen says. "Let's acknowledge that you're in a stage of *ing*. You are lear*ning* how to do things differently."

As I drive home after our session, I pray for surrender anew: "God, when the time is right, please release me from living my life through others. Please release me from fixing them." *As if they needed fixing—and as if I could fix them!* "Please, God, help me to be caring of others—and yet to take care of myself." I'm filled with regret for not yet having moved past this socially acceptable addiction.

What I hear back is "Progress, not perfection, Child."

But even armed with this latest wisdom from Ellen, wise counsel of past therapists, one therapy group, the *introvert aha moment* of Myers-Briggs, "personal growth work" from chakras to chanting, self-help books, AsiaWorks, Landmark, Midlife Meaning, tarot readings and more, I still tumble into my old stories when under duress. It's never more so than with Patrick. When we get into an argument, I feel all the old roles clawing me back down. At the first sign of what I like to think of as a "constructive request" (would he be willing to floss over the sink—and not into the bathroom mirror?), Patrick retreats into "I guess I'm the worst husband ever," accompanied by a hang-dog look. This triggers in me a residual feeling that I should comfort him. Followed immediately by a burst of fury as I stand, regally erect, pronouncing, "I can't do this right now!" and storming out of the room.

In sixty seconds flat, Patrick and I have retreated into the roles my parents played out over six decades of marriage. My husband and I are no longer in the room. In our place are Sad Dad and Cold Mom. Now, though, I realize, *I see the pattern and recognize the ancient tidal pull. I take responsibility for my part.* I remind myself that I am learn*ing* how to do this differently.

After I walk back into the room and sit down next to Patrick, he may still be sad and I may still be cold, but we both want an adult relationship. We both say, "I'm sorry. Let's try again. Let's stay in the conversation together. Let's try to be more honest and awake." Sometimes we agree to table it and talk again tomorrow, but—in any case—we correct course, remembering that we're in it together (even if we *hate* each other right now). We turn towards one another, not away.

We also seek our own comfort afterwards: Patrick soaking for a bit in the pity pool, and me on the phone with girlfriends indulging with them in what I call IMT (I'm married, too). But ours is not my parents' marriage, mired in The Handbook and its platitudes—traps that neither of them recognized, let alone knew how to change.

On New Year's Day 2017, Patrick leaves consulting for Four Seasons in order to start his own business. He'll continue facilitating global leadership training around the world, but now he'll also be handling his own accounting and airplane tickets, not to mention securing his own clients. I'm excited for him, but I've told him I'm unwilling to slide mindlessly into the role of Perfect Assistant to him.

I think he's heard me, but I'm not certain—until we're choosing our New Year's "motto." These are not resolutions-to-be-broken-at-the-least-provocation, but a catch phrase to inspire us when times get tough. I announce that I'm keeping "Here and Now"—the motto that's served me well for the past few years.

Patrick takes my hand, saying "No, *chérie.* This is the year you declare, 'Me, First.' And by that I mean Margaret first."

My tears brim. I've come a long way towards feeling what I feel—and learning to say no—but I'm still putting myself last too often. One of our wedding vows was, "Of all the people in the world, I choose you." Over and over, I have fulfilled that with Patrick—and with everyone I love, choosing them and their dreams.

"Amore mio," I ask, "you *do* understand what putting Margaret first would mean, right?"

"Yes," he says with a laugh. "It means that you won't be putting Patrick first. I know I'm going to live to regret the day I suggested this to you, but it's time." He pauses. *"Chérie,* do *you* understand what putting Margaret first will mean for you?"

"It will encourage me to take up more space. It will also take away my very valid excuses to not follow through on my commitments to myself."

Patrick says, smiling. "Brava! Sounds like you're up to something big, *chérie.*"

"Oh-oh," I respond, thinking, *Big and new and scary.* But I'm ready.

In January, I add to my prayers, "Please help me, God, to keep setting goals for each day, but also to set goals for my *life:* exploring the world, loving the world, and sharing the world through my creative expression." I draw a breath. "Then please help me, God, to take steps to achieve them."

"I'm on board, Child, if you are. So, do you know the first thing you're gonna do about it?"

"I do."

I sign up for a course in Solo Show Development at Chicago Dramatists and workshop a piece about growing up with my mom over the decades and re-finding my voice. I share to the class, shyly, that I'm afraid that it's too late to become an artist in my mid-fifties. Our instructor, Arlene, larger-than-life champion of artists, sails over to me, grabs me by the proverbial lapels, and says, "Do as I say, Margaret! Submit your show for consideration to Jason at SOLO Chicago Festival. It's not too late to put your work out there, girlfriend. But it's *getting* to be too late."

I'm ecstatic when my solo show, "Fierce," is scheduled for the winter 2017 season at the Berger Park Coach House Theater. As my director, I hire Emmi: petite in stature but ferocious in her commitment to me. She draws me out—over and over—as an actor. "You can do louder," is a frequent refrain.

"No I can't!" I wail. "This is as loud as I get."

"C'mon, Margaret, this is not the time to hold back."

I whisper another new prayer. "God," I say. "I can be excessively self-effacing. Please help me to make my voice *heard*."

Emmi also draws me into my own light. Literally. When we're at the theater for the final run-through the afternoon before my show, I ask, "Can we please turn the spotlight down?"

Emmi laughs and says, lovingly, "No, Margaret, we cannot. Just a reminder that your audience is coming to see your show. *The spotlight stays on you*."

I know she's right; my prayers for creative expression are being answered, and I never want to turn my back on an answered prayer.

On the day of my solo show, Amy—having moved away from Chicago—sends a bouquet with a card reading, "Dearest Marghi, Congrats my friend on this big accomplishment. I know you will be fierce! Much love." As my friends and family file into the theater, chattering to one another, I'm backstage doing jumping jacks to try to calm my nerves. I take one more sip of water, apply another layer of lip gloss, and pee for the nth time.

Then I ask, "Please God, help me to honor Mother and the love we shared and how hard we worked at growing up together." I feel a familiar pressure on the small of my back, ready to nudge me into the light. When my intro music comes on, I stride onto the stage. Over seventy minutes, my audience laughs at the funny parts and sighs at my "dirty laundry" just as I hoped they would.

One friend does say afterwards, "Oh, I could never share what you did!" and I believe that for her—but no longer for me. College soccer buddies Paula and Laura apologize for having "heckled me" with their sobs. Before I leave the theater, another friend hugs me, saying, "It's been too long since I've seen my mom. I'm going to go see her." And I feel just so satisfied.

When SOLO Chicago invites me to reprise "Fierce" in May, I pray again backstage to honor my mom, but what I hear back is, "Child, you've already done that. This time, just have fun." When a five-year-old bumbles innocently in from the park outside and onto the stage mid-show, I laugh and sweep my arm in her direction, "My co-star!" Even in this act of devotion, God helps me not to take myself too seriously.

After my solo show is behind me, I dive back in with my writers group: brilliant, talented Laurie, Jen, Jan, and Rita, who is my fellow storyteller and often my first reader. We meet monthly in one another's homes, each of us willing to share her truthful observations on one another's writing. They are all insightful editors, making my work stronger and inspiring me with their struggles and successes.

I hire writing coach MT to help me in the struggle to develop my next project—to find the heart of the piece. After the most recent elections, I feel a desperate need to share how living on four continents and visiting almost fifty countries has challenged and changed me. I keep telling everyone, "The world is not my enemy!" I'm imagining another solo show—a compilation of my travel stories—but when I realize that I've been on not only a physical journey but an emotional one for seventeen years, I say, "Oh. Sounds like a memoir."

With tremendous relief, I realize that I couldn't have written a memoir without living my life. My long dreamt-of book has been creating itself. Now it's up to me to write it down and send it out into the world.

I check out StoryStudio Chicago's website and—when I see that I'm scheduled to be in town for every class of Memoir in a Year—I murmur, "This is not a coincidence." I tell Patrick about the course, adding that it *is* a big commitment.

"Sign up!" Patrick says without hesitation, and I do.

I know the instructor, Nadine, from other writing classes and from seeing her present on a She Writes Press author panel. When I ask her to sign my copy of her memoir *Of This Much I'm Sure,* Nadine draws a heart and writes, "Margaret, I can't wait to see your book on the shelves." I can't wait for that either.

I love the structure of Memoir in a Year: learning craft from Nadine and getting feedback from her and my fellow writers. My cohort helps me to wrangle the arc of the story, sometimes unwittingly. When I read aloud the passage in Paris where I finally say no to the umpteenth potential visitor, one classmate objects: "I just don't understand why the narrator didn't want to make her friend's dream come true!" It's a comfort to me to see the other students rolling their eyes, but it's clear I have a lot of work to do to get across my story, my journey.

I've once again started dreaming of the cover I envisioned in Paris 2000: a map, a journal, and Margaret Davis Ghielmetti in a bold yet elegant typeface. "Glad you're dreaming again, Child," I hear, "but are you really all in? Are you really going to write your book?

Yes, I am.

But it's challenging for me to focus on writing. By 2018, Dad's been moved into the highest level of assisted living. He slumps in his hospital bed, no longer bothering to put in his false teeth or take off his Mister Magoo glasses when he drifts off to sleep. *He's in his nineties,* I remind myself. I pray for acceptance to love Dad not as I remember him and not as I would wish him to be. "Please help me, God, to accept each new normal of Dad's as he declines. Help me to stay present to how he is *now*." This was always Mother's advice to me, so I call on her, too—her celestial self—to stand by me.

For months, I resisted reading to my father, trying instead to compel him to participate in conversation. Now, though, as we're clearly near the end, it's my turn to delight Dad with his favorite books just as he delighted me as a little girl. I savor each word of *The House at Pooh Corner, Stuart Little, The Wind in the Willows.* I get most of the way through *Charlotte's Web* but have to stop: we both know how that one ends.

For a while, Dad can still fill in the blanks when I read; he has our favorites memorized. We've read Kipling's *Just So Stories* together a hundred times so when I start, "Them that takes cakes that the Parsee man bakes . . ." I wait for Dad to say, ". . . makes dreadful mistakes." Instead, he just mumbles, "Little Jack Horner." Dad would never, ever, have been confused like that until now.

He's losing his ability to converse, but in a burst of clarity, he says to my husband one day during a visit, "I'm glad for the unexpected pleasure of Patrick." We both know Dad doesn't just mean today.

I'm grateful for the four years with Dad since Mother died. But he's becoming increasingly distressed. He yelps, "Help! Help!" so often and so loudly that other residents on his floor complain. The nurses tell me that he adds "I'm sorry" and "Thank you" when they respond to his call button, but they can't seem to comfort him, and neither can my brothers or I.

Compassion is itching to set the needle down to play my old song, but I practice benevolence. When I'm putting on my jacket at the end of a visit and Dad whines, "Stay!" I settle my jumpy heart, which is so used to leaping up and reassuring him.

Taking a deep breath, I say, "Charlie's coming tomorrow and Pete the day after, Dad, but I'll phone you every afternoon."

He yells, "Don't forget my cookies!"

Another deep breath. "Dad, please remember that the nurses can bring you cookies any time. They have them at the nursing station. Just ask them, OK?" He bleats something about how they're not the *right* cookies and I say, "*Papà*, I have to go now. I have class tonight. I'll see you soon."

A very old Handbook voice whispers that I'm not doing enough, but I know that I am. I wish my father well, but I no longer choose to be so deeply in his drama.

By spring, Dad can no longer be relieved from the pain of bedsores. His doctor finally brings up the subject of hospice and Charlie asks Dad if he has any questions before he signs the paperwork. Dad manages to say, "I remember those little blue vials you had for your mother." We promise Dad that he'll get morphine.

When the hospice nurse shows up, she asks my father what's not working in his life right now. "Everything," my dad responds, plaintively. She responds that she's sorry for that, and isn't there anything good at all in his life? My father gently says, "My kids." I feel anointed. I might as well have a crown placed on top of my halo.

As soon as Dad begins hospice care, he takes a steep drop-off. His eyes are now half-closed and glassy, largely unseeing. Up until just a week ago, the nurses were still, somehow, maneuvering him into a Four Seasons polo shirt, one of the many that Patrick and I brought him from around the world. He no longer gets out of bed and only wears a hospital gown, but one morning he asks for help getting up and dressed. "I'm going golfing," he declares. In his mind, I guess, he's thirty-four years old, or even sixty-four—not ninety-four. I gently suggest we can golf together another time. I loved walking alongside him on summer days, joking and swearing over errant drives and pitiful putts. Another day, he asks, his voice panicky, "When are we boarding?" and I don't know if he means boarding a plane to Italy with Mother and me or boarding in a spiritual sense. I reassure him that he can board any time he likes. He pleads that he needs to get better.

I swallow hard and say, "Dad, the nurses are doing a wonderful job taking care of you. Please try to rest."

My heart breaks when he asks, "When am I going home?"

"Soon, Dad," I tell him, and I pray really hard that—even as an atheist—he will find home. I picture him as molecules roaming the universe. I'll be breathing him in, the way I breathe in Mother and everyone who ever lived.

One afternoon, as I'm sitting in a chair next to his bed, reading as he rests, he reaches his hand toward me. I think—I hope—he's going to caress my cheek, but instead he says, "There's a string across your face." There's not. I know from watching my mom that Dad has started on his journey to another place, another dimension.

After that, he can only moan "Ahhh"—a long whoosh of air from one of the most articulate men I've ever known. I place my hand lightly on his skeletal breastbone: what I hope is a comforting presence.

I can never thank his caregivers enough; they now give me hugs each morning before I can even say hello and tell me, "I know; it's hard." So hard.

The end is near. Dad's fingers are too cold for the nurse to get a reading with the little hand-held Puls-o-meter. Every day, I pray for mercy for my father and an exit as free from pain and anxiety as possible. This is so unfair! Dad's a good person. Why does he have to suffer?

I don't understand how his heart keeps pumping. I don't understand why his body won't release him. I remind myself that I don't need to understand. This is life on life's terms. Death on death's terms. A mystery not to be solved, but surrendered to. For almost two decades, I've been aware that I'm not in control of much at all, but that I still need to pray for patience and trust.

"I am with your father, Child. And with you." When I feel that grace, I'm calmer.

On some days, though, I cry so hard I'm sure the neighbors in our apartment building will call security. I howl, "My dad! My *dad!*"

I ask Patrick if he thinks I'm completely crazy for loving my father so much. "No, *chérie,*" he says. "It's not crazy. It's perfect."

For the thousandth time, I silently murmur thanks to my father for having shown me—by his example—what a good man to choose.

Charlie phones at five in the morning on March 22. "I got the call," he says. Patrick and I dress and drive to Evanston. Dad looks mummified: so rigid; so skinny, even though he's still slightly warm when I kiss his cheek. I am grateful to the nurse who shaved him before we arrived, clipping the elfin hairs from his ears into which I have whispered nonstop these past days, "I love you, Dad. Thank you. Go when you're ready to go."

Charlie and Patrick and I gently wash Dad's face, carved by dying into almost a skull. This ancient ritual is a balm for me. I brush his sparse white hair with a toothbrush because I can't find his old wood-handled hairbrush.

When hospice arrives, we gently ease Dad's skeletal arms into the sleeves of a yellow Four Seasons polo shirt. The shirt has been slit up the back so we don't manhandle his poor, shrunken body. We drape olive-green corduroy pants over his legs, and tuck them around him. We slide on bedroom slippers; we have no desire to jam his ancient feet into shoes. If my mom greets him at St. Peter's Gate, she'll be furious that we decided against the shiny black dress shoes she'd made him buy, but she'll just have to get over it. We slide his big black glasses on one more time. Lastly, we place a knitted Green Bay Packers cap on his head, a game towel under his hands, and a chocolate Easter bunny on top of that to sustain him on his onward journey. "We took him all the way home," Charlie says as he wraps me in a hug.

When the woman from the funeral home arrives, Patrick helps her to ease Dad onto the gurney from his hospital bed. She zips the black body bag around him and we follow her out. As we pass Dad's elderly neighbors, gathered at the communal table for lunch, one calls out, "There but for the grace of God go I!" and I think, *Would it have killed you to wait until the grieving children had passed?* Outside, in the clear cold daylight, the gurney is eased into the shiny black hearse, then Dad is gone.

In his now-empty room, we raise the window blinds Dad always wanted closed, letting in blazing spring sunshine on a blue-sky day. I feel like I'm emerging back into the land of the living after many months and back into a certain freedom after six years, since Mother first got sick. It's been a long road and I wouldn't do a thing differently, but I am grateful it's done. I walk out my father's door for the last time.

A week later, Patrick's and my entry table is covered with Easter bunnies: ceramic, wooden, fabric, felt—collected by my mom and treasured by me. Life is returning to the Midwest, and Patrick and I are hosting a Bratwurst Bash to honor and celebrate Dad. Charlie and Mary Ellen arrive after church. Don and Daniel fly in and other close friends file in, hugging us and greeting Dad's ashes, which are now resting inside a green lacquered box from Thailand, the green silk tassel on top of the box at a jaunty angle. I know my dad is getting a kick out of the fact that many of our guests are wearing green and gold to honor our Packers.

My brothers and I had decided against the Presbyterian Home chapel for a memorial. I'd asked Dad a few months ago if he'd had a change of heart about religion, and he'd said no. I pressed a little. "So you still believe it's done more harm than good?"

Dad replied, "No, I feel it's done *as much* harm."

I asked, "Is that a softening of your stance?" at which point Dad gave me the hairy eyeball and I stopped my not-so-subtle end of life questions. But our brief conversation helped confirm that holding a ceremony tinged by glowing stained glass would not be the way to go. It would not be respectful of my father, nor of the church.

For Mother, we'd asked the clergyman to keep the service as, um, non-religious as possible so as not to irritate my dad. The minister had responded, "Don't worry. I knew your mom, and I know your dad. They're good people, and that's all that matters to me." He did ask, "As we'll be in a chapel, would it be OK if I mention God—maybe just once?" which made us smile.

For this celebration, Charlie and I had conferred and chuckled over what celestial menu Dad would most appreciate. On the table is a centerpiece of favorites (which will double as party favors). Spam nestles next to King Oscar sardines, corn meal mush, Velveeta slices for grilled cheese, baked beans, and corned beef hash. It's food for After an Apocalypse, but—hey—Dad lived to ninety-four on frozen and canned foods, an ex-smoker who loved a couple of Scotches in the evening and loathed exercise. Who am I to argue with success?

For lunch, I've ordered Dad's favorite bratwurst from Bobby Nelson's in Wisconsin. They're the best brats in America from the friendliest small-town people. They ship them with a handwritten note: "We remember your dad. These are on us."

After everyone's had their fill of brats, Pik Nik Shoestring Potatoes, Jay's and Lay's potato chips, we ply them with ice cream and chocolate sauce with Planter's peanuts sprinkled over the top—Dad's favorite midnight snack. After that, we hand out the old blue mugs we used for years around our family table, and fill those with strong coffee. So many people who loved my dad now hold these mugs in their hands.

Choking back tears, I look around our living room. "I'm so grateful to each of you for being here today to honor and celebrate Dad. And thank you a million times over for all the support and love you've given me over the past days and weeks and months and years. Thank you, Charlie, for being—again—my absolute Band of Brothers partner in caring for our parents. We were committed to taking them all the way home, and we did it. Thank you, Patrick, for all the years of supporting me in doing this and for loving my parents and my family and our friends so much. I love you all."

Then I read out loud what I've written:

"Dad's name was Richard, but everyone called him Dick.

"*D is for Dear.* I was a little tomboy who dreamed of growing up to be the first female quarterback for the Green Bay Packers. Dad let me be me on the football field, and also when he read to me before bed. In *Fifty Famous Fairy Tales,* Dad would read the role of Beauty so I could have the role I really wanted: the Beast. His example to us was to lead a decent life. So D is also for Decent.

"*I is for Intelligent.* Dad retained a brain full of knowledge and he loved to *share* what he knew. When Mother and he and I traveled to Rome together, Dad would seat us at a café with a cappuccino and he'd deliver a lecture he'd prepared. If you'd ever like to learn about the Eternal City's fountains, aqueducts, or a *lot* about obelisks, let me know. I'll be happy to share his typed and bound pages with you. Dad also loved to learn. We took adult education classes together when we both worked in downtown Chicago. That was when I realized in my twenties that I really didn't know my own father. The time together over dinner before class helped us launch our friendship as adults.

"*C is for Caring.* Dad was not exactly demonstrative; he didn't say that he loved me. He did show me, though. When I was hurt or bewildered as a little girl, Dad would wrap his arms around me from behind, and I'd put my little paws on his forearms and know I was loved. As an adult, when I was hurting, he would gently pat me on the head. I'm also proud of my father for how much he truly cared for the people I love best.

"K is for Kooky. Dad was the consummate story and joke teller: embellishing with endless details, always landing the punch line. And he was a master at improv. That man could riff! When I told Dad earlier this year that I had just written about him for my Memoir in a Year class—and had shared about him with my fellow writers, and now everyone just loved my father—he said, with a straight face, 'Well, since it seems like I'm an essential part of your book, maybe it's time for us to talk royalties.'

"'Sure, Dad. What do you think is fair? Throw out a number.'

"'Fifty percent.'

"'Um, OK, Dad, let me think on that.' And—smiling to myself—I dropped the subject while we noodled for a while on a crossword. After we'd finished the puzzle, I said, 'Dad, I have to admit, that percentage doesn't feel quite right to me. You know, on the royalties. Could we talk some more on that? Would you be willing to throw out another number?'

"'OK,' he said. 'Fifty-one percent.' That was my father: my dear, decent, intelligent, caring, kooky Dad—I will love you forever. *Ciao ciao, Papà.*"

Once I'm done, Charlie shares his remembrances, and others who knew my parents offer tributes: how they felt welcomed, safe, seen, and honored in our home. My parents weren't perfect. They were flawed and frustrating, ridiculously rigid, but they were also—sometimes—magnificent. I am beaming with pride at how my parents made a difference in the world.

I still know their stoic language; it's my mother tongue. It's just not the language I choose now.

I'm grateful to have inherited their values, but I'm no longer beholden to their Handbook.

After Dad has been gone a month, I'm taking long naps every day, sleep so profound it feels like death. Does part of me think that if I sleep deeply enough, I will be rejoined to my parents? Or am I just exhausted after running for six years and having my heart broken?

I hate that they're really not coming back. It's not just a game of Hide and Seek. I tell Linda that I also hate how my dad feels inaccessible to me, like he's being ferried over the River Styx en route from the land of the living to the underworld. Then I ask her, "And what about my mom? Why is she gone, too?" I had developed an intense relationship with the spirit of my mother after her death: talking with her, enjoying visions of her, receiving her blessings.

Linda says, "Maybe your mom is the one rowing your dad over." I feel a tremendous relief as I picture my mother standing up and poling rather than rowing—as though it's a Venetian gondola and not just a row boat. She is confident, young, barefoot—no need to worry that her Ferragamos will get scuffed or wet. My father is seated in the back of the boat, a white-grey shadow slightly aglow—sitting tall like he hadn't sat for years, his lean frame restored to him.

When I'm talking with Don and Daniel in April, I describe my experiences and say, "We journeyed so often and so well. I can't bear the thought that they have pulled away from my shoreline—that they have separated from me."

Don says, "Maybe it's *you* who needs some separation from them right now."

My shoulders slump, but I also say, "That's true. I want to be in the land of the living. I'm not meant to be on their journey with them."

Then, two months after I became an orphan at fifty-eight, I'm on FaceTime with Patrick; he's just waking up in the Seychelles, where he's been facilitating leadership training. He's yawning in the million-thread-count Four Seasons sheets, before he packs to fly on to Mauritius, where he'll do more training and everyone will fall in love with him—on another gorgeous desert island. He tells me, "A participant in my training came up to me at the end and thanked me for changing her life."

I snap, "I want to change lives, too, Patrick!"

He's surprised by my outburst—usually my response is how happy I am for him—and he pauses before saying, "You do change lives, *chérie*. Just look at all you did for your parents."

"Patrick," I say, "my parents are dead. Perfect Daughter is done, and I'm no longer a Perfect Trailing Spouse, Expat, Tour Guide, or Hostess to the World. So, it appears that I'm jumping into Perfect Assistant to *you* to fill the void. I spent all day working on our taxes and confirming your international travel insurance and now the damned photocopier's out of toner. I'm still doing the chores first, even if that means sacrificing my own work. I have a coaching session with MT tomorrow, and I haven't gotten any writing done."

Patrick resists my passive aggressive lures, saying, "Thank you for all you've done for us and do for us."

I mumble *you're welcome* but it's really a low growl.

He asks, "Could you consider just going to MT's, trusting that she might have something to share with you that you're not even aware of?"

I feel my face getting hot with the frustration of a thwarted perfectionist who still wants to do it all perfectly, yesterday, without any help, thank you very much.

But aren't I now awake or at least struggling to stay awake? Do I really *still* feel that I don't have the right to exist if I'm not a saint, savior, and sentry? I want to be making choices instead of blindly listening to The Handbook's threats, "Don't you dare change. I will bring you down."

One thing I know is that this is mine to handle. "I'm sorry,

Patrick," I say, "I'm not angry at you. If I keep changing the damned photocopier toner versus writing, well, that's on me."

"Whatever you choose to do, or not to do, *chérie*, please be very gentle with yourself." He adds, "Before we hang up, are you OK?"

I tell him I'm fine, and he coughs, because by now I've confided to him that—when a woman says she's fine—she's almost always not.

"So how are you *really*?" he asks, and I know that he really wants to know.

"I'm done," I say. "Done sacrificing my creative dreams in favor of the payoff of taking care of others. Done with the guilt of having gotten off track because of that. Done with hiding behind the articulate excuses I'm so good at crafting to avoid living my life."

"I'm proud of you, *chérie*. You're on your path."

"Thanks, *amore mio*. I am. So are you. I wish us both bon voyage."

With another layer of old story peeled from me, I find myself again on my metaphorical knees, where I am closest to my Higher Power. "Help me, please, God, to know that my life has meaning and to love myself for who I am."

"Check and check, Child."

I already have one Moth GrandSLAM under my belt from two years ago. The theme that night was "Out on a Limb." I told a story about caring for my mom at the end of her life, about doing everything I could for her, then letting her go. I basked in the support of Daniel, who'd flown in, and SuperFan friends and family in the audience. I didn't win, but I didn't care; I'd shared a tale of big love.

Now, in October 2018, "Never Again" is the theme for my second GrandSLAM. I tell a story that leaves me shuddering with sadness— about how I repeatedly gave away my self-respect to try to hold men to me. I'm delighted by two high scores from the judging teams. The third score devastates me; it seems unreasonably low and knocks me out of contention.

On the way home afterwards, I tell myself that I crafted the story well and told it from the heart, and I like the story of the woman who won. The Handbook would have me leave it at that, but I keep fantasizing that I'll get a phone call. "Come back to the theater. We double-checked the numbers and that third score was actually a 9.9 out of 10. You've won after all!" Needless to say, that call does not come.

Before bed, I babble, "God, I don't have it in me right now to start the process all over again of getting to StorySLAMs, hoping my name gets called, praying to win to qualify for another GrandSLAM." (Lots of detail to the Divine, who is well aware of all this.) After drawing a breath, I ask, "What would You have me do?"

"Child, I would have you share your unique journey. Get it?"

I get it, God.

With Memoir in a Year drawing to a close, I hire Nadine as my developmental editor, saying, "I swear to you, I will write my book if it's the last thing I do!"

She chuckles. "Margaret," she says, "Everyone who knows you *knows* you're going to write your book now."

I trust that all the words and sentences I'm writing will add up to my memoir. I take it one day at a time and one page at a time and—by February 2019—I've polished my first twenty pages to submit to the publisher She Writes Press for consideration. This act feels so vulnerable, I tell only Patrick and a few friends. In fact, this feels like one of the biggest moments of my life. She Writes Press emails back that my submission has been received and that I'll hear back within six weeks, so I keep on writing.

In March, Patrick and I visit Marc and his wife Lucia on the island of Koh Samui, Thailand, where Marc has co-created Kamalaya Wellness Sanctuary. Palm trees sway overhead and the Gulf of

Thailand blues the horizon as we catch up with these dear fellow travelers and dream of upcoming trips together (over my final espresso before our detox begins). Afterwards, as the naturopath does my intake session, she says, "I sense that you didn't give yourself time to convalesce after caring for your dying parents. It's time to give yourself a break." She recommends a personalized program of superhealthy food (no carbs, sugar, or caffeine) plus treatments to energize me (which I'll need, with no carbs, sugar or caffeine!).

Over the next nine days, a massage therapist tells me that I swallowed pain for so long that my belly got full and transferred the pain to my back to carry around. He says that's why my lumbar is so tender.

During Reiki, I feel a tremendous heat in my hands. I tell the therapist that I'm writing a book. She says that's why my hands are on fire.

An emotional release practitioner starts our session by asking me to share something of my family. I tell him that I still feel that I could have done more for my father. He considers for a moment. "Please imagine picking up your father in your arms," he says and—once I do—I'm so happy. I've missed Dad so much! "Now carry your father over to God as you understand God." As I carry my dad, he's telling me stories and we're both laughing. "Now place your father gently into God's waiting arms."

There's a part of me that doesn't want to let Dad go, but I hand him over to God, saying, "I know this is where he belongs—in Your loving care, not with my claws dug into him."

I'm fairly sure I hear a gentle "Duh!" from the Divine before Dad starts telling jokes to a deity he never believed in. "Have you heard the one about the priest, the minister, and the rabbi?" *They're good*, I think, and I walk away.

At the end of our session, the practitioner observes that I can use this technique with anyone or anything I'm carrying. "But," I say, "Some people don't *want* to be handed over."

He laughs and says, "That's true. And you seem to believe that love equals caretaking. But you can still *choose* to hand them over."

When I share all this with Patrick afterwards, I add, "*Amore mio*, I'm just realizing that you never actually *complained* about my caretaking you."

"You bet I didn't," Patrick says, and I'm grateful for his honesty. "It's been *very* comfortable for me, but taking care of me can't be your focus now."

He reminds me that he's the one who suggested "Me, First" for me, then he laughs. "I did assume that was limited to 2017, but here we are—two years later—and you're still putting Margaret first!"

At twenty-six years married, we both know that our relationship is a work in progress. I still tend to snarl "I'll just do it myself!" when Patrick may simply be mentioning a task to me in passing. He may still secretly love it if I do it—but it's *my* choice. He still tends to complain about how he's overwhelmed with work, even when it's been *his* choice to take on too much. I force myself to say, "I respect your experience and your feelings, Patrick, but I'm going to choose not to pick up on that right now," instead of "How can I fix it?"

I'm still tempted by the gleaming hooks that The Handbook sometimes dangles in front of me: *Just a nibble of enabling, Margaret?* But I know now that the emotional payoff has to come from inside me—not from the praise of others for my people pleasing. I'm retraining myself not to bite, no matter how alluring the lures.

Still at Kamalaya on the first day of April, I'm awake early to enjoy the pre-dawn scent of jasmine on the air and birdsong as complicated as a diva's aria. Once I finish my detox tea (missing coffee every sip of the way), I open my inbox. There's an email from She Writes Press, the publisher I'd submitted to six weeks ago. My heart is beating so fast I think I'm having a heart attack as I open the email.

It's a yes!

I wake Patrick up to tell him, "*Amore mio*, it's happening!

Assuming it's not an April Fool's Day joke, my book will be published in 2020!"

He says, sleepily smiling, "I'm so happy for you, *chérie*, and so proud of you."

I'm happy and proud, too.

When Patrick's work takes us to Paris later in 2019, I'm back in the place where—almost two decades ago—we started our expatriate journey and where I started to write my book. Correction: where I *wanted* to write my book—but bought flowers for our guests instead.

This time in Paris, I write all day with a break at Mon Café for mineral water instead of too much wine (and I no longer care what anyone thinks of my shoes). On Patrick's day off, I take a day off, too, lunching at Les Deux Magots of de Beauvoir and Sartre fame, two of my college literary heroes. We visit Père Lachaise cemetery for the graves of Oscar Wilde (his tomb red with a hundred lipstick kisses), Proust (an unexpectedly unadorned marker), and Apollinaire (the letters of his poetry forming a lopsided heart). Back at the hotel, I pull out my dog-eared copy of Hemingway's *A Moveable Feast* to read in the late afternoon sun, *but I'm no longer just lusting after literature—I'm creating it.*

For a summer break, we return to our favorite former-farmhouse hotel overlooking a sea of Tuscan vines. Each day begins with an early morning walk alongside the ripening grapes (to work off the previous night's pasta). We visit Castellina in Chianti for their farmer's market—overflowing with stalls selling lemons blazing like the sun and crusty bread as big as a bushel. We lunch on *prosciutto e melone* on the hotel's terrace, then it's to work for me. I write in the shade while Patrick swims or reads or snoozes. After dinner in the garden, we're asleep by ten, *but I'm no longer just dreaming of writing. I have a book coming out soon.*

When Patrick gets an offer to work overseas for an extended assignment, he's over the moon with excitement. "*Chérie*, we'll be in Venice together for two whole months!" I protest that I still have so much writing ahead of me. He mopes, saying, "I just assumed you'd be thrilled. It's *Venice!*"

"That's the problem, *amore mio*. I'm not sure that I'll be able to resist her charms, or resist inviting everyone we know to visit." I do add, "I'm thrilled for you, Patrick, and I hope you'll say yes. *But I have to finish my book.*"

We're both clearly frustrated and agree to take some time to consider the decision.

I remember to ask for guidance, "God, Your will, not mine. Would You have me in Venice for two months—or here in Chicago?"

"Child, I know that—in the past—this hasn't been your strong suit, but here's an idea: Would you consider a compromise?"

Bingo! I think, and tell Patrick I'll join him for one month instead of two. He brightens, saying, "That would be perfect, *chérie!*" and books his ticket.

I'm just about to book mine when I hear one last rumbling question, "Just want to make sure, Child. Are you ready to defend your writing against every possible temptation?"

"You mean like welcoming back-to-back house guests?"

"For example," God replies.

I protest, "I have been writing! I'm even postponing storytelling until after I hand my manuscript in!"

"Well done," God replies. "In Venice, though, will you be willing to say no to comfortable, familiar Perfect Hostess and Italophile Guide?"

Oooh! Those shiny hooks dangling right in front of my face! Two of my favorites!

"Child," I hear in an impatient voice. "We've been through this. I am talking about your *destiny*."

"You're right, God," I say (which elicits significant divine eye-rolling). On the spot I buy my airline ticket and compose a very different email than I have in the past. "Patrick and I would love to see you in Italia! As we won't have a guest room, here's the website of a cozy hotel we love and the email address of the owner. Tell him we sent you. Patrick will be working and I'll be writing, but we'll meet you for your welcome espresso, and join you for dinners, too."

As planned, Patrick flies to Venice a month before me. When I join him there, we indulge in a coffee at the Café Florian in Saint Mark's Square, the seagulls stealing sandwiches right off the plates of tourists and the orchestra playing waltzes and schmaltzy show tunes. We're sitting where Dickens and Byron sat, but we won't do it more than once; the music surcharge is ruinous. Patrick offers us a gondola ride. We climb on and hold hands as our gondolier sings soft traditional Venetian songs, taking corners—between crumbling brick walls and his sleek black craft—with only millimeters to spare. At the Hotel Danieli's rooftop bar overlooking the Venetian lagoon, Patrick orders a *spritz* cocktail of *prosecco* and sparkling water; I have a mint and ginger mocktail. This is the hotel where seven-year old Patrick announced to his parents that he would become a hotel general manager one day. So we're back where it all started for his career—the career that has taken us around the world together.

On all the days after that one, I work nonstop, taking a break midday for a long walk and picnic-shopping at the local grocery store (plus one more espresso before I knock off writing at sunset for dinner with Patrick).

I resist all sightseeing until the visits of Marc and Lucia, Jetti and Otto, and our very last weekend in Venice, when Patrick and I visit the Basilica di San Marco during Sunday Mass, its Byzantine mosaics glowing even in the dim incense-smoky light. The congregation sings a minor key hymn of gratitude, and my heart strains toward this ancient link between humans and the Divine.

I add my whispered, "Thank You, God, for everything. Especially my book." *And finally I'm no longer just praying to be an author. I am one.*

When Patrick and I are back in Chicago, it's full steam ahead on my manuscript, which is due to the publisher in February 2020.

I'm shocked by how difficult writing a whole book is (and embarrassed to admit that I still somehow thought it would be easier). When Linda observes that I'm not just writing a book, I'm making sense of my life, I try to take heart from that. But I struggle every day: typing, deleting, editing, revising, tearing my silver hair out, and finally sighing with pleasure when even one sentence finally feels right.

"Killing my darlings" is also harder than I thought, even for someone who's used to editing lean and mean for storytelling. I figured I'd be able to trim several hundred pages of Trip Reports down to three hundred pages of memoir in a jiffy—but instead I'm obliged to steel myself daily to coldheartedly cutting words, passages, and entire chapters (saving juicy tidbits for a future book).

Reading for pleasure is forbidden (except the *New Yorker*—yes, for the cartoons). Also *verboten* are all the tempting rabbit holes for a first-time author: how to develop a website? Hire a publicist? Maximize social media? All must wait.

I hate saying no to storytelling requests, but—when I explain to show producers that I need to conserve my energy for my memoir—they tell me, without fail, "We'll book you after you turn in your book. Write now, woman!"

Nadine's on call as my writing coach—and my writer's therapist. She tells me, "When I get an email from a coachee with the subject line all in caps—and with more than three exclamation points—I know it's time to pick up the phone."

I see her name on caller ID and say, "Hello! Is this Doctor Kenney Johnstone calling?"

"Yes! How can I be of service?"

"Nadine, I'm just not sure that all this crap is ever going to turn into a book!"

"I understand," she says. "You're in the forest, but I'm in the treetop. I see your book coming together." I remind myself that I'm braiding together a physical journey with an emotional awakening, and that's complex. My brain hurts. Both sides of it.

Another time I tell Nadine that it's killing me to be looking back at when my parents were dying. Now it's my heart hurting. "Writing a memoir can mean reliving trauma," she says and suggests that I write something less devastating for a bit. I sculpt travel tales—instead of mining grief—until I'm no longer crying for hours.

A month later, I reach out to her, panicking that I'm never going to get my manuscript polished enough to turn it in on February first. Doctor Nadine replies, "Never fear. You can do this, you will do this, and I'm here for you." That's all I need to hear to take a deep breath and get back to work. And, while I trust her words, I struggle to get new revisions to her with enough different from the previous version so to make a read-through worth her time (and my money).

Patrick gently points out that—when I should be revising—I seem to distract myself with crossing each "t" and dotting each "i" (which really can wait for the proofreader). "*Chérie*, might this have to do with your subtitle?"

"Just a reminder, *amore mio*," I respond. "I'm a *recovering* perfectionist."

At least now I also accept help: the offer of proofreading from Pink Bubble Amy, self-care prompts from wise owl Kimetha, insightful editing suggestions from Rita, a women authors mug from Sally G. to keep me caffeinated, multiple mazel tovs from Karen, book tour VIP lanyards from Deb, and weekly "Stay strong!" admonitions from my friend Nellie, just entering her ninety-sixth year. Friends and family invite us for meals when I'm too tired to even consider cooking. They email or call to check on me when I'm too tired to even think straight.

Don, who long ago taught me to love reading and is now my book guru, offers me laser-focused coaching on bookselling; Daniel and he offer their guest room in Alexandria as a peaceful place for R&R&Writing. (Not so peaceful, though, that I release my constant fear that—somehow—I'll delete my whole manuscript. I email a copy to Patrick almost hourly.)

Daily, I tell myself, *Listen up, word nerd: Ideal word choice must wait 'til the final polishing!* That particular joy will be the cherry on top—I'm saving it to savor it.

When I feel writer's block, I'm tempted to postpone my publication date until next year, next decade (or perhaps posthumous would be best). Instead, I regroup, revise my timeline, and recharge with my peeps: my writers group, my Women and Children First book group, at StoryStudio, and the Chicago Writers Association.

Writing all day, I'm tired all the time. I feel spacey and untethered like a bobble-head. I finally wave the white flag and go see my doctor. She knows I'm writing a book; she also knows that I'm always watching my waistline. "Salads are commendable," she says, "but they can't be all you eat. This is hard work for your brain and it needs carbohydrates for fuel." When she adds, "I want you to go home tonight and eat a pizza," I promptly tell her that I liked her before, but that now I'm in love with her.

My book gets juicier over the months, as do I. Possibly due to the pizza, and also because snacks seem to fly into my mouth each time I enter our kitchen (when I thought I was just coming in for a glass of water). In an effort to stay in (almost) the same size of jeans, I remain religious about my daily lakefront walks—and I begin working out twice a week with a strength trainer. Cris understands women my age, but also respects that I'm a former athlete. On the day she teaches me bicep curls, I'm ecstatic. I'm lifting weights at sixty! When she slides boxing gloves over my hands, calling me Xena, Warrior Princess, I glow with pleasure. "Hit me with your best shot!" she says. *Kapow!*

It's all helping to keep me going, but I'm still very tired. Eyes burning from staring endlessly at the computer screen, I jot on a stickie, "Buy stock in eye drops."

My old instinct, of course, is to push harder, but there's grace in getting older: I simply don't have the strength to power through. "Help me, please, God, to pause now—and start again when I have energy."

"You've got this, Child, and I've got you."

By autumn 2019, I've gotten more honest about my dreams for the book. My mantra used to be a righteous, "I write for my own pleasure." I graduated to modestly saying, "If I sell just one copy to my closest friends, I'll be happy." That's no longer true (if it ever was). When I realize just how much I want this book out in the world, I hear a derisive snort from The Handbook, "Ridiculous!" But my goal has always been to connect, and it's also now to start a conversation and help inspire others. Even I know that's not ridiculous at all.

When the publisher requests a head shot, my first instinct is to take a shyly smiling selfie. Instead, I book a photographer and— inside his studio, I'm still riddled with nerves—but emboldened by the presence of my stylist-friend Frankie, who holds my hand—and tames my hair. When I hear The Handbook sniffing, "Vanity!" I remind myself that this—all of this—is in the service of spreading hope. In my favorite photos, I hold a globe in my arms. The world is not my enemy.

I'm fighting this fight without the need for a suit of armor—or a mask—because I no longer feel like an impostor. I'm an artist struggling to fulfill a dream I've had my whole life. I'm determined to show up for myself as I try to show up for others: fully committed to their aspirations, believing in them 100% if they're willing to put in the work. I want that for myself. I give that to myself.

I'm honoring my heroine's journey: from unconsciously incompetent to consciously incompetent, and on the never-ending odyssey toward consciously competent. I've been discovering myself as I discovered the world then sailed back to port.

I still love to travel, but I'm finally reunited with home: not just Chicago or Patrick, but me.

And my turquoise journal is now never out of my sight.

It's all satisfying but—*damn!*—this is hard work: my beloved book is kicking my butt.

That's OK, I think.

Because this is MINE.

EPILOGUE

So where's The Handbook in all this?

It's still with me: safe at home or tucked in my carry-on when I travel, next to my even-more battered passport, still *far* too many guidebooks, and my next writing project in a new turquoise-blue journal.

I've grown grateful for The Handbook's fierce stoicism. It helped me to get out into—and around—the world. But I do things differently now. It took me awhile, but I discovered that it wasn't too late to learn how to live my own life.

Mostly, I've swapped out The Handbook's rigid rules for my prayers, which I try to recite first thing in the morning—but which work just as well at one minute before the clock strikes midnight. "Thank You, God, for this beautiful day" is how I always begin. Several "Please help me" specifics follow, before closing with gratitude, including, "Thank You for making my *love-the-world* and *write-the-book* dreams come true."

"My pleasure, Child."

Pristine twenty years ago when I first packed it for Paris, The Handbook's cover by now is scuffed from Sahara-dusty Egypt, warped from tropical-steamy Singapore—and is that the waft of garlic from Thailand? A hint of rich butter from a Parisian croissant? A splotch of spicy mustard from atop a Midwestern bratwurst?

It's a slimmer volume than it used to be, too. My New York shrink had told me long ago, "You can choose to tear pages right out of your Family Handbook. You know that, right?" I most definitely did not know that then, but I know it now.

The Davis Family Handbook—REVISED

I solemnly swear to abide by the rules, but only when they feel right for me.

Repeat "How lucky am I?"

My cup runneth over, but—like everyone else's—it has some dings on it: I see my life in its battered glory. I don't let anyone tell me how to feel and—guess what?—as lucky as I am, I allow myself to want *more*.

If you want it done right, do it yourself.

Nah. Do it with help: from Patrick, friends, family, strangers, the spirits of those gone before, and—for me—a gently-nudging (occasionally eye-rolling) loving God.

I don't need to do life alone. There's help if I ask for it—and accept it.

Always put others first.

In my 2000 journal, I'd written, "I like to help people enjoy life fully and guide them to make it richer." I still do. But now I claim the same respect for me.

Don't air your dirty laundry in public.

How could anyone have known that things were not as rosy as I depicted them—if I never told them? I try now to be honest and vulnerable, so, here goes: I have not, in fact, loved every single place I've visited and every single person I've ever met. (There: I've said it and no one died.)

The people who love me have long told me—and shown me— that they want not just Perfect me, but all of me.

It's what I want, too. Be real with me and I'll be real with you.

Above all, JUST DO IT.
I started my journey brave and learned how to be brave(ish). Now I'm genuinely brave when that's my truth. I Just Do It when I choose to (and don't do it when I choose not to).

In Paris all those years ago, I asked, *What about my life? My dreams? What about me?*

Back in Chicago now, I know that it's never too late to fulfill my own dreams.

I'm putting my own life first. At last.

Acknowledgments

I am grateful to every single person who loves me, cares for me, and lifts me up to be my best self. You've fed me emotionally, spiritually, and literally and—when my courage in the writing failed me— you buoyed me up with your pride and belief in me. I could write a whole 'nother book filled with appreciation for each of you.

To my husband, Patrick Ghielmetti: This book would not exist without your having taken me with you around the globe and back home again. Your support and love mean the world to me. After all these years, *amore mio*, "of all the people in the world, I choose you."

To both my families—American and Swiss: Thank you for sharing your homes and hearts and tables and lives with us. *Mammà* and *Papà*: For setting me on the journey and sharing so many together. Freddy and Monique: For helping to make our dreams come true.

To my artistic and creative community: Nadine Kenney Johnstone: Couldn't have done this book without you, dear Doc, and wouldn't have wanted to. Ditto to writing coach MT Cozzola and my writers group: Rita Balzotti, Laurie Kahn, Jen Cullerton Johnson, and Janice Deal. To Linda Braasch: For helping reveal my heroine's journey. To Don Henderson: Team *Brave(ish)* Book Guru Extraordinaire. To artist Amy McCormac: For begging to read my work from the first word written.

To the authors who showed me how a book gets written: with

butt in chair, plus Susan Paul Ecto-chocolate, and Niva Piran Pocka Pocka Egg! To Brooke Warner: For championing women writers. To the She Writes Press team and sisterhood: For your good counsel and warm encouragement. To the Books Forward publicity team: For boundless enthusiasm in helping me connect to a wider audience.

To each storytelling producer who has invited me on stage to connect with your audience. To my fellow tellers and solo show artists who offer me insights and who also dig deep to share themselves authentically. Rock on!

To every GM and hotel team around the world who ever welcomed me—and us: Thank you for sharing your cities and countries, traditions and customs, meals and laughter. I appreciate the good desk lamps to write by and the endless Nespresso to keep me going. To our Four Seasons Family: What a joy and privilege it was to be among you for twenty-two years.

To those who've opened up new spiritual and personal growth pathways: Thank you for breathwork and Badass Women, couples retreats and chakras, tarot and trainings, Midlife Meaning and Mastery, *Your God is too Small, Love Poems from God,* and even reassurance on mysterious *vayus.* In short: all things wonderfully woo-woo.

Lastly but not least: I thank You, God. And, to every perfectionist—recovering or not quite yet—I see you.

Discussion Questions

1. What was written in your family's Handbook?

2. What rules were in The Handbook?

3. What roles did you take on?

4. What do you think you were protecting yourself from?

5. What are your greatest strengths?

6. How are they your greatest weaknesses—when used in excess?

7. Does perfectionism (or something else) keep you from living your fullest life?

8. What dreams have you postponed?

9. Where have you given up your own voice?

10. What would you like to discover (or re-discover) in yourself?

11. What emotional payoff(s) would you be willing to forego – in order to fulfill a dream or reclaim your voice?

I'd love to stay in this conversation on www.margaretghielmetti.com.

About the Author

© Brian McConkey Photography

Margaret Davis Ghielmetti has lived on four continents and has visited nearly fifty countries. She is a Live Lit Storyteller who has won two StorySLAMs with the Moth. She wrote and performed a solo show, "Fierce," about re-discovering her creative expression, and is passionate about sharing the beauty of the world through her photos. Nothing delights her more than genuine connection. She and her Swiss-born husband, Patrick, can be found in Chicago when they're not out exploring.

www.margaretghielmetti.com

SELECTED TITLES FROM SHE WRITES PRESS

She Writes Press is an independent publishing company founded to serve women writers everywhere. Visit us at www.shewritespress.com.

Renewable: One Woman's Search for Simplicity, Faithfulness, and Hope by Eileen Flanagan $16.95, 978-1-63152-968-9
At age forty-nine, Eileen Flanagan had an aching feeling that she wasn't living up to her youthful ideals or potential, so she started trying to change the world—and in doing so, she found the courage to change her life.

Godmother: An Unexpected Journey, Perfect Timing, and Small Miracles by Odile Atthalin $16.95, 978-1-63152-172-0
After thirty years of traveling the world, Odile Atthalin—a French intellectual from a well-to-do family in Paris—ends up in Berkeley, CA, where synchronicities abound and ultimately give her everything she has been looking for, including the gift of becoming a godmother.

Motherlines: Letters of Love, Longing, and Liberation by Patricia Reis. $16.95, 978-1-63152-121-8. In her midlife search for meaning, and longing for maternal connection, Patricia Reis encounters uncommon women who inspire her journey and discovers an unlikely confidante in her aunt, a free-spirited Franciscan nun.

Broken Whole: A Memoir by Jane Binns $16.95, 978-1-63152-433-2
At the age of thirty-five, desperate to salvage a self that has been suffocating for years, Jane Binns leaves her husband of twelve years. She has no plan or intention but to leave, however—and there begin the misadventures lying in wait for her.

Learning to Eat Along the Way by Margaret Bendet $16.95, 978-1-63152-997-9
After interviewing an Indian holy man, newspaper reporter Margaret Bendet follows him in pursuit of enlightenment and ends up facing demons that were inside her all along.

Notes from the Bottom of the World by Suzanne Adam $16.95, 978-1-63152-415-8
In this heartfelt collection of sixty-three personal essays, Adam considers how her American past and move to Chile have shaped her life and enriched her worldview, and explores with insight questions on aging, women's roles, spiritual life, friendship, love, and writers who inspire.